MECHANIX ILLUSTRATED
HOW-TO-DO-IT
ENCYCLOPEDIA

Edited by the Combined Staffs of MECHANIX ILLUSTRATED
FAWCETT BOOKS and ELECTRONICS ILLUSTRATED

IN SIXTEEN VOLUMES

VOLUME 3

COMPLETE CONTENTS
AND INDEX IN VOLUME 16

No part of the text or illustrations in this encyclopedia may be used without the written permission of Fawcett Publications, Inc. All rights reserved under Pan-American Copyright Convention and the International Copyright Convention.

COPYRIGHT 1961 FAWCETT PUBLICATIONS, INC.

Well-known reader services of Mechanix Illustrated are extended to readers of this encyclopedia to the extent of blueprint and plan offerings as indicated throughout the various volumes. Inquiries relating to such services and communications regarding the editorial material in this encyclopedia should be directed to Fawcett Publications, Inc., Encyclopedia Service, 67 West 44th Street, New York 36, N. Y. Printed in the United States of America.

GOLDEN PRESS • **NEW YORK**

BOATING

How To Sail

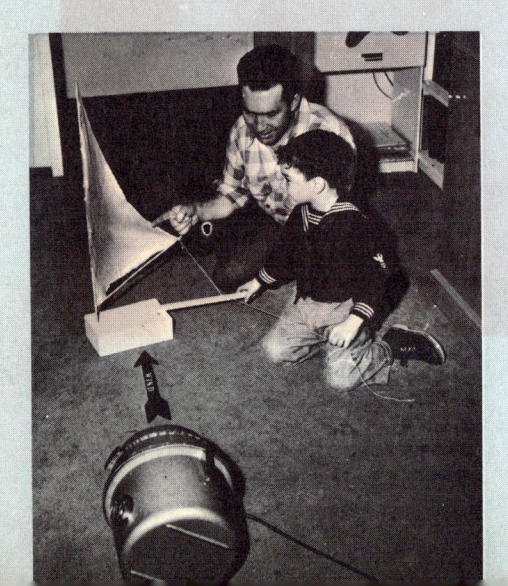

A living room trainer helps teach you how to handle your sailboat.

By Mike Drucker*

SAILING is by no means difficult and the fundamentals can be learned by the average person in a matter of hours. An obvious question arises at this point. "Can we learn to sail from a written text?" In most cases the answer is "No!" Generally nothing more can be gleaned from an article of this type than a knowledge of how it should be done.

An electric fan or the blower on a vacuum cleaner provides wind for practicing with cigar box boat.

*Director, Cap'n Mike's Sailing School, Jamaica Bay, N. Y.

The easiest way to begin to sail is on a reach. Keep the wind coming over the side of boat at about 90° from the center line. Pennant or smoke from stack can be used as wind indicator. Note direction.

In order to sail back over same line—or reach—turn boat by **pushing the tiller toward boom.** Draw sail in as boom swings in. When on new course let sail assume same angle as on other course.

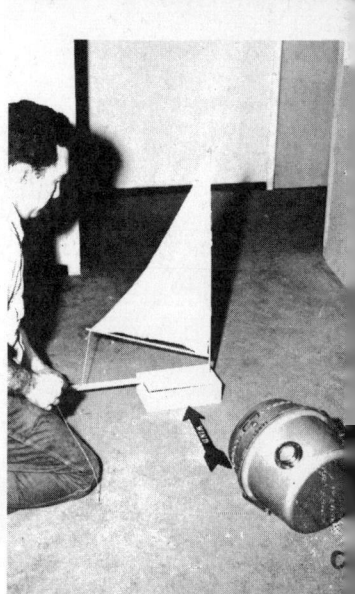

By sailing a zig-zag course into the wind we are able to make headway in that direction. To change your tack (turn), push the tiller toward the boom. Handle on cigar box boat acts same as tiller on sailboat.

BOATING

Musts before sailing: oars or paddles, life jacket, anchor, bailer, hat, sun glasses, and a good lunch.

However, I am attempting to do more than just that. By constructing a simple cigar box trainer and utilizing it in conjunction with an electric fan, the action of the wind on the sail can be studied at first hand. The tiller or rudder control on the trainer will act exactly as it would on a sail boat. You will be amazed at the ground you can cover without ever having cast off a mooring. A nautical purist will cringe at my obvious omission of nautical language. The use of nautical terminology in an article written for the benefit of the would-be sailor, will only add to his confusion. An individual interested in sailing will, once he has gotten his "sea legs," quickly enough acquire a nautical vocabulary, but let us get him sailing first.

The maneuvers are described in numbered sequence so they may be followed and referred to, with ease.

YOUR FIRST BOAT

If the question were put to a dozen sail boat skippers, as to their recommendations for the ideal beginner's boat, you will probably receive twelve different answers, each one using his own early experience as a basis for his choice. Therefore, I maintain that the best boat for a beginner is any sailboat he can beg, borrow or rent. Of course, it would be unwise for him to try to learn to sail on a 75-ft. schooner. Therefore, the only limitation I place is that it be a single-masted vessel of such size that an individual can handle it easily alone. The sailboat should have a fixed counterweight in its bottom (a keel) or one with a pivoted steel plate called the centerboard. The centerboard and keel serve to prevent the boat from drifting sideways. For simplicity of description, I will assume that the boat being used is similar to the one used in the demonstration photos; that is, a single-sailed dinghy. Any additional sails will only increase the confusion. Once the basic principles are mastered, there is no problem in adapting the use of the additional jib sail. The vessel depicted in the photographs is Midge constructed from plans (No. 927) published in MECHANIX ILLUSTRATED. It is a 7½-ft. flat bottomed pram, with 27 sq. ft. of sail and a dagger type centerboard.

Before getting under way there are certain precautions that must be taken These rules should apply for the balance of your sailing career.

1. Never enter the boat without having on board an approved life jacket.
2. Do not take passengers until you are proficient in sailing.
3. Determine as best you can the weather conditions for the day and continue to observe them for the balance of the day.
4. Always have aboard a secondary means of propulsion; either oars, paddles or a small horsepower outboard motor. While in some quarters this is considered heresy, it nevertheless can save a lot of hard work for the beginner.
5. A suitable pump or bailer should be kept on board.
6. Never tie down the rope used to control the sail. Hold it in your hand at all times.
7. Face the boom when steering.

As far as clothing is concerned, I recommend a hat as a must and the balance depends on your morals, your pocketbook or your social standing.

It can safely be assumed that the person from whom the boat was commandeered will instruct the beginner in the proper method of raising sails for that particular boat.

We can now proceed to the actual mechanics of "making the boat go."

INSTRUCTIONS PRIOR TO CASTING OFF

Before casting off your first mooring, it is necessary to acquire the "feel" of the boat. By this I mean, getting to know its limits of stability, the sensitive or sluggish action of the rudder, etc. All this can be done while still safely tied to the mooring. Proceed as follows:

1. Lower the centerboard and keep it down while you are learning.

When dead into wind, sail will shake violently. Shift weight to other side and boat will continue to swing. On new course now, draw in boom close to centerline, then set at an angle of 45° to direction of wind.

When sailing downwind, keep the wind over the shoulder which is away from the boom. Tack downwind by bringing the sail in over center of boat, allowing wind on both sides as in tacking, only from rear.

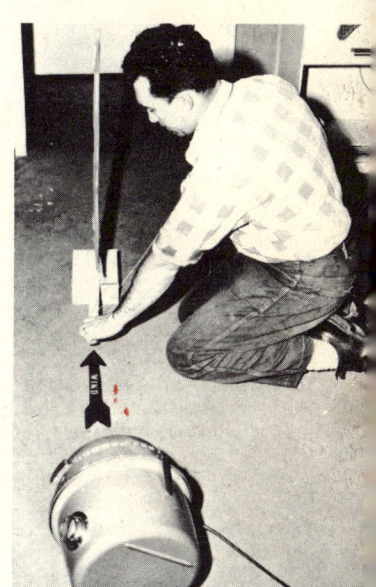

Now swing the boat to the opposite side, being careful to bring the wind over the shoulder once more. Permit the sail to swing over to the new side. To get full power from wind, set the sail at about 90° angle.

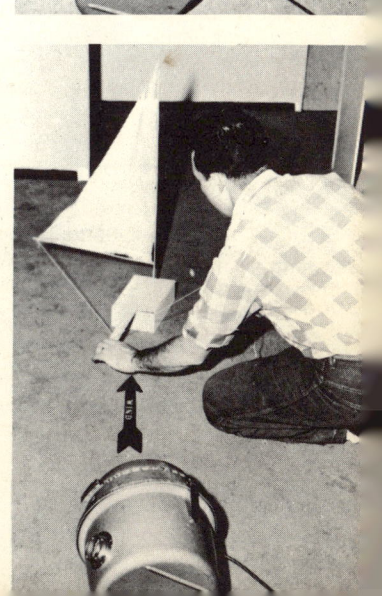

BOATING

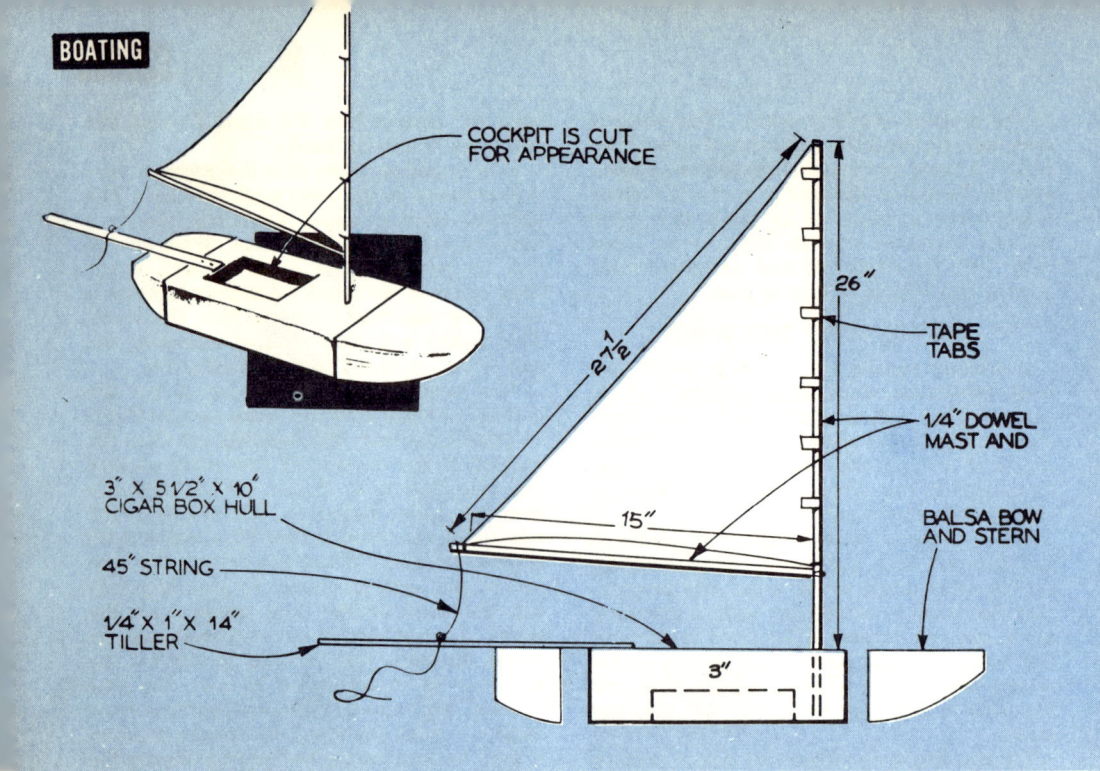

Diagram labels: COCKPIT IS CUT FOR APPEARANCE; 26"; TAPE TABS; 27½"; 15"; ¼" DOWEL MAST AND; BALSA BOW AND STERN; 3" x 5½" x 10" CIGAR BOX HULL; 45" STRING; ¼" x 1" x 14" TILLER; 3"

2. Take your position at the tiller.

3. Bring the sail over the center of the boat and hold it there.

4. Gradually push the tiller away from you, then with force pull it towards you. This will swing the boat to one side. The wind will then strike the sail and impart a forward motion to the boat.

5. Permit the boat to sail until it has reached the limits of the anchor line.

6. Then release the sail and the tiller and permit the boat to settle back to its previous position at the end of the mooring line.

7. Repeat this until you feel more relaxed about handling the boat and until a measure of control is achieved.

Assuming that you have mastered the above, let us now actually get under way. By simply casting off his mooring and assuming that his boat will start sailing, the beginner runs the danger of permitting his boat to collide with other moored boats. Therefore, I recommend that you row the boat to a clear area, drop the anchor, then proceed to set your sails. Once this is done, haul in the anchor and get under way. If while hauling in the anchor, you do drift back, you will then have plenty of sea room.

I recommend that all the following maneuvers be practiced with the home trainer so that you will have a good mental picture of the procedure. When using the trainer in executing a change of direction, do not simply swing it around, but try to impart a forward motion so that a more accurate demonstration will be achieved.

SAILING ON A REACH

One of the simplest and most delightful ways of sailing is known as "a reach." When sailing in this manner, the vessel is able to sail from one point to another and return with no complicated maneuvering. A vessel is considered to be sailing on a reach when the wind is coming directly from the side of the boat. The wind indicator, a flag or a bit of ribbon in the rigging, would be pointed 90° from the center line of the boat.

1. Let us assume that we have cast off our mooring with the wind coming over the left hand side of the boat.

2. Our objective is to sail a distance away, and then to turn around and come back to the original starting point. It is always a good idea to pick an object on the shore to steer by. Proceed along with the boom tip about two feet away from the rear corner of the boat. When we have reached the point where it becomes necessary to turn the boat, push the tiller firmly to the side of the boat upon which the boom is located. Do not jam the tiller over because the boat will then lose considerable speed.

3. As the boat swings gradually around to the left, steadily haul in on the sail. Permit the boat to swing until it is headed back

to the original starting point. The wind is now coming from the right-hand side of the boat. A hard and fast rule to follow, whenever it becomes necessary to turn a boat completely around, is to push the tiller toward whatever side the boom is on. That rule will be demonstrated several times during the course of our cruise.

SAILING INTO THE WIND

Continue sailing on a reach until you have achieved complete control in making turns. This will prepare us for the next step which is the always interesting technique of sailing the boat in the direction from which the wind is blowing; that is, sailing into the wind.

It is a physical impossibility for a boat to sail directly into the wind. However, by sailing at an angle to the wind and permitting the wind to strike our sails a glancing blow, we can impart a forward motion to the boat. The procedure involves a series of zig-zag courses during which time we are able to sail approximately 45° into the wind.

Let us return to either our home trainer or our boat afloat. Assuming that during the course of our cruise and while on a reach, we decide that we would like to sail to an object which is located directly into the wind.

1. The wind while sailing on a reach is striking us directly over our left-hand side. Our boom is located on the right-hand side of the boat.

2. Following the golden rule in changing direction, we push the tiller to the boom.

3. The boat continues swinging in a windward direction until it is approximately 45° into the wind.

4. Haul the boom in to a point where the boom tip is just inside of the right hand edge of the boat.

5. Trim the sail in until all sail flapping stops.

6. Pick an object ashore as a steering guide. Continue sailing along this tack until the point we wish to reach appears to be at right angles to our course.

7. Now prepare for the next zig-zag leg which will bring us closer to our objective. Execute the maneuver for turning, i. e., ease the tiller in the direction of the boom while simultaneously drawing in the boom over the center line of the boat. The boat will then swing around. For an instant the boat will be pointed directly into the wind with the sails shaking violently. As the boat continues to swing around, the wind will strike the sail more fully and the boat will begin to gather headway. Once again sail on a 45° course into the wind, holding the sail rope firmly in hand.

When sailing close into the wind, a boat will achieve its greatest angle of heel. The method used to avoid a capsize due to a sudden puff is to release the strain on the sail by permitting it to swing out freely, thus spilling the wind. Another method is to swing the boat directly into the wind. This safety valve method of releasing the sail is the quickest and most effective.

The method of determining if we are sailing as close into the wind as possible is to gradually turn the boat up into the direction of the wind until the outer edge of the sail begins to flutter. This indicates that we have sailed so directly into the wind that the wind is now blowing on both sides of the sail. When this occurs, the boat can be put back on course by simply pointing the nose of the boat away from the wind. Do not, under any circumstance, tie down the rope that is used to control the sail, nor is it advisable to loop the line around your hand. Should it become necessary to spill the wind, to avoid a capsize, it may be impossible for you to release the control line fast enough. Avoid sailing the boat too close into the wind since the forward motion will be considerably reduced.

SAILING DOWN WIND

After having arrived at our windward destination we now wish to go in the opposite direction, that is, with the wind on our back. A boat sailing in this manner can best be compared to a sled sliding downhill. The wind now "pushes" the boat in the downwind direction. In order to obtain maximum power from the wind, our sail is let out until it is approximately 90° to the center line of the boat. This is done to obtain full pressure of the wind against the greatest possible sail area. Extreme caution must be observed when sailing in this manner. If the person at the tiller is not alert and permits the boat to alter its course enough to allow the wind to blow behind the sail, there is the danger of the sail being flung from one side of the boat to the other. An action such as this is called a "jibe" and in this case an accidental jibe. The velocity reached by the boom during this swing is enough to cause a serious injury to anyone unfortunate enough to be caught in its path. The result of such an accident can do a great deal of damage to the boat such as a dismasting or can, in a rough sea, possibly capsize the boat. This can be avoided by a simple precaution.

Let us assume that we are sailing before the wind with the boom on the right-hand side of the boat. Rather than permit the wind to blow directly over to stern, veer the boat to the left so that the wind then blows over the left-hand shoulder of the man at the tiller. In this manner a safety zone is created which would permit a certain amount of wind shifting. Sailing with the wind striking the sail from over the shoulder of the helmsman is the best way to avoid an accidental jibe. By executing a series of controlled jibes it is possible to "tack downwind" in order to reach our downwind objective. We can best describe this maneuver by comparing it to the tacks we completed into the wind. In this case the wind is behind us rather than in front of us. Let us go through such a maneuver.

1. Our boat is sailing with the wind just over our left shoulder with the boom far out on the right side. We continue sailing on this tack until we find it necessary to change our direction in order to sail closer to our target, which is located to the right of our present course.
2. The next step is to haul in the mainsail, steadily and gradually, until the boom is directly over the center line of the boat.
3. Then swing the tiller away from the direction of the boom, drawing it toward the helmsman. The boat will then veer off to the right.
4. The man at the tiller swings the boat to the right until the wind is blowing directly from the back of the boat on both sides of the sail. At this point the boat is sailing on its momentum.
5. Continue to swing until the wind comes over your right shoulder.
6. At this point the sail is let out to assume the 90° angle on the left side of the boat.

In the beginning, this maneuver should be practiced only in the lightest breezes. It is difficult to execute this maneuver in a strong wind. The combination of steep waves and high winds make sailing before the wind a little tricky. Since you are traveling in the same direction as the wave, the boat behaves somewhat like a surf board.

There is a tendency on the part of the boat to swing broadside to the waves. When this happens, the boom which is extended out over the water, touches the wave, causing a tremendous drag on the rudder. This makes the boat unmaneuverable permitting the next wave that comes along to roll the boat over. By moving all ballast (passengers) as far back as possible the tendency of the boat to bury its nose and lift the rudder out of the water can be avoided.

In the beginning it is recommended that the centerboard remain down at all times to give the boat greater stability. Later, when you have achieved greater skill, the centerboard can be raised when running before the wind.

When it becomes necessary to return to a windward direction, it is a simple matter to swing the boat just as we do in tacking, by pushing the tiller to the boom. As the boat swings closer to the wind, haul the mainsail in gradually so that the boat does not lose forward motion. It is only necessary to continue the swing until the desired windward course is reached.

LANDING AT A MOORING

Basically, the principle involved in learning how to land at a mooring is that of being able to stop the forward motion of the boat.

The methods of landing at a dock or at a mooring are the same except that in the case of a mooring more speed can be tolerated since it is snagged with a boat hook and in this manner its forward motion can be checked.

1. Landing with the wind behind you: Assuming that you are approaching a long pier with a float at the end. Sail down wind until you are just about a boat length past the float; then tack up, heading the boat into the wind and utilizing the momentum to coast up to the float.
2. Landing with the wind coming from the dock: This requires that you sail on a reach (i. e., with the wind coming from your side) until the dock is about 45° from your course and about two boat lengths away. Then simply head up directly to the dock.

CAPSIZING

Distance is very deceptive on water and a shore line that seems apparently near could be miles away. The proper procedure in the event of a capsize is to:

1. Don your life preserver.
2. Get the anchor over to prevent drifting.
3. Remove sails from mast and boom.
4. By placing weight on centerboard and using it as a lever you can right boat.
5. Stuff the centerboard slot with a shirt or rag to prevent the boat from filling while you try to bail her out.
6. If this is not possible, hail a passing boat and you will be towed to shore and safety.

The willingness to help in time of distress is characteristic of seagoing folk.

By being aware of potential danger and observing the appropriate precautions, such danger will not readily materialize. •

Sail Slide Magazine

By S. S. Rabl

IF you've ever wished that you could slap a sail against the mast and hoist away without feeding the slides on the track one-by-one, here is a gimmick that will do the job for you.

The track on a new mast should be set away from the stick on a ¾x⅜ in. spruce liner along its entire length. On a mast already in use the lower end of the track should be linered out from nothing to ⅜-inch for about two feet. The drawing below shows the simple construction of one magazine. Where the sail is fastened also to the boom with slides, two magazines will be needed. •

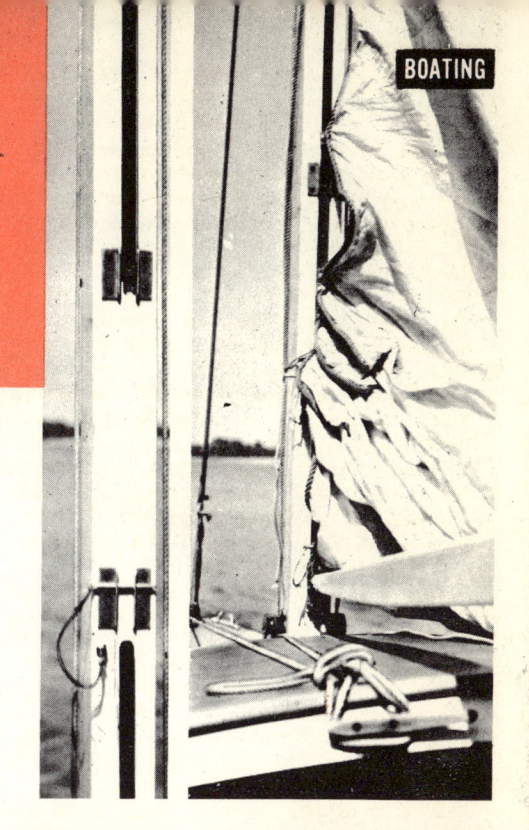

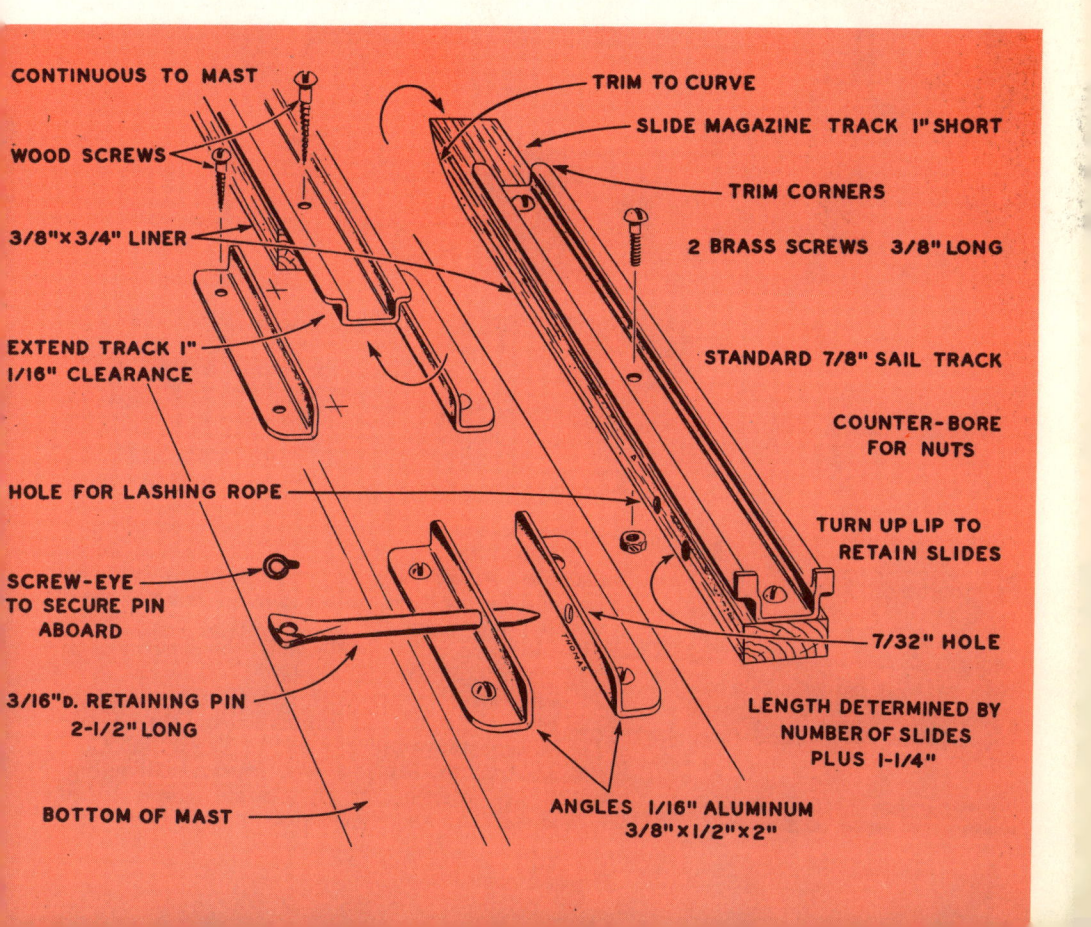

BOATING

- CONTINUOUS TO MAST
- WOOD SCREWS
- 3/8" X 3/4" LINER
- EXTEND TRACK 1" 1/16" CLEARANCE
- HOLE FOR LASHING ROPE
- SCREW-EYE TO SECURE PIN ABOARD
- 3/16"D. RETAINING PIN 2-1/2" LONG
- BOTTOM OF MAST
- TRIM TO CURVE
- SLIDE MAGAZINE TRACK 1" SHORT
- TRIM CORNERS
- 2 BRASS SCREWS 3/8" LONG
- STANDARD 7/8" SAIL TRACK
- COUNTER-BORE FOR NUTS
- TURN UP LIP TO RETAIN SLIDES
- 7/32" HOLE
- LENGTH DETERMINED BY NUMBER OF SLIDES PLUS 1-1/4"
- ANGLES 1/16" ALUMINUM 3/8" X 1/2" X 2"

BOATING

Sail Care

Taking care of your sails properly will bring big rewards for very little effort.

By Ike Manchester

Properly broken in sails on Seagull above show perfect air-flow curve.

HOW many people realize that as much as one-fourth of the value of a small sailboat is invested in a good suit of sails? Probably not many, for despite a lot of good intentions, quite often sails are not given the simple but necessary care they must have in order to last out the life span built into them. Most owners of small boats willingly work hard to keep their crafts shipshape, but unfortunately, the same care is rarely given to a good set of sails.

To demonstrate a practical and effective routine of sail care, MECHANIX ILLUSTRATED asked the advice of Ike Manchester of the Manchester Yacht Sails Co., South Dartmouth, Mass., a well-known sailmaking concern. Mr. Manchester gives some simple rules for good sail care and shows how to carry them out.

BOATING

New sail must be stretched gradually to make its specified length in order to acquire proper set.

Sails which are improperly broken in will never acquire a good set or operate really efficiently.

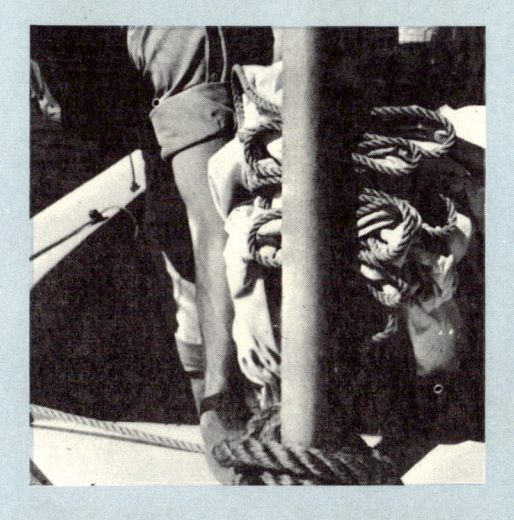

Feeding a sail into grooved mast is eased by furling the luff of the sail on top of the boom first.

Boom should come down amidships, preferably into boom crotch. Never lower your sails into water.

Especially if sails are left on spars, use water and mildew-proof preservative for longer life.

Always remove battens after a sail. They cause rips and tears in sails, can be broken if left in.

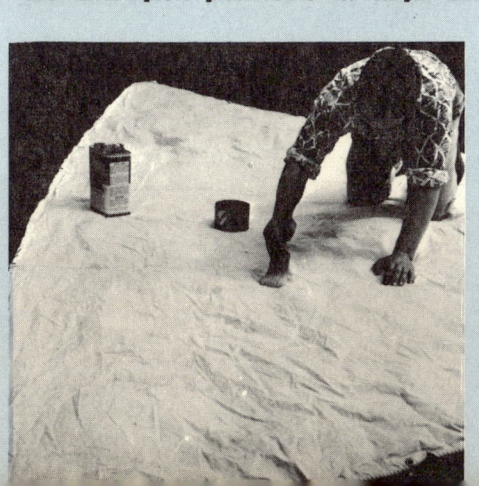

BOATING

IF your boat hull is poorly maintained, it is quickly and obviously unseaworthy, and unsafe. But a neglected set of sails will still drive a boat after a fashion—not with much efficiency, though, and not for very long. A sparkling new paint job on your hull or a newly sanded deck will probably draw more attention than a well-maintained set of sails, but good sail care pays off in big dividends—maximum efficiency and substantially longer lasting performance for a very small cost in terms of time and money.

Any new sail should be stretched gradually to the length specified by the designer or sailmaker. If it is forced to its full length immediately, it will never acquire the set

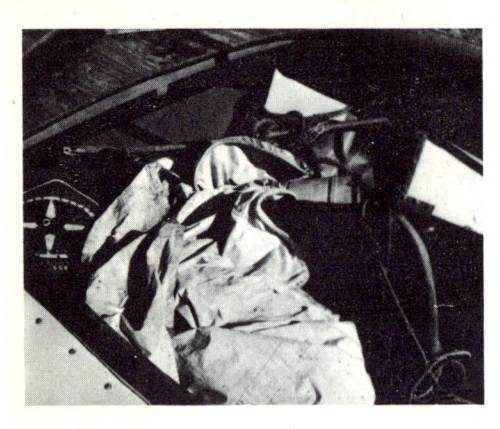

Nothing will cause sails to deteriorate more quickly than mildew. Sails left in boat bottom ask for it.

Mildew fungus (above) needs dampness for growth, but does not affect synthetic fabrics like nylon.

To prevent mildew as well as other sail damage, take sails off spars, carry ashore in sail bag.

Spread out on lawn to dry, hosing them off about once a month if they've been used in salt water.

Dry sails indoors on rainy days. Hang them from line edges and in open position to keep shape.

When sail is dry, examine it carefully for rips, chafed spots, and loose fastenings (slides, etc.).

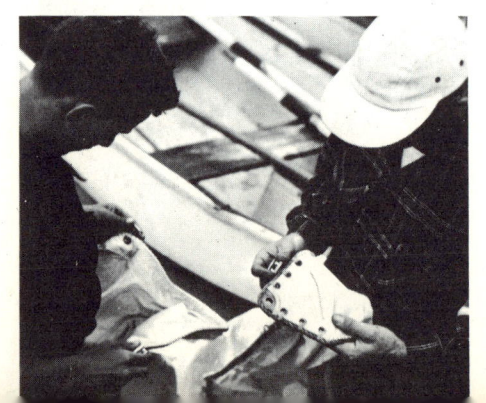

BOATING

necessary for a perfect air-flow curve and top efficiency. Don't heave too heartily on the halyards the first few times out. Each sail should be stretched to size by the wind, not by the bully-boy action of a too-enthusiastic masthand. If you stretch your sail gradually in this way, it will automatically assume its proper set after a few sails.

When raising sails, careful feeding of the bolt rope or slides will help to prevent wrinkling and chafing of the sails.

Don't ever permit your sails to flap wildly if you can help it, for it causes severe wear and tear and can quickly do enough damage to require extensive sail repairs. You can avoid this unnecessary expense

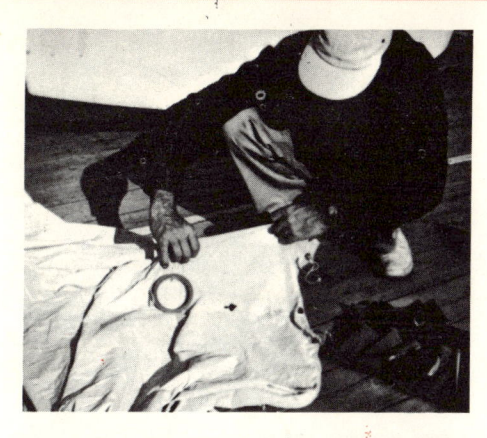

Good sailors carry handy kits with waterproof tape, needle, and twine to make temporary repairs.

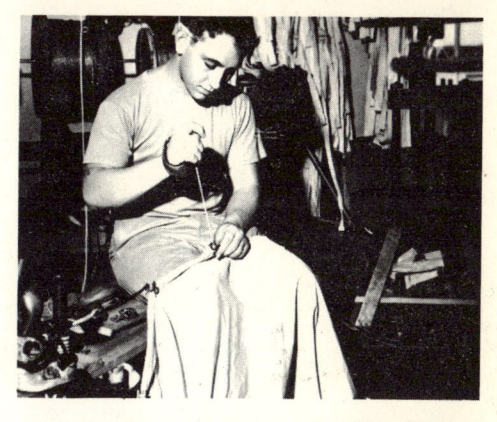

Check thoroughly at season's end to see if major repairs are needed. Have professional make them.

Folding sails properly, even thoroughly dry ones, is important to maintain shape. Make long folds ...

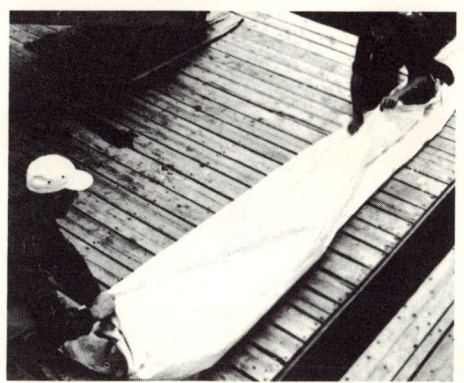

... then roll neatly with as few creases as possible. Don't stretch the canvas. Leave lines exposed ...

... like this, as oil and tar in them stains the sail. The neatly rolled sail is then tucked into sail bag.

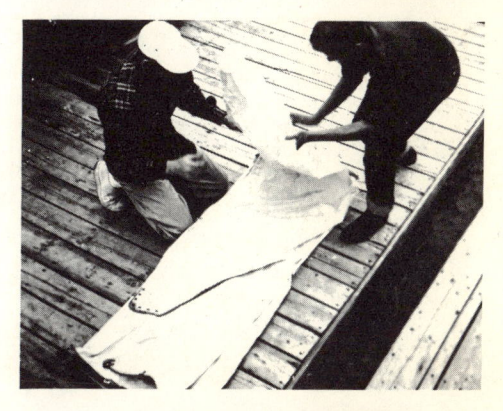

Suspend bag from attic beam or in locker to keep rodents off. Wire is better than rope shown here.

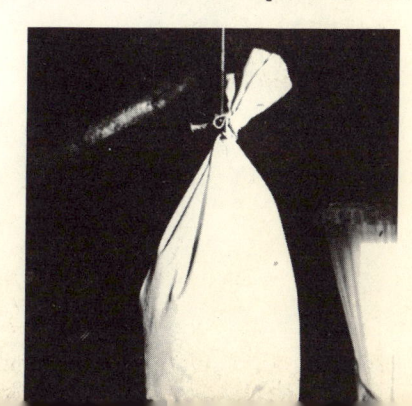

by simply controlling your sails, especially in high winds.

Proper procedure in handling your sails after you've been for a sail is important. The boom should come down amidships, preferably into the boom crotch.

Remove your sails from the spars and take out the battens. Left in, they can cause rips and tears as well as be broken themselves. Sails should then be taken ashore and spread on the lawn or hung indoors to dry thoroughly.

Sails should be examined frequently for small rips and tears which, if mended immediately, will save more extensive repair-work later. This is another very good example of the proverbial ounce of prevention being worth many dollars of cure, for little rips can be whipped into giant tears by just one sail on a blustery day. A sail-mending kit which contains needle, twine, and waterproof tape is a very convenient item to keep around. At the end of each season, you should examine all your sails carefully.

Sails should be dried, folded, and stored as shown in the photographs. Leaving them in heaps at the bottom of your boat, folding them before they have thoroughly dried, or letting them remain on the rigging during rain, morning fogs, etc., is just asking for them to mildew. This fungus growth which thrives on dampness is most detrimental to any canvas, silk, or cotton sail, for it causes very rapid deterioration. Mildew does not affect the synthetic fabrics like nylon, but poor treatment of even such hardy fabrics will wear them out much more quickly than is necessary.

If you use your sailboat so frequently that you want to leave the sails rigged, you should give them a good coat of one of the water and mildew-proof preservatives which ought to be brushed on sails at the beginning of the season for best protection.

Lastly, store your repaired and carefully folded sails in your sailbag which should be suspended from a wire (it precludes any possibility of rats or mice getting at them) and hung in a dry place. •

boating hints

Practical Scupper Strainers. The commonly used flat strainer with holes in the top clogs up with trash and small particles very quickly. This results in a large pool of water on deck and more in the bilge. To eliminate this annoyance, I designed and built a brass cone, hammered a flange around the edge, soldered a 1/8-in.-dia. brass rod across the top for a handle, and drilled the cone full of 1/8-in. holes. The bottom of the cone forms a basin where trash can collect without stopping the flow of water. The strainer is easily lifted out for cleaning. The pattern is for a cone that will fit a 1½-in. scupper.—George Brook Taylor.

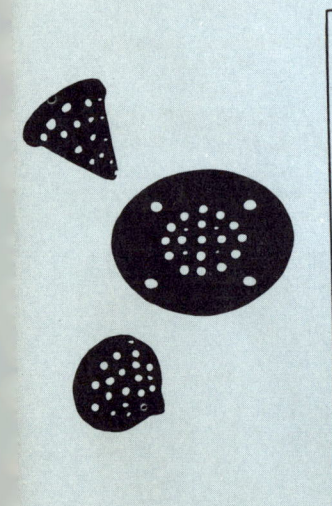

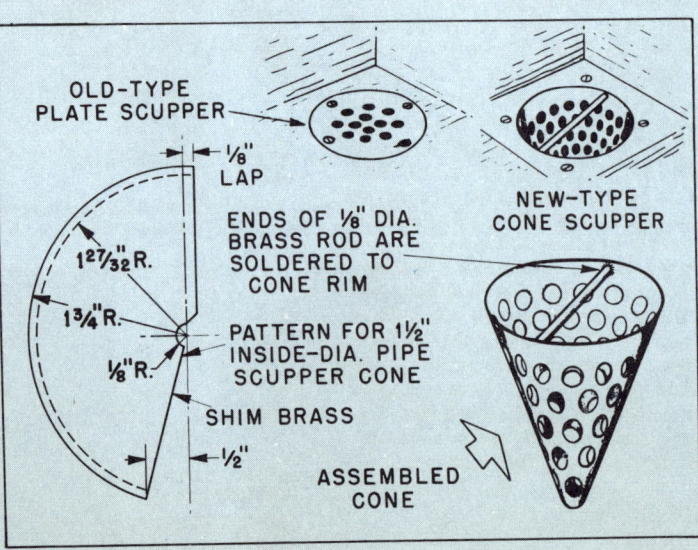

Inertia-Operated Pump

WEEK-END sailors will enjoy peace of mind if they know the water from normal seepage during the week is squirting overboard with every roll of their boats. With an average of six strokes per minute, this pump will move 30 gallons a day.

Purchase a secondhand fuel pump without a vacuum-booster chamber. Disassemble and thoroughly clean it and add new valves, valve springs, diaphragm, and gaskets. Omit the diaphragm return spring. Solder up the rectangular hole in the diaphragm rod; then drill a No. 9 hole for the reach rod. Drill a ½-in. hole in the pump housing for insertion of the reach rod. The reach rod and collars are taken from Junior's Erector set. Bend the rod as shown and silver-solder a small washer at the bend. Thread the short end of the rod for a nut. Replace the pump screen with one cut from bronze window screening, which will provide sufficient protection for bilge service. Assemble and check the pump.

The lever is 12¾ in. long; drill it as shown. Make the collar striker and fasten it to the top of the lever so it is free to rotate. The counterweight can be cast from lead or built up from 3-in. plate washers. Make the pump stand to suit and bolt it to two adjacent frames so the lever swings athwartships. Bolt the pump in place and add the lever support, the lever-support bracket, the awning-slide lever bearing, and the lever. Set the reach-rod collars ⅛ in. from the ends of the striker.

Pipe up the pump with 5/16-in. rubber hose over 5/16-in. copper tubing fitted to the pump ports. Use bronze screening to form a bonnet over the end of the suction line.

—R. Lieto

BOATING

Rigging a Small Sailboat

Make a boat safer and easier to handle by leading all lines close to the tiller.

By John Wolbarst

IT often happens that small sailboats aren't rigged for maximum safety and ease of handling. The jib and mainsail halyards, for instance, are usually cleated to the base of the mast. This means that it's necessary to get up, leave the tiller and go forward if you want to drop sail in a hurry. Then too, dual jib sheets, used with an overlapping jib, often lead back to cleats along the rails. In a stiff wind, with the crew up to windward to keep the boat down, the jib sheet in use is cleated out of reach across the cockpit. Trouble may arise in a sudden squall or if the boat grounds and the helmsman can't act quickly and smoothly. After a near accident in my 14-ft. plywood centerboarder, I re-rigged the boat as follows:

Halyards: Two small cheek blocks were added, one each side, near the base of the mast. The jib and mainsail halyards run through these and aft to the cleats.

Mainsheet: This formerly came down from the boom to the rear of the centerboard box, was in the way when coming about and led off in different directions, depending upon which tack the boat was on. A pulley on the boom was moved forward two feet and a swivel pulley mounted on the centerboard box directly beneath it. The sheet now goes forward along the boom, down to the pulley on the box and aft to a jam cleat.

Jib sheets: The dual sheets now pass through swivel pulleys on the rails and lead to a cleat at the center.

Jib downhaul: A light line was run from the head of the jib, along the jib-

BOATING

All lines lead back to a central location atop thwart mounted at the rear of the centerboard box. It's easy for lone sailor to drop sails quickly when necessary.

Downhaul is run down jibstay inside snaps and then passes through a shackle at the bow.

stay inside all jib snaps, through the shackle at the bow and aft to a cleat. This was done because the jib is too light to fall by itself. Now I turn the boat into the wind briefly, center the sail over the boat, let go the jib halyard and give a few pulls on the downhaul. The jib comes into the boat and I never leave the tiller.

Now, having everything at hand when an emergency comes up, both sails can be dropped within 45 seconds. The cost of this added safety and convenience was only a few dollars. •

Manner in which the boat was rerigged is detailed below. Jib sheet in use is cleated.

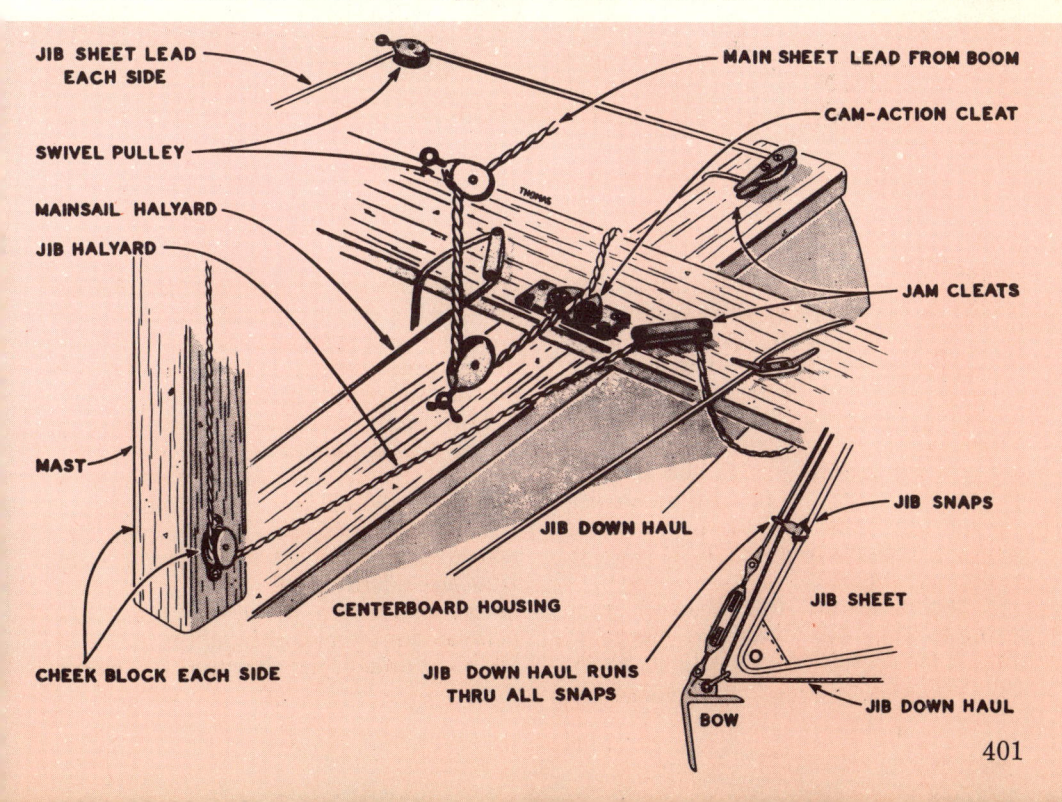

- JIB SHEET LEAD EACH SIDE
- SWIVEL PULLEY
- MAINSAIL HALYARD
- JIB HALYARD
- MAST
- CHEEK BLOCK EACH SIDE
- MAIN SHEET LEAD FROM BOOM
- CAM-ACTION CLEAT
- JAM CLEATS
- JIB DOWN HAUL
- CENTERBOARD HOUSING
- JIB DOWN HAUL RUNS THRU ALL SNAPS
- JIB SNAPS
- JIB SHEET
- BOW
- JIB DOWN HAUL

401

BOATING

Outboard Motor Cart

Those big, heavy outboards are easy to handle with a cart like this.

By Howard Rozelle

THIS outboard motor cart has everything. It's strong enough to handle a 40-horsepower engine; it's rigid enough to allow it to be used as a repair stand, even to cranking; it hauls a gas tank, with room left for a tool box; it's so well balanced that a child or a woman can move a big engine easily; and it folds compactly in 10 seconds by removing one pin which also locks it in the folded position. What's more it's light, easy to build and cheap.

If the materials are salvaged from scrapped toys and discarded pieces of pipe, it can be built for as little as $1.75.

Even if used materials are purchased and spot welding is paid for, the cost shouldn't exceed seven dollars. A cart incorporating all its features would sell for a good deal more.

The simple construction is detailed in the drawing. Beyond what is shown, little information is required. Note, in the illustration at the upper right of the next page, that the handles are bent outward. The width at the pivot is only 19½ in.—slightly too narrow. A few inches above the pivot, the pipes are bent so that the width at the ends of the handles is 22 in. Another thing that bears mention is that the hole in the outer pipe at the pivot should be reamed slightly larger to allow for the bolt wobble caused by the bend of the pipes at this point.

Wheels are 10-in. diameter, but 8 or 12-in. may be used if slight alterations are made in the dimensions. The axles are mounted in holes drilled through the support pipes and then spot welded. Hub caps are used as dressing.

Pipes must be threaded where elbows are used at the joints. Spot welding is used elsewhere. The crosspiece beneath the wooden mount is cut to size and welded in position where the U brackets will engage it when the cart is folded.

Vertical tabs, welded at the ends of the platform, prevent a gas tank or tool box from sliding off. •

BILL OF MATERIALS

Used Pipe: ¾" dia., 20'
Electrical Conduit: ½" dia., 9'
Bolts: 4, ½"x2"
2, ⅜"x3"
Strap Iron: ⅛"x1", 5" long
Pipe Elbows: 4, ¾" I.D.
Axles: 2 long bolts (or a steel rod) at least ½" dia.
Plywood: 1 piece, ¾"x5"x18"
1 piece, ¾"x5"x16½"
Wheels, 10" dia.; hub caps; grips

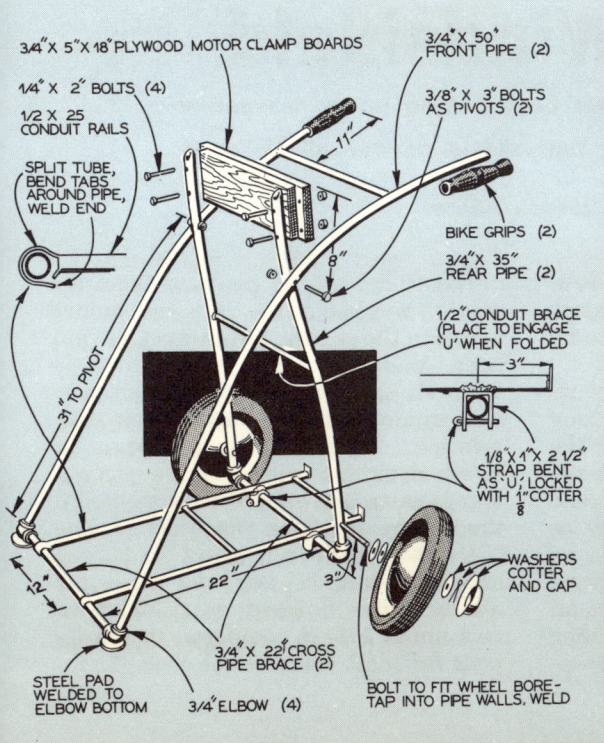

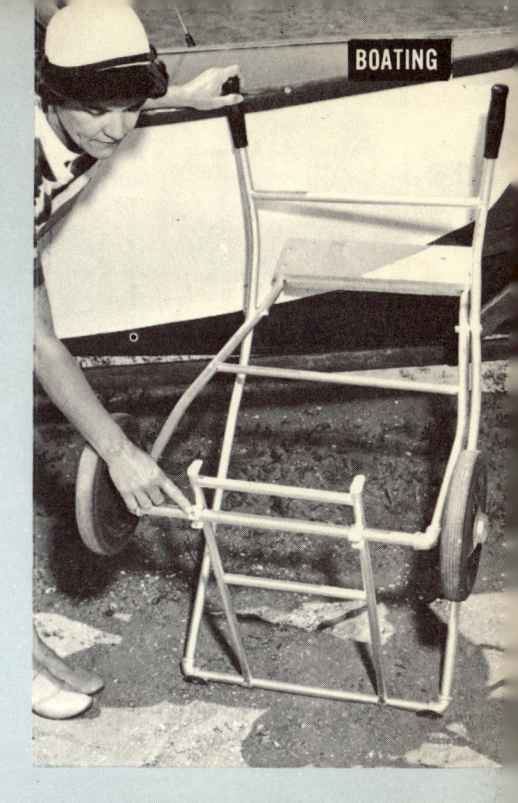

Cart is tilted up to show how single cotter pin (through U bracket) locks platform to bottom rear crosspiece.

Remove cotter pin, lift platform and swing sections together to fold cart. Pin is replaced at center crosspiece.

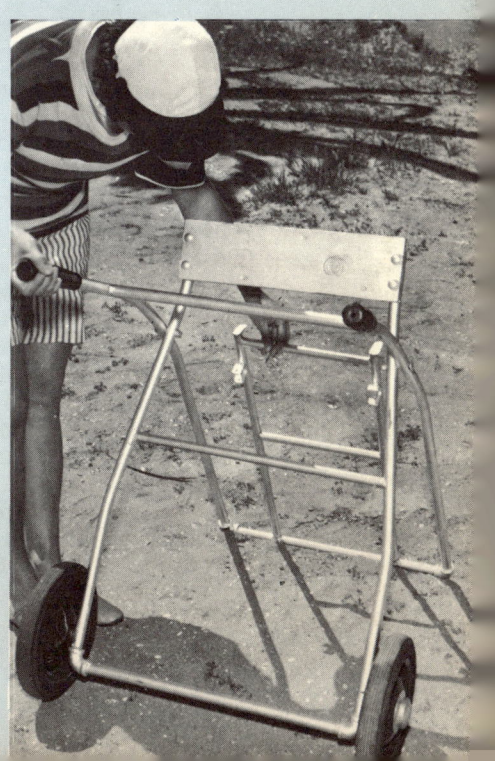

BOATING

BOATING

Boat Windshield

For the boatman who has been looking for an inexpensive windshield, here is one that should answer all his needs.

By Joseph Adams

A windshield on an outboard runabout has two purposes; it keeps out spray and is a must if a top is to be installed in the boat.

The dimensions shown on the drawing are for a broad 16-footer and they should be adjusted according to the length and width of your particular boat. The glass is V-type, shatterproof auto glass, obtainable from auto wreckers for about $2 a section. Score the glass on both sides, and with one edge raised slightly, tap along the score with a hammer. The inner gummy layer is then cut with a razor blade.

The frame should be made from the same type wood as the deck and stained to match the general appearance of your boat. Waterproof glue is used throughout. To avoid moisture between glass and framework use elastic seam composition. To make a good contact between deck and windshield, a piece of electrician's tape should be cemented to the underside of the windshield frame.

Marine grade plywood and brass screws should be used for best durability. The finished windshield will cost about $10 as compared to the $50 paid for most commercial ones. •

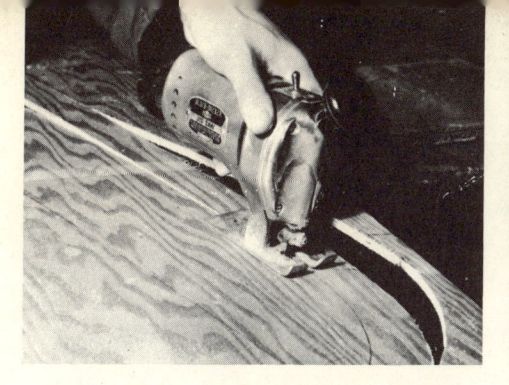

A band saw or portable jig saw will easily cut the plywood frame to the desired shape.

To get the proper contour, set frame up as shown and trace deck shape with a compass.

Front and center sections are permanently joined. The back section is removable.

After frame is sanded to conform to deck, the side braces are attached with brass screws.

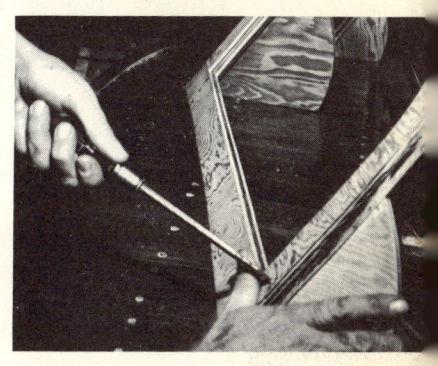

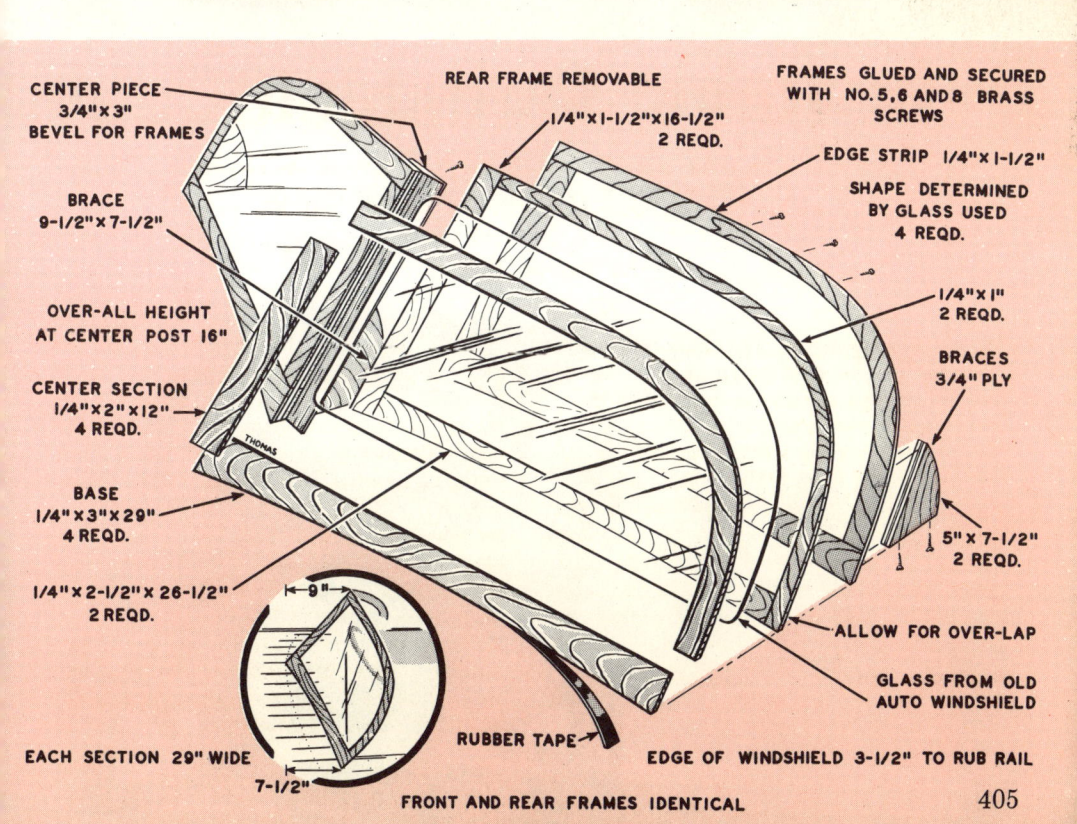

CENTER PIECE
3/4" X 3"
BEVEL FOR FRAMES

BRACE
9-1/2" X 7-1/2"

OVER-ALL HEIGHT AT CENTER POST 16"

CENTER SECTION
1/4" X 2" X 12"
4 REQD.

BASE
1/4" X 3" X 29"
4 REQD.

1/4" X 2-1/2" X 26-1/2"
2 REQD.

EACH SECTION 29" WIDE

REAR FRAME REMOVABLE
1/4" X 1-1/2" X 16-1/2"
2 REQD.

RUBBER TAPE
7-1/2"
9"

FRONT AND REAR FRAMES IDENTICAL

FRAMES GLUED AND SECURED WITH NO. 5, 6 AND 8 BRASS SCREWS

EDGE STRIP 1/4" X 1-1/2"
SHAPE DETERMINED BY GLASS USED
4 REQD.

1/4" X 1"
2 REQD.

BRACES
3/4" PLY

5" X 7-1/2"
2 REQD.

ALLOW FOR OVER-LAP

GLASS FROM OLD AUTO WINDSHIELD

EDGE OF WINDSHIELD 3-1/2" TO RUB RAIL

405

BOATING

Detachable Outboard Cabin

Now you can convert your open runabout into an outboard cruiser using this inexpensive design.

THIS lightweight cabin will provide you with a dual-purpose boat, an open craft for calm inland water, or weather-and-spray protection where the going is rough. It can be lifted off by removing seven bolts. The original was built on a farm with a circular saw the only power equipment available.

Front view of the easily built cabin shows framed plate glass windshield.

BOATING

By Hi Sibley

Three-quarter view shows amazing roominess of the portable cabin. Note plywood forward deck.

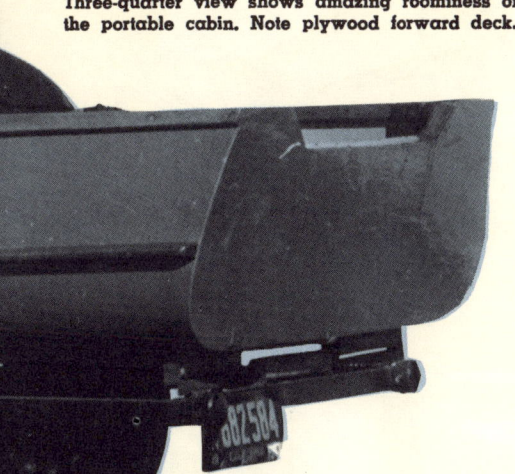

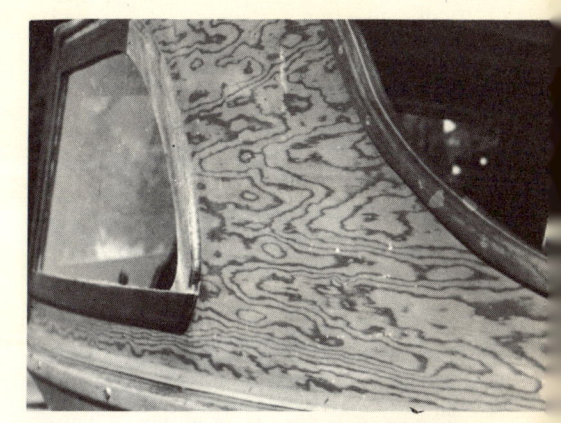

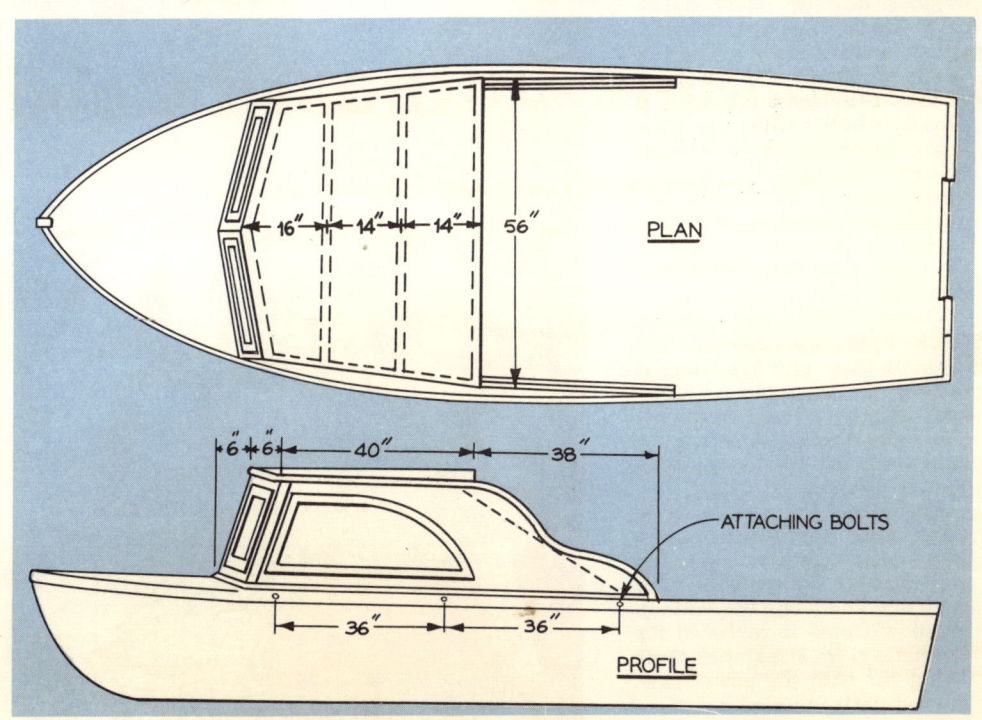

PLAN

16" 14" 14" 56"

6" 6" 40" 38"

ATTACHING BOLTS

36" 36"

PROFILE

407

BOATING

General over-all dimensions are given in the plan and profile drawings as adapted to a standard 15-ft. Fiberglas hull. Dimensions can and should be adjusted to fit your own boat. Assembly details are shown also in the drawings.

Sides are ½-in. marine plywood reinforced with ¾-in. mahogany framing with 1⅛-in. carlins supporting the cabin roof. This is the same material as the sides and is secured with seven ovalhead screws in each beam. Apply waterproof glue to all contacting surfaces.

Application of retaining bolt also is illustrated. Brass toilet bolts are used in the original, with nuts on the inside. The only preparations necessary on the hull are to drill holes for the bolts through rub rail and sheer stringer, and deck over the bow end with a 2x2-in. stringer underneath, running fore-and-aft, to which the seventh bolt is secured, as shown in the drawing. This view also gives locations of bolts with nuts on the inside and heads countersunk and plugged over with shipwright's dowels. Note bulkhead which is secured to ribs, either existing in this location or added. Ample storage space is thus provided and, with a Fiberglas hull, will be dry. This type of hull just doesn't leak. In case your hull is open forward, deck it over with ¼-in. marine plywood, installing beams similar to the carlins of the roof. Seal the joint at the sheer line with marine glue.

The windshield sash consists of mahogany framing with ¼-in. plate glass and are hung at the top with brass piano hinges. Catches are provided on the inside with folding brackets to hold them open when ventilation is desired.

Profile on the side wall is given in the last drawing. One-inch half-round molding is installed along the top edge with cove molding along the bottom. Window frame is rabbeted for the plate glass, straight sections being cut with the power saw, curved parts chiseled out. •

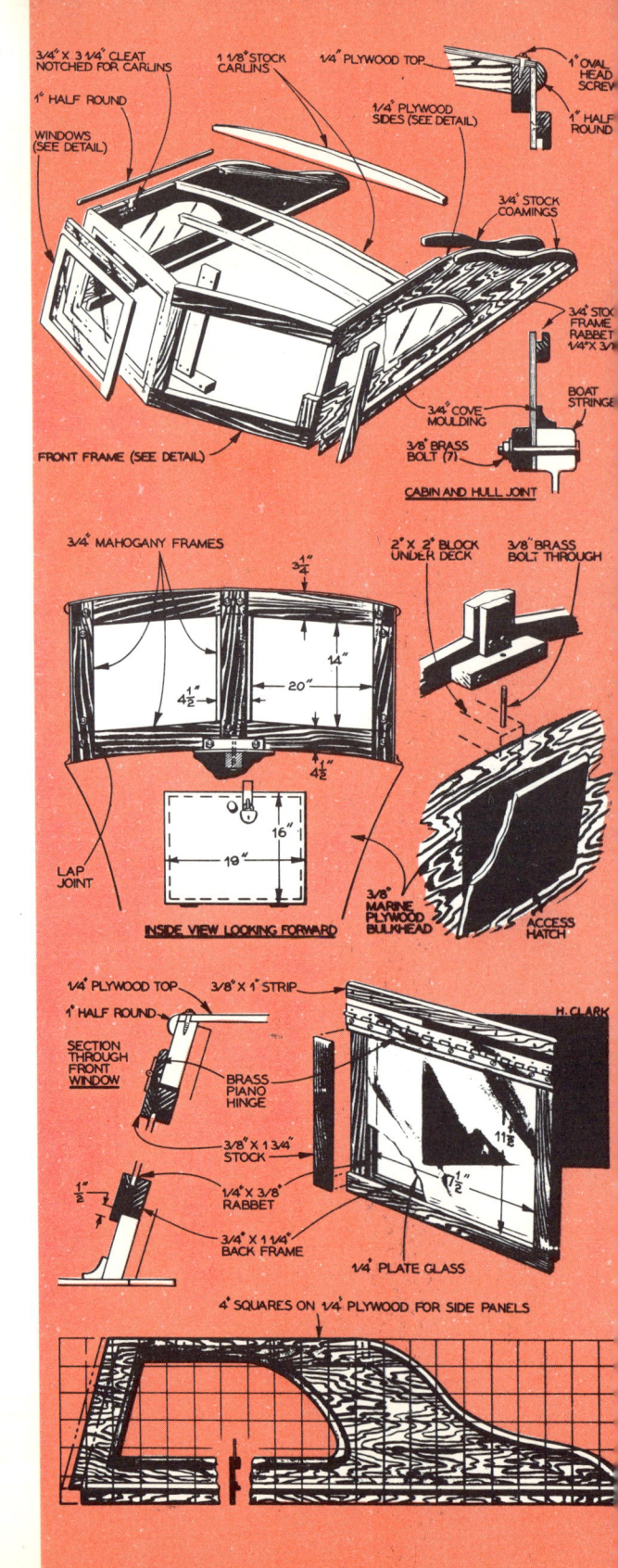

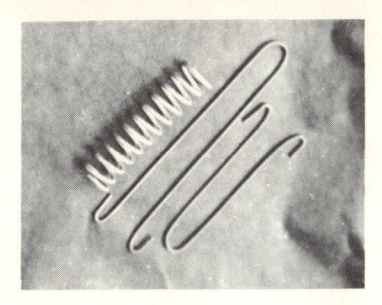

You can keep your canvas boat cover snug with this simple gadget made out of a strong compression spring and two pieces of wire or bronze welding rod as shown in photo left.

A rope buffer on your dinghy will protect the paint of your sloop or cruiser. Rope should be stretched prior to attaching it.

Ordinary garden hose, 12 to 18 inches long, and split spiral fashion can be slipped over mooring line to make a good chafing gear.

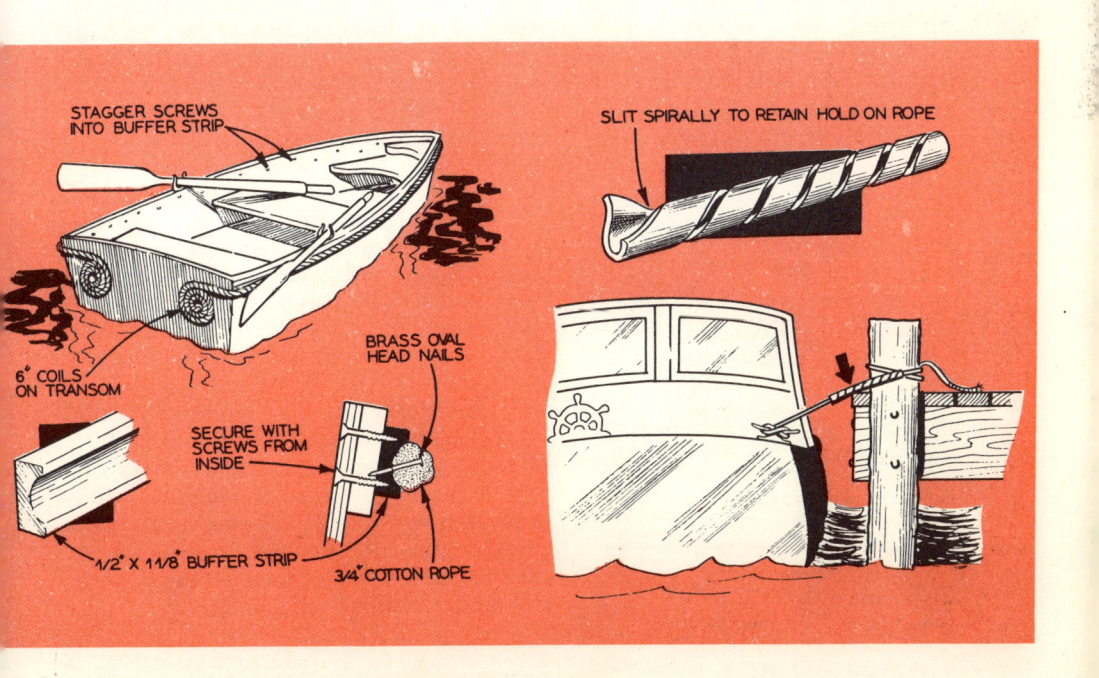

STAGGER SCREWS INTO BUFFER STRIP

SLIT SPIRALLY TO RETAIN HOLD ON ROPE

6" COILS ON TRANSOM

BRASS OVAL HEAD NAILS

SECURE WITH SCREWS FROM INSIDE

1/2" X 1 1/8" BUFFER STRIP

3/4" COTTON ROPE

409

Enclosing the Outboard

Keep out a following sea and tone down the noise by enclosing the outboard in a self-bailing well.

By F. C. Clark

THE transom cut for the engine on many an outboard cruiser is so low that a following sea has no trouble climbing into the boat. No matter how good the skipper's intentions, there are times when he's caught out in rough weather and the low cut becomes dangerous.

I've found that the best answer is to merely enclose the engine on three sides with lockers and a self-bailing well. At first thought, an enclosure running the full width of the cockpit, and extending some 20 in. inboard of the transom, may seem to take up too much space in an area already small. In practice, however, such an arrangement actually added to the size of the boat by providing for the orderly housing of cables and gear. In addition, appearance was improved and motor noise deadened. Fiberglas or Styrofoam insulation in the well will deaden the noise even more.

Dimensions of the enclosure will vary, depending on the boat and motor. Just mount the motor (or motors) on the transom and run through all tilts and swings—size of the enclosure will be obvious. Remember drain holes at rear of well and ventilate properly, else the engine will cough and die. •

BOATING

Gas line and steering cable holes. Shape opening so that steering cable won't rub.

Top panel of false transom is folded down, outboard clamped inboard for trailer move.

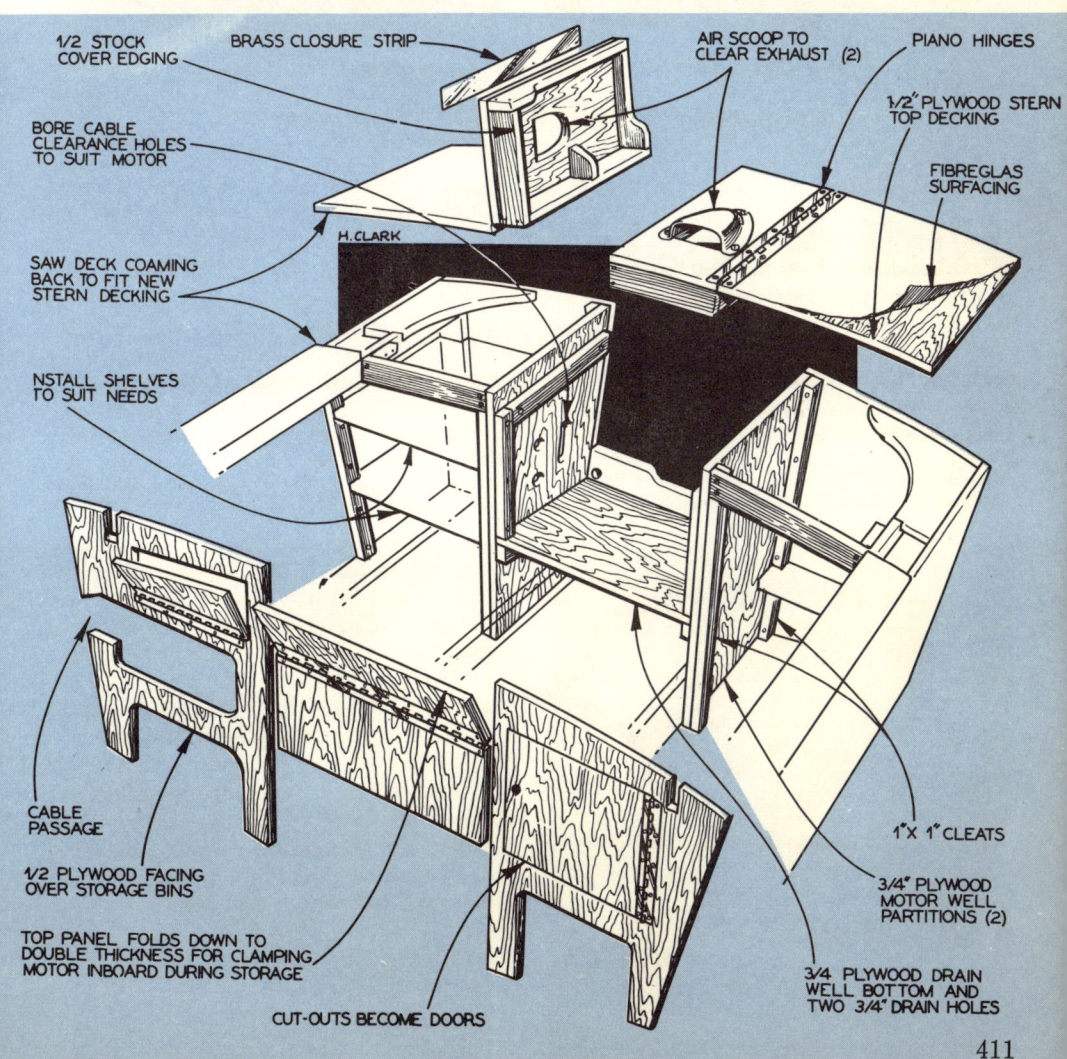

- 1/2 STOCK COVER EDGING
- BRASS CLOSURE STRIP
- AIR SCOOP TO CLEAR EXHAUST (2)
- PIANO HINGES
- 1/2" PLYWOOD STERN TOP DECKING
- BORE CABLE CLEARANCE HOLES TO SUIT MOTOR
- FIBREGLAS SURFACING
- SAW DECK COAMING BACK TO FIT NEW STERN DECKING
- H. CLARK
- INSTALL SHELVES TO SUIT NEEDS
- CABLE PASSAGE
- 1/2 PLYWOOD FACING OVER STORAGE BINS
- TOP PANEL FOLDS DOWN TO DOUBLE THICKNESS FOR CLAMPING MOTOR INBOARD DURING STORAGE
- CUT-OUTS BECOME DOORS
- 1" X 1" CLEATS
- 3/4" PLYWOOD MOTOR WELL PARTITIONS (2)
- 3/4 PLYWOOD DRAIN WELL BOTTOM AND TWO 3/4" DRAIN HOLES

411

BOATING

Hull Repair

Above a plywood runabout is shown in action. Usually driver takes more punishment than boat.

By Hal Kelly

Here is a simple procedure for replacing a plywood planked bottom. The only power-driven tool you need on the job is an electric drill.

Photos by the author

As can be seen in a stern view of badly damaged bottom, the aluminum fin was completely torn off.

Wood dough over screw head must first be removed with ice pick or other sharp instrument.

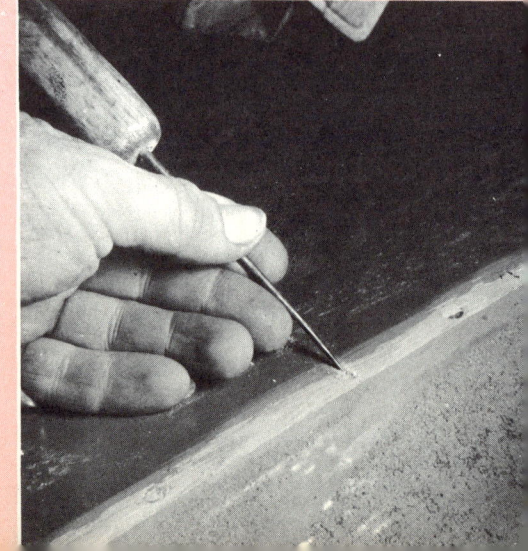

BOATING

DURING the past ten years, plywood planking has been used on more and more boats. Better waterproof glue and improved manufacturing methods have turned plywood into a very durable material. The small runabout pictured, which is capable of doing over 50 miles per hour, has only ¼-in. thick plywood on the bottom and weighs less than 140 pounds. This little boat flipped the driver and ran up on a rocky shore line. Although not punctured, the bottom was ruined.

The repair time on the project was 15 hours—from removing the old bottom to replacing the new one and finishing it off. Cost was $14.00 for 4x10-ft. mahogany plywood and $8.00 for paint and screws. The bottom on this particular boat was glued and screwed to all the battens and chines, and in some places Anchorfast nails were used. Most small boats are built the same way except that Bedlast or some other sealer may be used in place of glue. In any case the procedure for repairing remains the same.

Place the boat, bottom up, on a pair of padded saw horses of a good workable height. Then remove all screws and nails. Dig out the wood dough over the screw heads with a sharp instrument such as an ice pick and unscrew them. Anchorfast nails are best handled by cutting the wood from around them with a sharp chisel and using a claw hammer to pull them out. If the screws are brass, the chances are that you can use them again, but the nails are a total loss.

With the boat right side up on the horses, pound the bottom out with a blunt block of wood and a husky hammer. Be sure that the part of the bottom you are working on is not directly over the horses. After the bottom has been loosened from the frame, turn upside down and remove the entire bottom. With a little care it will remain in one piece, and can be used as a pattern for the new bottom.

Turn the boat upside down again and clean off all the battens and stringers which the bottom will contact. If the bottom was glued you will have one layer of the plywood adhering to the frame. This is best removed with a hand plane. The plane blade will easily cut off the remaining plywood without going through the glue. Using a straightedge, check the frame to see that it is flat and true.

Using the old bottom as a template, cut out your new bottom to size leaving a little extra to be trimmed off after it is attached in place. I used ¼-in. thick mahogany instead of the old ¼-in. fir plywood. The mahogany costs more but stands up better and does not require the sizing fir plywood needs. I used Sealer 900 between the plywood and frame. The bottom is carefully fitted in place and notched up front where it comes to a vee. All the pilot holes for the screws or Anchorfast nails are drilled now.

Remove the bottom and dust off the sawdust from the pilot holes, and generously coat the battens and chines with Weldwood glue or a good sealer—whatever you prefer. The bottom is now quickly screwed or nailed in place, about every two inches on the chines and transom and 4 inches apart on all battens. If screws are used, a

After the slit in the screw is completely clean, it's easy enough to remove screw with screwdriver.

First cut wood dough from around heads of Anchorfast nails with chisel, then pull with claw hammer.

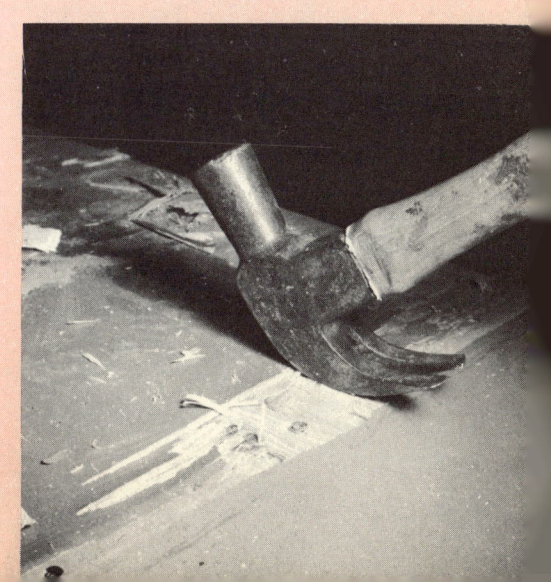

BOATING

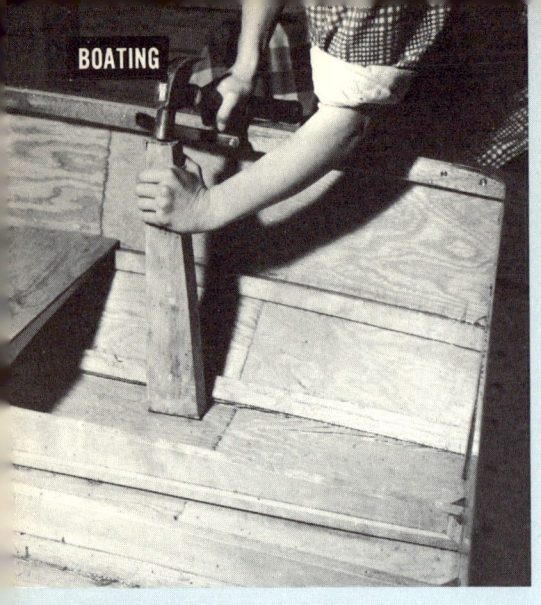

Pound out the bottom with block of wood and hammer. Make sure saw horse is not directly beneath.

After loosening bottom from frame, turn boat upside down and remove bottom, keeping it intact.

Plane off pieces of plywood which are stuck to frame. Use your steel straightedge as check on level.

Screw holes are drilled with a "screwmate" which drills tapered holes and countersinks for heads.

Oscillating sander is handy for smoothing bottom and wet sanding it, after the last coat of paint.

screw attachment for a small electric drill will save time and blisters on your hands. Wood dough is used over all the countersunk screwheads, or nails.

When the wood dough and glue is dry, trim off the excess and sand down the entire bottom with a medium fine paper. If the bottom is fir plywood your best bet is to use a sealer like white Firzite before painting. Use a good boat enamel. I used Boat Life, and after two coats I wet sanded to a slick finish. If the boat is to be used in fresh water only a good outdoor enamel will do the trick.

If mahogany is used no sealer is needed. Don't forget to give the inside of the bottom a coat of varnish or paint. Your Runabout is now as good as new and ready for action. •

Bill of Materials

4x10 ft. sheet of ¼ in. marine plywood (mahogany or fir)
3 gross of ⅞ No. 7 screws or 1 pound of 1 in. No. 12 Anchorfast nails (350 nails per pound)
1 pound of Weldwood glue or one quart of Sealer 900
1 quart Spar varnish for inside of boat
1 quart Boat Life or Spar varnish for outside
1 quart of Firzite if fir plywood is used
Small can of wood dough

Here finished bottom gets its final coat of paint. Inside of bottom will take either paint or varnish.

BOATING

PEANUT

BEVELING entire frame for application of plywood skin. Stanley Surform file does precision job easily. Note fairing stick, above, used for checking out the bevels.

YOU CAN KILL TWO BIRDS with this project: Learn how to go about this business of making a boat from plans—and also to provide your little guy with one of the proudest life-size "toys" a kid ever had. You can build this little nifty in a couple of weekends and for less than twenty bucks. My boy is only eight and he loves it. With a helmet on he's a king at the controls, the envy of every kid in the county—and the darling of the ladies. I nearly busted my bib with pride when I first saw him take off in it.

With the "Fisherman's Friend," the 3 hp Evinrude kicker which usually trolls, this baby takes off like a hydro. Does a smart 15 mph or better.

Built of 1/8-inch plywood, the boat weighs about 35 lbs. With the motor off it

BOATING

Diagram labels: DECK FILLER, 1/2" MAHOGANY FINS, TRANSOM ASSEMBLY, FRONT DECK, HANK CLARK, REAR CLAMP BOARD, SIDE PANEL, MOTOR CLAMP BOARD, BOW HARPIN, CHINE, SHEER RAIL, BOTTOM BATTENS, SAW KERFS, RIB 2, KING PLANK, STEM, FOREFOOT, DECK RIB, BOTTOM PANEL, RIB 1, FIN BATTENS

1/8" X 30" X 80"
FLUSH DOOR PANEL
(2 NEEDED)

Panel layout labels: SIDE PANEL, DECKING, BOTTOM

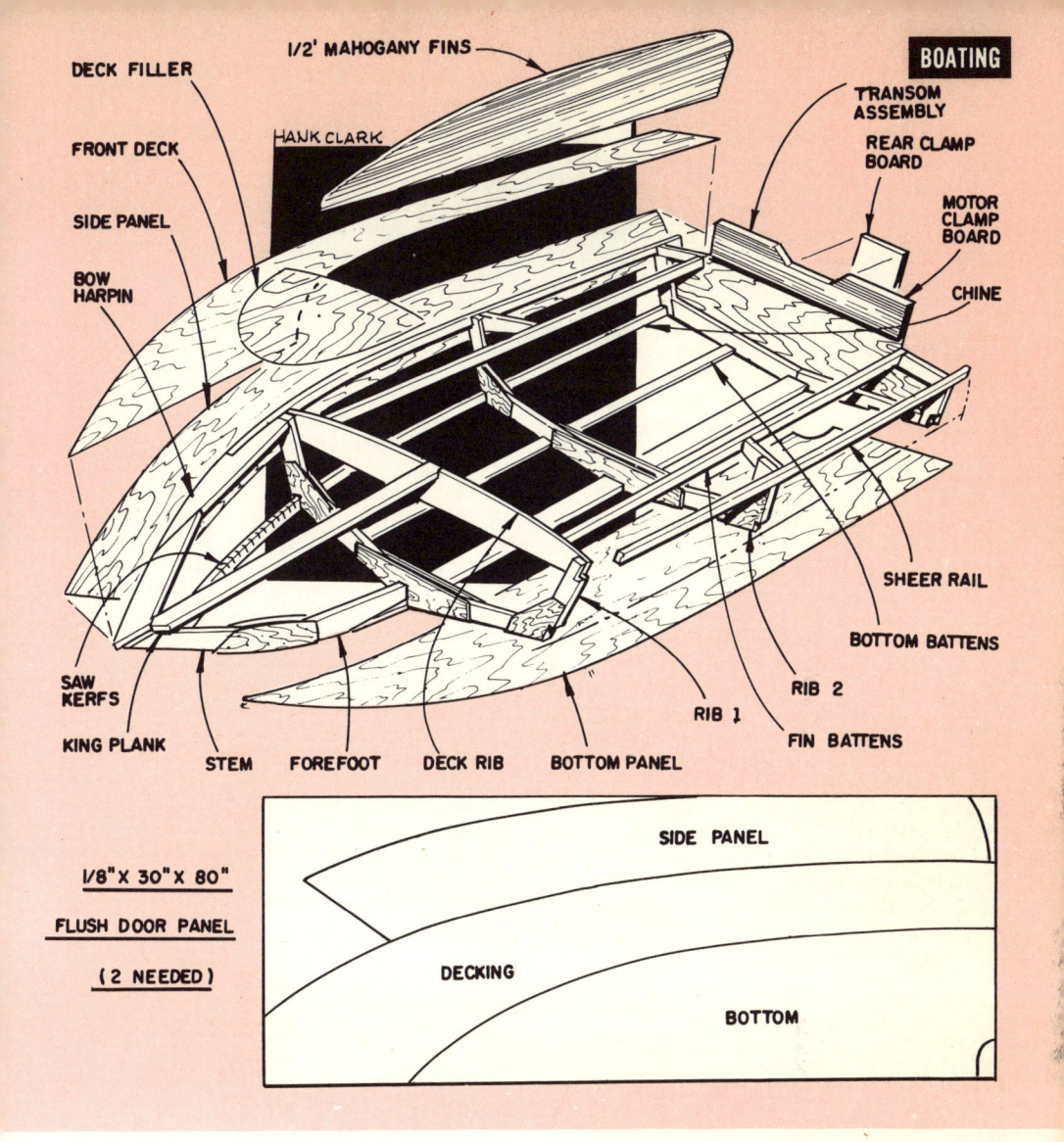

can carry an adult, the action gained by holding onto a tow rope a la water skiing. Lots of fun here. Foreward driving is obtained by re-rigging the fuel feed, substituting a car choke cable to create a remote fuel feed.

Assemble the two little ribs first (about an hour's work) and you will find there's still time to make the transom in one evening. Lay out all the cut stock over the full-size rib plans, then put together with gussets, glue and nails. Transom is 1/8-inch ply plank, edged with 3/8-inch fir. Nail through the ply into the fir, using glue. Now cut the stem and forefoot stock, with band or jig saw, to curve, and join with ply gusset. Bow harpin is next, and is used because the sheer rail could never bend so sharply. Jig saw solid fir into curve, and join halves with plywood web under. Now for the jig setup. This is two rails of 2x4 onto which are placed all ribs, transom, stem, and harpin. Nail a 1x2 across both ribs for support upside down on the rails. Space ribs, using keelson piece with clamps. Screw stem top to harpin, nail harpin to jig, join with keelson, which goes back to transom notch. Transom tilts 5 inches forward. After checking line up, drive a screw into each rib through the keelson, using glue liberally. Now add the sheer rails, screwing first to harpin's edge. Then bend back to transom notch with one screw per rib.

Now comes a more difficult area of work, bending on the chines, over which the side and bottom panels join. From transom to Rib 1, o.k. but from there to stem the bend

BOATING

is too much for the ¾-inch mahogany. You could use fir, but this doesn't hold nails like mahogany. Solution is to cut a series of saw kerfs along the inside face of the chine, relieving the compressed grain. Then it bends readily. Water won't help. Space the cuts about ½ inch apart. As you bend toward the stem, plane on the bevel where the bottom ply lays, then secure with screws and glue to all ribs and stem. Now bevel all the chine, stem, and transom for good contacts of bottom and side ply panels, using a flexible stick to check your planing. Keelson also gets beveled in the process. Actually, you must fuss with this job as you would on any larger boat hull, since this is meant to keep water out with tight joints.

Now cut and place the two bottom battens into their notches, and secure using glue and screws. For planking, we used ⅛-inch mahogany plywood from flush door stock, getting all parts out of two sheets, 30x80 inches. Use a 4 by 8-ft. panel if that's available, and get all parts except deck out of one sheet. If ⅛ is not available, use ¼-inch plywood, but this will make the boat heavier and overly strong, and require much wetting around the stem bend. But it can be used. The side panels go on first as usual and are blanked out by following the figures given on the large scale art. Clamp a side panel to the frame, check for fit and lay, then put in about four pilot screws, as a position gauge. Then remove, swab with Weldwood glue along chine, sheers, and stem, then replace panel with the pilot screws. Immediately start driving in the aluminum nails every two inches along chine, stem and transom, and 3 inches along sheer. Anchorfast nails are fine, too, but the glues does the real holding job. Repeat this process for the other side, and for the two bottom panels. Bottom panels extend about 5 inches aft of transom bottom as afterplane. Use a back-up block when nailing into the chine forward of Rib 1, as the kerfs make it somewhat flexible until the glue all sets. Later when turning the boat over, work filler into these kerfs with a putty knife, a good Weldwood and saw dust mix, with water. Knock off the jig now, along with rib ties, and set the hull upright.

After taking pictures of Junior in it, remove the boy, and beg him to let you install the deck dash, followed by the fin battens back to the transom. Install the motor clamp now using plenty of glue, and back this up with the rear clamp board. Avoid nails here, and use clamps. Cut the decks out of the ⅛-inch plywood remaining and lay on with glue and nails. Trim, when dry, along the gunwales, and along fin batten. Plane the fin batten to a vertical plane, so that fin stands erect or vertical

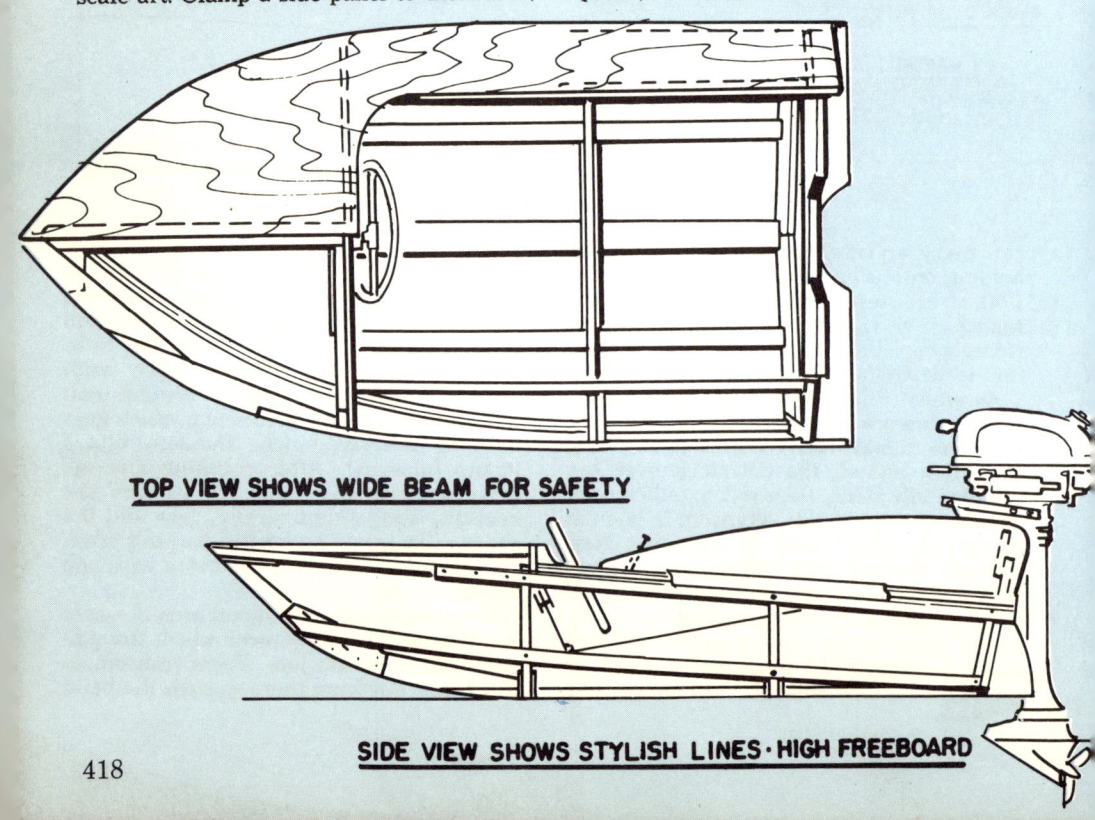

TOP VIEW SHOWS WIDE BEAM FOR SAFETY

SIDE VIEW SHOWS STYLISH LINES · HIGH FREEBOARD

418

BOATING

when glued and screwed in next. This fin also braces the transom motor board. Two long screws driven through it into the board, along with generous glue, do the job. Thus you have adequate freeboard for safety, and the new finny look. Screws go every 8 inches along each fin into batten. Now place glue blocks along the seams behind the transom, at bottom and sides to assist in waterproofing. Now you can varnish the hull if mahogany, or paint to taste.

Clamp on the 3 hp Evinrude, hook up the choke control, the steering, a quick removal device on drawings, and Junior can take off just like dad does. Watch the gas, because one pull sends the engine into drive, as there is no gear shift. Just aim away from everything, and in idle, the boat maneuvers slowly and surely.

One caution: Do not lean back against the motor at idle, since the boat will be end heavy then. Balance with the bricks. Under all circumstances, an elder should be watching. The boat is capable. Be sure the boy is. It's tremendous fun when all hands know what's what. •

SPECIFICATIONS

Length	6 ft.
Beam	35 in.
Depth	12 in.
Freeboard	9 in.
Weight	35 lbs.

BILL OF MATERIALS

FIR

¾"x2"x12'	Ribs-Transom
1⅛"x2"x36"	Stem-Forefoot
¾"x3"x88"	Harpin
¾"x1"x80"	Fin Battens
¾"x3"x32"	Dash

Weldwood Resin Powder

MAHOGANY

¾"x4"x22"	Motor Clamp
¾"x6"x12"	Rear Clamp
½"x1"x16"	Sheers-Battens
⅝"x1"x12"	Chines
¾"x2"x48"	Keelson
½"x8"x5'	Fins

PLYWOOD (Mahogany)

⅛"x30"x80"	(From Flush Door)
(or 4'x8' panel)	
⅛"x12"x33"	Transom
⅛"x12"x20"	Gussets
¼"x6"x32"	Bottom Gussets

HARDWARE

1½" No. 7	3 Doz.
1" No. 6	1 Doz.
1 Lb. ½"	Brads
5 Lb. ⅝"	Aluminum Nails (Planking)

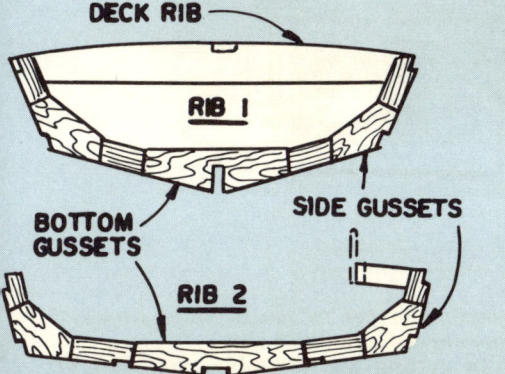

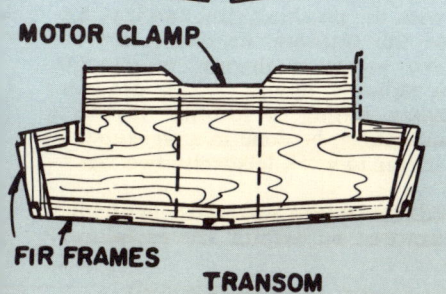

LARGE SCALE PLANS

with full size half ribs are available for building this boat at $2.00 per set. Send orders to Henry Clark, 36 Highwood Drive, Dumont, N. J. Specify FB-PEANUT.

BOATING

ROWBOAT

Make it for $35 from one piece of plywood

THIS 11-foot hull will cost you only $35 to build and comes out of a single sheet of ⅜-inch plywood. We used Weldwood Royal Marine Plywood for the job. It can be put together by almost any workshopper with a minimum amount of tools and time.

It rows smartly and gets a real burst of speed from a 3 to 5-hp outboard, actually planing like a runabout. It won't tip or trip with its generously flared sides and will take a rough clop. It can be lifted on top of a car by one man. It will carry up to four persons. The editors feel that it's impossible to get so much water transport anywhere for so little cost.

In cutting and assembly, you deal directly with the planking, first and last. Except for the transom, no other ribs are used. No precision jigging, alignments, plumbs, squares, angles, rakes, deadrise, coordinates, lofting or full-size layout is necessary. It can be done in a weekend, or if you prefer to work leisurely, two weekends.

In addition to the materials mentioned, tools required or helpful are as follows:

BOATING

Glue bottom batten for assembly to the transom bottom. The top batten goes on the same way, is screwed from the back.

Photo at left shows the transom as seen on a jig, with the two side panels screwed lightly to it for bend trials; cord tacks front end, as shown here.

a rip saw or saber, plane, ratchet screwdriver, Stanley's Surform (extremely handy for planing jobs), an electric drill with Screwmate.

The author tested the boat on Long Island Sound, using a 3-hp Evinrude Lightwin and a 5-hp Evinrude Fisherman. With the 5 attached, the boat climbed right out on a plane and clocked 17 mph with two persons aboard! With the Fisherman at full bore, the bow was rammed through every large wake available; it either parted through or planed right across the ridge of each. As a small scale runabout, this is a superb boat; it handles easily and offers real boating thrills, yet isn't overly much for even a child to handle. It makes a dandy second boat for every member of the family to enjoy.

When finishing, seal all plywood with Firzite or other filler and varnish or enamel to suit. Before beginning, study the drawings carefully, then study the step-by-step photographs. It's a simple boat to construct. And it'll offer a summer full of fun. Why not begin now? •

421

BOATING

BILL OF MATERIALS

3/8"x4'x14' marine plywood (one)
1"x3"x13" mahogany (keel and lower transom batten)
1"x1½"x10' mahogany (2) (chines)
1"x1¼"x11' mahogany (2) (shear)
1"x1¼"x10' mahogany (1) (keel)
2"x2"x12" inner stem (1)
1"x6"x60" transom top and knees
1"x10"x48" seat (1)
1"x12"x48" seat (1)
1 lb. Weldwood waterproof glue
¾" no. 7 Screw-mate
2 gross ⅞" no. 7 brass screws
40 1¼" no. 8 brass screws

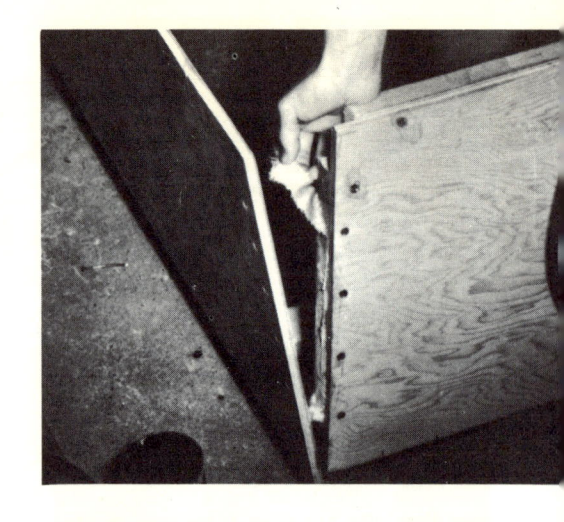

After drilling the sides for screws, glue them to the transom batten. Into the glue bed, lay linen strip which compresses, distributing the Weldwood marine glue entirely over the surfaces.

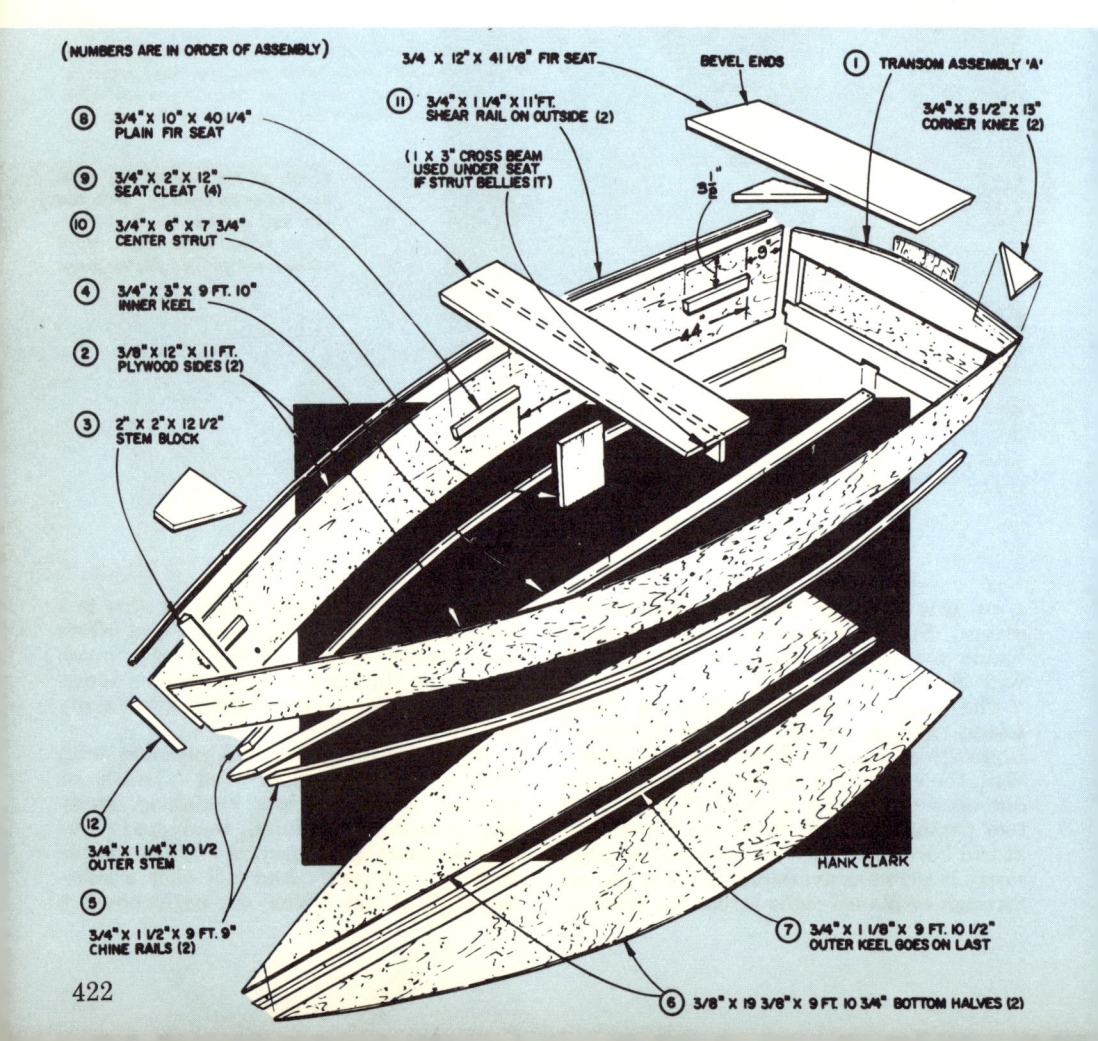

(NUMBERS ARE IN ORDER OF ASSEMBLY)

① TRANSOM ASSEMBLY 'A'
② 3/8" x 12" x 11 FT. PLYWOOD SIDES (2)
③ 2" x 2" x 12 1/2" STEM BLOCK
④ 3/4" x 3" x 9 FT. 10" INNER KEEL
⑤ 3/4" x 1 1/2" x 9 FT. 9" CHINE RAILS (2)
⑥ 3/8" x 19 3/8" x 9 FT. 10 3/4" BOTTOM HALVES (2)
⑦ 3/4" x 1 1/8" x 9 FT. 10 1/2" OUTER KEEL GOES ON LAST
⑧ 3/4" x 10" x 40 1/4" PLAIN FIR SEAT
⑨ 3/4" x 2" x 12" SEAT CLEAT (4)
⑩ 3/4" x 6" x 7 3/4" CENTER STRUT
⑪ 3/4" x 1 1/4" x 11 FT. SHEAR RAIL ON OUTSIDE (2)
⑫ 3/4" x 1 1/4" x 10 1/2" OUTER STEM

3/4 x 12" x 41 1/8" FIR SEAT
BEVEL ENDS
3/4" x 5 1/2" x 13" CORNER KNEE (2)
(1 x 3" CROSS BEAM USED UNDER SEAT IF STRUT BELLIES IT)

HANK CLARK

BOATING

Inner stem joins two sides at the bow, as shown here. This is planed to a bevel for a good fit, then glued and screwed in place. Get the stem absolutely vertical to avoid nose that is askew.

With the front bow aligned and drilled, glue and screw it closed, as described. Note that two chine rails with planed bevels are now ready to be wedged into place. Study the diagrams for details.

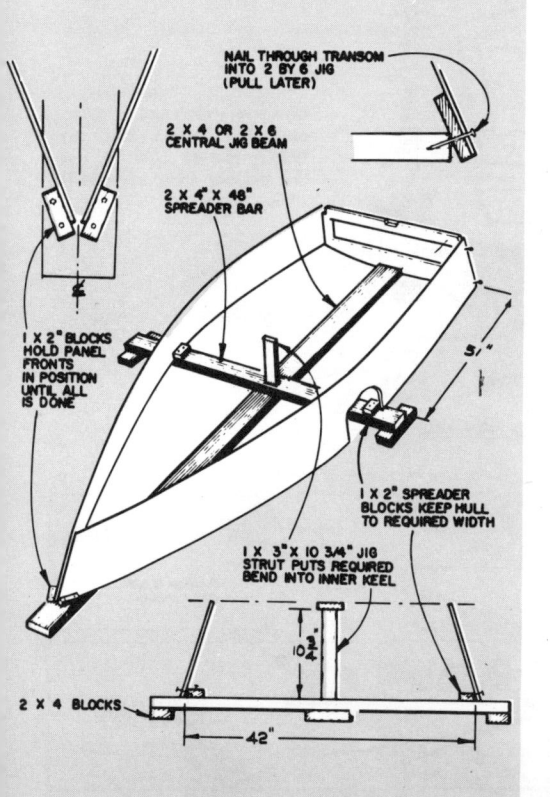

With inner keel secured to side panels, front end glued and screwed, chine rails are then bent in (as shown here), ready for securing to interior sides; the 3/16-inch exposure is to be planed.

Diagram labels:
- NAIL THROUGH TRANSOM INTO 2 BY 6 JIG (PULL LATER)
- 2 X 4 OR 2 X 6 CENTRAL JIG BEAM
- 2 X 4" X 48" SPREADER BAR
- 1 X 2" BLOCKS HOLD PANEL FRONTS IN POSITION UNTIL ALL IS DONE
- 1 X 2" SPREADER BLOCKS KEEP HULL TO REQUIRED WIDTH
- 1 X 3" X 10 3/4" JIG STRUT PUTS REQUIRED BEND INTO INNER KEEL
- 2 X 4 BLOCKS
- 10½"
- 42"
- 5"

BOATING

Chine goes into notch cut for it in transom. Note the two screws joining the inner keel to transom.

With 3/4-inch No. 7 Screwmate, predrill all holes for all panels two inches apart, as shown in photo.

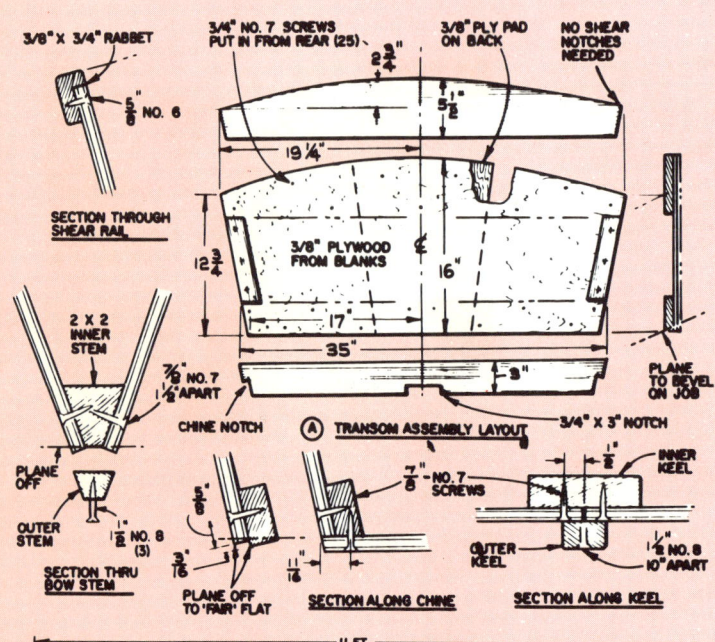

Diagram at left shows stern assembly details. Diagram below shows how to cut the panels from plywood.

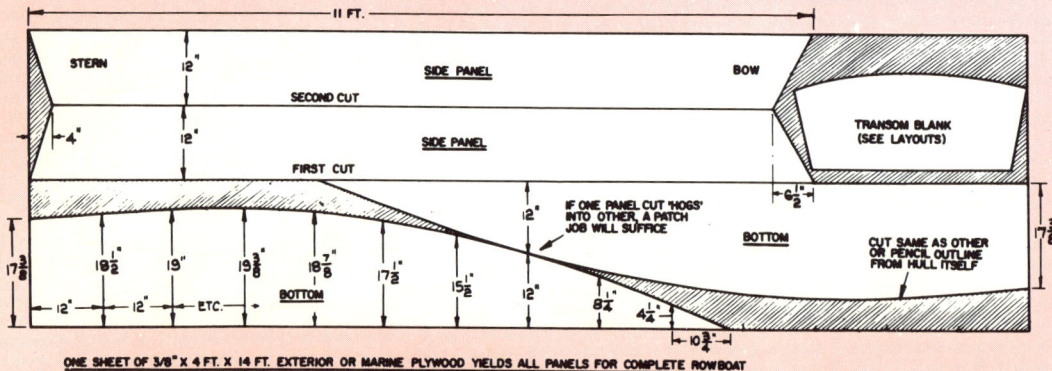

ONE SHEET OF 3/8" X 4 FT. X 14 FT. EXTERIOR OR MARINE PLYWOOD YIELDS ALL PANELS FOR COMPLETE ROWBOAT

424

BOATING

Ratchet screwdriver makes short work of setting the screws; no linen strips are used on the glued side joint since chine face is milled at factory.

The final job before the bottom goes on is that of checking the planing job with a "fairing" stick, which measures flatness for installing the bottom.

Stanley's Surform tool, with its many small chisels, makes baby-skin smooth surfaces, is ideal for job.

Weldwood mix is brushed on at this point. Note that half of bottom is already secured in place.

Schedule for screwing the hull is shown in diagram at right.

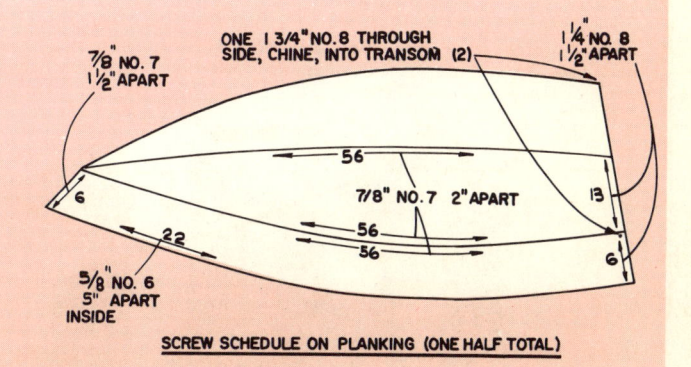

SCREW SCHEDULE ON PLANKING (ONE HALF TOTAL)

425

BOATING

Linen strips are laid into Weldwood glue before securing bottom. Again compress glue onto surface.

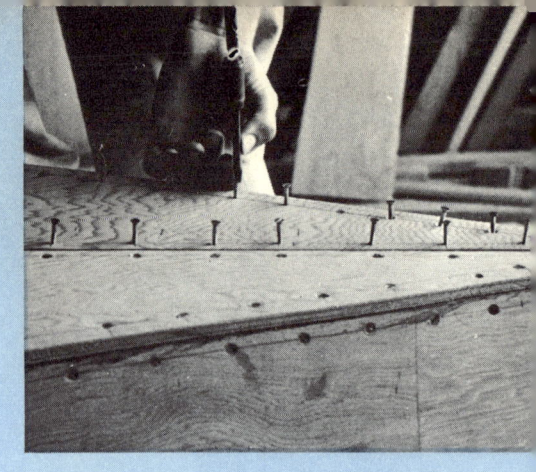

To strengthen hull, cover exposed bottom side joint with a strip of lumber for chafing guard.

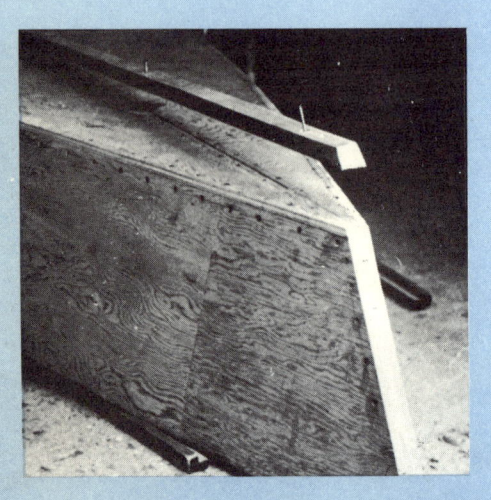

Outer keel goes on last, covers any gap between bottom halves, seals bottom, good launching skid.

The final touch for the nose is the outer stem. It will be planed to a taper after screwed into place.

Seats are now screwed to cleats placed on sides with glue. Screws are driven in from the outside.

Sheer rail is rabbeted to mount atop side panels, serving as frame plus rib rail. Screw holds batten.

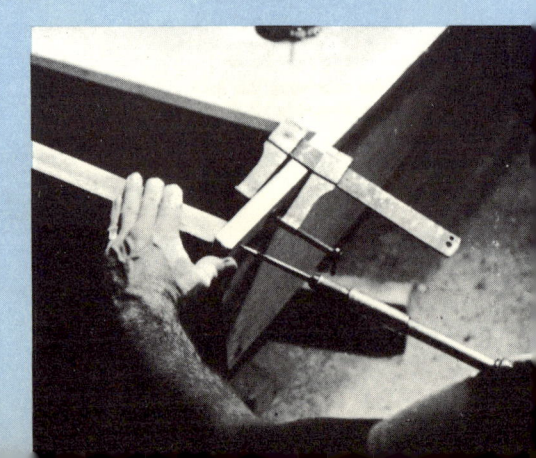

BOATING

Rest of sheer rail is secured from inside every six inches. Note how side panels fit flush into rabbet.

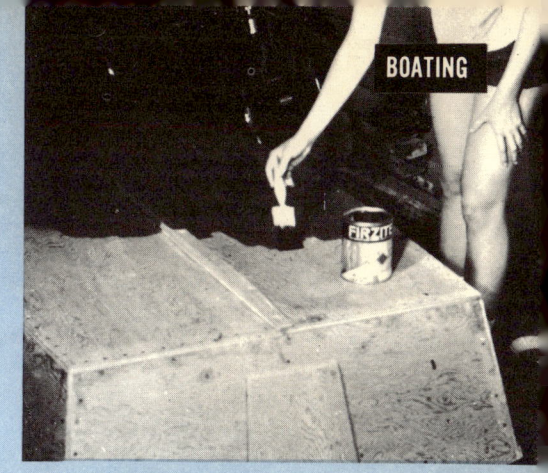

Before painting boat, apply two coats of Firzite which seals outer plys, is solid base for paint job.

Final result of all your effort will be this fast moving, highly attractive rowboat, shown here with motor.

427

BOATING

FOO-LING

By Hal Kelly

Build this class "A" or "B" runabout.

DRIVER got her to 45 mph and she is riding light for "A" despite his 170-pound weight.

FOO-LING will qualify under the A.P.B.A. rules for both "A" and "B" Stock Runabout and is very fast in both rough and good water. Highly maneuverable, she will bank in a tight turn right up on her side due to the fact that the upper chine is placed on the OUTSIDE of the non-trip which keeps the boat from sliding out. This type of construction I have never seen attempted on a plywood-planked hull. On a wider turn she can be made to ride the outside chine. As a marathon boat she is great. This strip of wood on the outside of her non-trip keeps her from diving into a big wave without offering a great deal of wind resistance. She rides beautifully when going into a headwind, won't wander all over the course, and runs as straight as an arrow. She will take any motor from 7 to 25 hp, but for motors other than the Champ Hot Rod and Mercury Quicksilver units, the transom will have to be made 17 inches high. Check with dealer for height.

Most important is getting the proper propeller for your outfit. This must be done before you try any hopping up of the motor. If you will give me the motor make, year, hp, and model number, and the weight of the boat with passengers, and what use you want to put your outfit to, I will tell you the make and kind of propeller you should use.

When building FOO-LING, please stick to the materials listed. With Fiberglas bottom all hardware and cushions she will weigh under 130 lbs. If you use Fiberglas on the bottom, you can use fir plywood—so what you save on plywood you can put into Fiberglas. With Fiberglas and all hardware she should cost about $130.00 and take about 80 hours to build.

After accumulating the stock listed in the bill of materials, you are ready to start on the ribs. Full sized rib drawings are available. Due to space limitations only half of the ribs are shown, but since the ribs are the same on both sides this will offer no problem. Cut out all of your rib components and place them on the full-size rib drawings using Anchorfast nails and screws as indicated on the drawing. A piece of thin tracing or wax paper will keep the glue off your plans.

The bottom of each frame is continuous from chine to chine; check drawing for size and shape. The sides of the frames are 1½ inches wide and straight-sided; the large gussets form the non-trip chines. Place the frame components on the layout and hold them in place with temporary fastenings. Place two plywood gussets over frames (one on each side) and fasten with glue and ¾-inch No. 16 Anchorfast nails. You will not have to drill pilot holes for this size nail. Use as many and about the same placement as illustrated on your full size rib drawings. When all 4 gussets are in place, carefully inscribe the center line on both sides.

Assemble the transom and transom frame. Cut transom from ¼-inch thick plywood. Transom framing is $1\frac{3}{16}$ inch or ⅞ inch thick. Assemble transom frame. All lapped joints should fit snugly. Coat mating surfaces of the joints and fasten together with ⅞-inch No. 8 screws. Carefully notch for battens, keel, bottom chine, and sheer before assembling transom frame to transom. Glue and fasten transom to transom frame with ¾-inch No. 16 Anchorfast nails placed about two inches apart.

The keel and stem are one piece, ½x1½ inches, but forward of Rib No. 1 it is backed by another piece ½x1½ inches. Both are glued together when the proper shape has been obtained, and steaming is not necessary. This can be done now or later on, when all the ribs are set up.

After the glue in the frames has hardened, cut the notches for the bottom chine and sheer. Note that only in Rib No. 2 do the bottom stringers go through, on transom, Rib No. 3 and Rib No. 1 they butt.

The boat should be built on a level wooden floor, or on a wooden cradle laid on a concrete floor (see step-by-step drawings) in an area about the size of a one-car garage. Lay out the center line and frame lines on the floor or cradle according to the spacings given in the drawing, using such temporary bracing as you feel necessary. Set up frames and transom; a couple of nails will hold each frame to floor or cradle. When all is securely erected, double check and make sure everything lines up. Remember, no hooks or rockers in the bottom. Coat the bottom stringers and notches with glue and slip into place. Then fasten to ribs and transom with small blocks; glue and fasten in place with

YOU don't have to use this type of jig. The one illustrated on page 432 is adequate.

TRANSOM with afterplane in place. Two drain holes proved ideal for marathons.

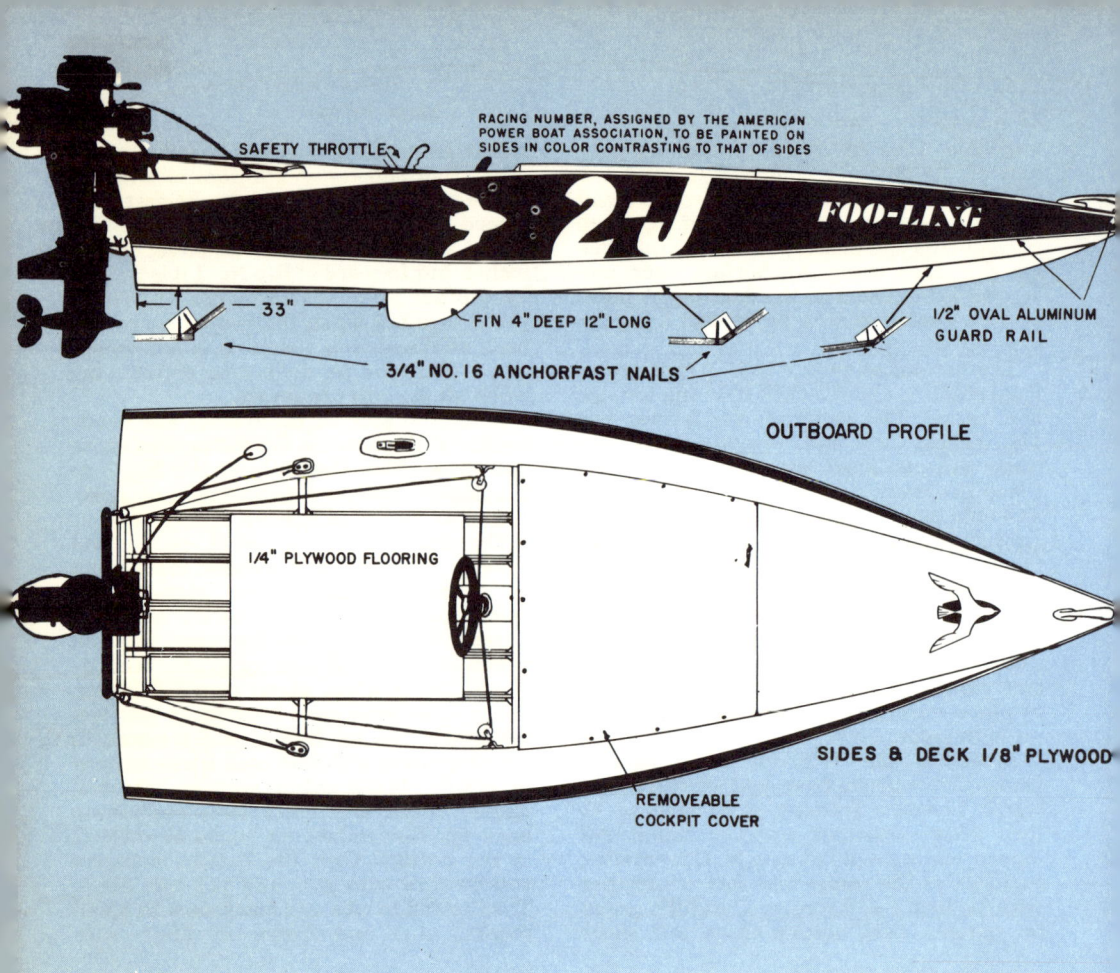

1-inch No. 16 steel brads. Next slip the keel in place with glue and 1¼-inch No. 8 flathead wood screws, using two screws to secure to transom and all ribs, and one about every 8 inches to the bottom stringer. The same procedure is used on all battens except that one screw is used to fasten to transom and all ribs. Next secure the bottom chine and sheers, using glue and 1½-inch No. 8 flathead wood screws. Where they butt against the stem and transom, bevel them to obtain a good landing; one screw at each frame, transom and stem. The bottom chine is cut thinner (⅝ inch thick) from the bow to Rib No. 1, where it gradually takes on its original thickness; this will allow it to bend easier and lighten the nose. Don't forget fin bracing from Rib No. 2 to Rib No. 3. Add 1 inch after plane to transom.

Fairing is probably one of the most important phases. If you have done a good job of setting up the frames, this should not be too difficult a task. Use a plane and a good wood file. Carefully trim and fair so the plywood planking will lie on all structural members. Check the fair from time to time as you progress by springing battens around the structure. Remember that from Rib No. 2 to the transom the bottom must be perfectly flat, and the plywood bottom can't be flat unless the structural members are faired flat. The non-trip chines are fitted first. A large sheet of wrapping paper will come in handy to give you a rough idea of their shape. Cut the panels a bit oversize, clamp in place and mark the outline of the bottom chine. Remove them and cut out a wee bit over size. Remember to glue and fasten in place the ⅛-inch thick by 1¼-inch square wood blocks at the top of the non-trip chine of each rib. The bottom goes over the edge of the chine except up toward the front where they butt each other. After the non-trip chine is fitted, glue and fasten it in place using ¾-inch No. 16 Anchorfast nails to transom, bottom chine and stem, and one nail at the top edge of the chine at the transom and each rib.

INBOARD PROFILE

1/4" PLYWOOD KNEES
DASH 1/2" THICK MAHOGANY
UPPER CHINE 7/8" SQ
SHEER 7/8" SQ
KEEL 1/2" X 1-1/2"
BOTTOM CHINE 7/8" X 1-3/4"
1 INCH SQUARES
ALL STRINGERS 1/2" X 2-1/2"
KEEL—FROM RIB 1 TO BOW 2 PIECES 1/2" X 1-1/2" BENT & GLUED TOGETHER

KEEL, BATTENS, CHINES, AND SHEERS NOTCHED INTO TRANSOM FRAME ONLY NOT TO EXTEND THROUGH TRANSOM. TRANSOM 1/4" PLYWOOD

DECK FRAMING

COMBING 1/2" X 1-3/4"
SEAT 10" BY 30"
TRANSOM FRAMING 7/8" THICK MAH.
FIN BRACE
17"
STRINGES 1/2" X 2-1/2"
BATTENS 1/2" X 1-1/8"

STRINGERS BUTT ON BOTH SIDES OF RIB 3

INCHES FEET
12 9 6 3 0   1   2

FRAMING SET-UP

FLOOR LINE
48" RIB 1 32" RIB 2 28" RIB 3 24" TRANSOM
14° ANGLE

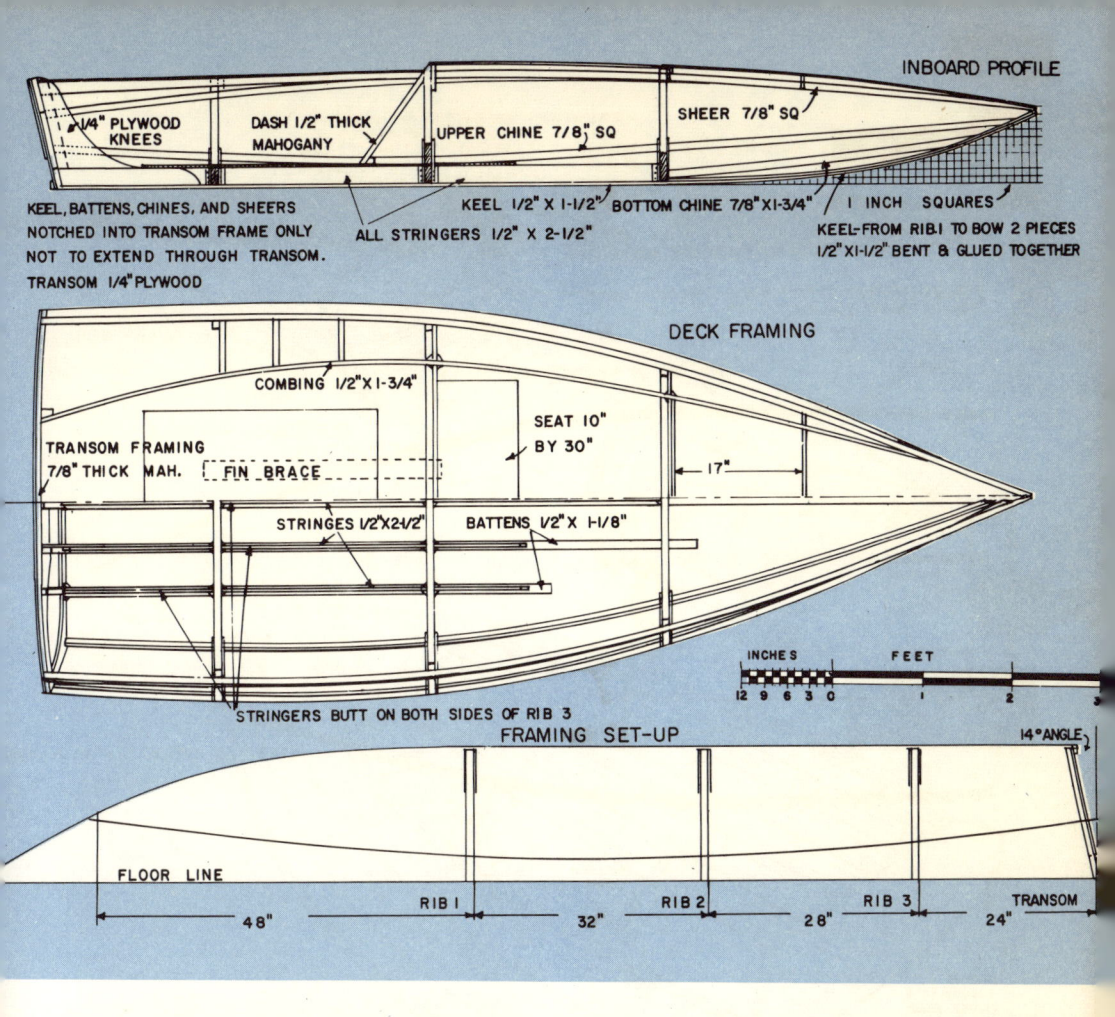

You will have to fair the bottom of the non-trip where the bottom will rest on it, and up toward the front where the bottom butts the chine. The bottom goes on much the same way and is all one piece with a V cut in the front to allow the bottom to come to a V. Up toward the front it will take a little careful fitting to make the bottom butt into the non-trip chine. Use a few screws to temporarily hold the bottom in place while you are fitting it. Mark on the bottom from the inside where all the battens, etc., come in contact.

Glue is applied to all structural members that the bottom will touch, and also to the bottom where you have marked areas the battens, etc., will contact. Put the bottom in place (a two-man job) and screw in the same screws that held it temporarily in place while you were fitting the bottom. Three-fourth-inch No. 16 Anchorfast nails are used to fasten the bottom to the transom, keel, battens and stem. Place about every 1¾ inches apart and countersink a bit (about $\frac{1}{16}$ inch). The bottom is best fastened to the battens forward of Rib No. 2 with ⅝-inch No. 8 flathead wood screws, placed about every 4 inches apart, and countersink about $\frac{1}{16}$ inch. After the bottom is dry, plane the edge at the same angle as the chine, except toward the back where it is allowed to remain square. This gives you a little lip to help grip the water on turns.

The upper chine is now fastened in place. This is ⅞ inch square and starts to taper toward the front to nothing at the very front. This taper starts about 5 feet from the front. Glue and 1½-inch No. 8 flathead wood screws are used to fasten the upper chine to all ribs and transom, well countersunk. From the inside the non-trip is fastened to the upper chine with ¾-inch No. 16 Anchorfast nails set 1¾ inches apart. At the very front this upper chine is best clamped in place until the glue is dry. At this point take the boat off the floor or jig and set it up on two well-padded horses at a good workable height. Saw off the extra piece on transom and ribs.

431

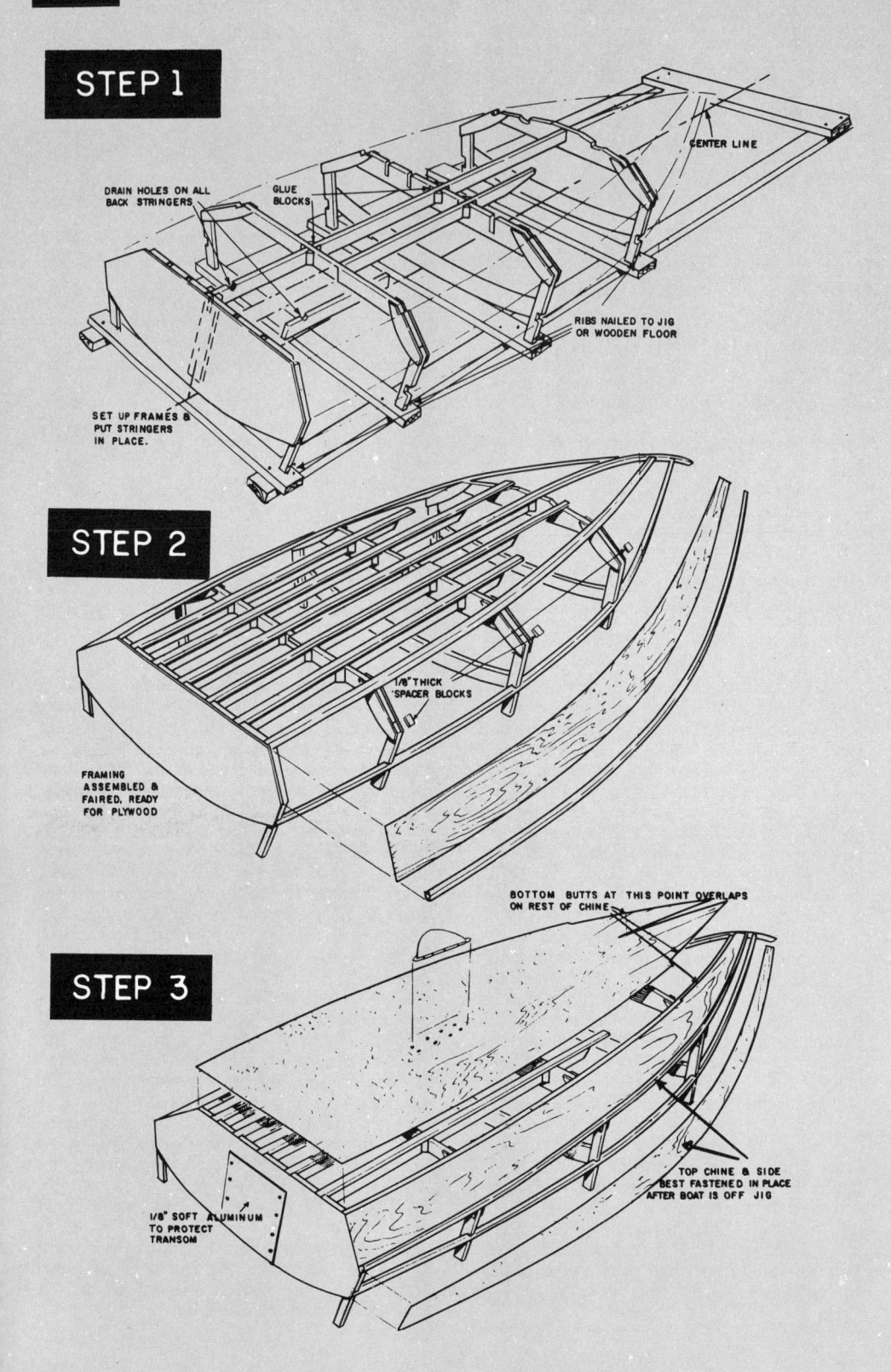

BOATING

STEP 1

- CENTER LINE
- DRAIN HOLES ON ALL BACK STRINGERS
- GLUE BLOCKS
- RIBS NAILED TO JIG OR WOODEN FLOOR
- SET UP FRAMES & PUT STRINGERS IN PLACE.

STEP 2

- 1/8" THICK SPACER BLOCKS
- FRAMING ASSEMBLED & FAIRED, READY FOR PLYWOOD

STEP 3

- BOTTOM BUTTS AT THIS POINT OVERLAPS ON REST OF CHINE
- TOP CHINE & SIDE BEST FASTENED IN PLACE AFTER BOAT IS OFF JIG
- 1/8" SOFT ALUMINUM TO PROTECT TRANSOM

NON-TRIP chines in place and ready for bottom planking, which is in one piece.

TRANSOM with all bracing in place. Varnish the inside at this time, give 4 coats.

Fashion the deck beam, cockpit coaming, and other braces according to the plan; all are ½ inch thick. The cockpit coaming runs from 3½ inches wide at the transom to ¾ inch wide where it is fastened to the inside of the sheer. Fit transom bracing and knees in place as indicated in drawings and photos. Knees are glued and fastened to the stringers and transom bracing with Anchorfast nails and screws. If you use a flush throttle, now is the time to put in the bracing for it.

Now fair off the upper chine and fit it to the sides. The side is glued and fastened in place with ¾-inch No. 16 Anchorfast nails spaced 1¾ inches apart. When the side is dry, fair off at the upper chine as shown in the full size Rib Drawings; also fair at the sheer line. The side decking is glued and fastened in place with ¾-inch No. 16 Anchorfast nails. The deck beam on Rib No. 1 is built up on one side so you can slip the removable cockpit cover in place after the front middle decking is fastened in place. Front middle decking is fastened in place in the same way as the side decking. Glue and fasten flooring in place with ¾-inch No. 16 Anchorfast nails. This forms a structural part of the bottom and will prevent it from warping or cupping.

The front seat offers no problem and is not glued in place. Use ⅞-inch No. 8 flathead wood screws. Sand the entire boat down and varnish or paint to suit your taste. Remember to varnish under the floor boards BEFORE you fasten them in place. Also, it is a good idea to varnish the entire inside before the decking is put in place. Give the inside 4 coats. The bottom, to the top of the non-trip chine, is fiberglass. Read fiberglassing instructions on page 68. Now screw fin in place and install hardware. I bolt my back lifting handles in place as I use them to tie down my motor.

Now for that first test run! If you are racing, be sure to have a good, sound, safe helmet. Always wear it and a good life jacket with collar, even when testing. Motor angle and height are very important for racing and a motor ⅛ inch too high or low has lost many a race. A marine speedometer is handy to have while making these adjustments. Spend a little time with your outfit; learn how to handle her; get the feel; find out where the best place is to kneel in her when turning, both in calm and rough water. The first turn in a race is no place to learn the feel of your boat. Remember, you have a great boat, but it is only as good as the driver.

BOATING

BILL OF MATERIALS

BRONZE, MONEL or EVERDUR FASTENINGS
- 2 dozen ⅝" #8 flathead wood screws
- 1 gross of ⅞" #8 flathead wood screws
- 2 gross of 1¼" #8 flathead wood screws
- 4 dozen of 1½" #8 flathead wood screws
- 3 lbs. of 1" #16 Anchorfast nails 950 to lb.
- 8 carriage bolts ¼" x 4" with nuts and washers

PAINT PRODUCTS
- 5 lbs. of Weldwood glue
- 1 lb. of Wood Dough or similar surface filler
- 1 gal. of Spar varnish for interior, decking, and exterior

PLYWOOD
- Decking and sides 2 sheets of marine grade plywood ⅛" x 4' x 8'
- Bottom non-trip chines, seat, and flooring 2 sheets of Marine grade Plywood ¼" x 4' x 12'

SITKA SPRUCE or WHITE CEDAR
- Sheers and upper chine .. 4 pieces ⅞" sq. x 12'
- Battens .... 4 pieces ½" x 1⅛" x 8'
- Keel .... 1 piece ½" x 1½" x 12'
- Bottom stringer .... 1 piece ½" x 2½" x 8'
- Bottom stringers .... 4 pieces ½" x 2½" x 7'
- Frames .... 1 piece ⅞" x 12" x 12'
- Deck frames, etc. .... 1 piece ½" x 8" x 12'

HONDURAS MAHOGANY
- Inside of keel at bow .... 1 piece ½" x 1½" x 5'
- Transom framing .... 1 piece ⅞" x 8" x 16'
- Bottom chine .... 2 pieces ⅞" x 1¾" x 12'
- Dash and dash beam ...... 1 piece ½" x 7" x 7'

HARDWARE
- 1 Steering wheel
- 1 piece of steering rope 26'
- 1 Safety throttle
- 1 Bowden throttle cable 5' long
- 1 Racing fin
- 2 Forward steering pulleys, with anchor straps
- 2 Rear pulleys
- 2 Steering line tieback
- 2 Stern lifting handles
- 1 Bow handle
- 24' of ½" oval aluminum
- 2 Steel 'S' hooks to hold rope block to steering bar

FIBERGLAS

The bottom of FOO-LING is Fiberglased, up to the top of the non-trip chine at the expense of 10 extra lbs. Costs ran me a little less than 40 cents a foot. I used a medium weight glasscolth, 50" wide, which left no seam on the bottom at all. A thin application of the plastic was applied to the bare wood with a brush. After it had hardened (the next day), I laid the cloth over the bottom and trimmed to fit. You need not cut out a V for the front as it drapes over the bow very well. A generous coat of plastic was applied to the bottom, the cloth laid over the bottom and smoothed out, and more plastic was applied with a squeegee to smooth. The cloth becomes almost invisible if applied correctly. The next day with a grinder I carefully ground down the surface so that it was smooth, flat, and even, and one more coat was applied with a brush, and carefully smoothed with a lot of elbow grease and wet sandpaper. Then a lacquer compound was used to give a plate-glass finish. Fiberglas is composed of a plastic and a hardener plus the glass cloth or mats. You have to work rather fast. It's a two man job as the "pot life" is short or long depending on how much hardener you use. By short "pot life" I mean that the mixture hardens in the pot before it hardens on the boat. One minute it is liquid, but then it starts to turn into a jelly and proceeds to get very hard in a matter of seconds. I would say that for the beginner it is a dog job. But the results are very rewarding. It is literally as tough as glass and just as smooth. This is not intended to be a full discussion by any means, but just a few words to let you know what you are in for if you would like to Fiberglas the bottom.

Some say it's luck that often wins a race, but you will note that the best drivers make their own luck. You have a good boat, but a well-tuned motor and the proper prop, plus good setup also help to win. Oh yes, and the driver counts, too—you know darn well he does.

To get your racing numbers for A.P.B.A. racing, write to the American Power Boat Association; 2534 St. Aubin Ave.; Detroit 7, Michigan.

A mistake many new drivers make is that in testing and adjusting their motor too early the day of the race—setting their motor for the best speed at that time. A few hours later their race comes up, and perhaps by now, a strong wind has roughened the water so that in the middle of the race they find they are much too high or kicked out too much.

It's always nice to test out on good water; it's nice riding and you go much faster.

BOATING

FIBERGLAS cloth cut to size. Notice how well it drapes over stem without cutting a V.

ALL SET up and ready to run. Note aluminum plate under motor to protect transom.

But I make it a point to do at least half of my testing on rough water. Try setting up some buoys and practice turns. I know a few fellows who set up their own course and practice out on it as if they were running a race; they even have a starting clock to practice on. I'll admit that there's nothing like an actual race for experience, but testing will be a big help.

Motor setup is not easy to learn. It's hard to know whether to kick it in (for rough water) or out (for calm water) or how high to run. You can look around and see how the better drivers are running their boats, but frankly this is of little help because boats and driving styles differ. I have seen two good drivers at a race both running the same make hydro, motor, and prop: one ran on the fourth motor notch, the other on the third. Both took a first and a second, and were tied on time. I'm sure this would confuse any beginner. When you practice for a race, don't just run around. Try all kind of setups.

Pickup means a lot in short-course racing and I often sacrifice a few miles of top speed for acceleration. As an example, before one race a friend of mine was passing me on a long stretch down the river. He was running faster than anyone else. With a beautiful start he hit the first buoy first in a three-buoy turn, but coming out of the turn five fellows passed him and I think he finally finished a sad sixth. I managed to steal a second in that heat.

The main thing you can do to a stock motor and remain legal is to carefully set up your reed cage and points. Run the exact amount of oil in your motor that the manufacturer recommends—no more, no less. In breaking a new motor don't run a rich oil mixture, but set your high speed jet a little richer for the first hour, with the spark on two-thirds. Run the motor at half-throttle for 15 minutes. Then give the motor a five-minute break and run again for 15 minutes. Do this for about one hour running time. Now take her out and boot it wide open for a stretch, but for the next two hours running time refrain from any continuous high speed runs.

I always run my motor with a full butterfly. In case of a flip it's much safer for you and the other drivers, and will save you from a blown motor.

All in all it's a great sport and I never met a finer group of people than those within the sport. We cover about 8,000 miles each year just going to the races. When I go, the whole family goes: wife, two kids and the dog. Win, lose, or draw, we all have a picnic. See you at the races. •

LARGE SCALE PLANS

with full rib drawings (plus six colorful decals) are available for building this boat. They are $10 post paid. Order from Hal Kelly's Plans, P. O. Box 2095, Fort Pierce, Florida. Specify Plan FB-FOO-LING.

435

BOATING

MALAHINI

By Glen L. Witt, N.A.

A 16-foot outboard runabout with generous beam.

MODERN STYLING, a deep vee and a wide beam give Malahini dry, safe characteristics.

A GENEROUS SIZE outboard runabout is the Malahini, 15 feet 11 inches in overall length, with an extreme beam of 6 feet 7 inches. She is a particularly versatile boat with the seats being of the floating type. That is, they may readily be removed, providing a flat area 9 feet long, and up to 5 feet 9 inches wide for carrying camping gear. The aft seat could be turned around and placed back to back with the front seat for trolling or for a water ski observer.

The generous vee in the fore portion, and the wide beam, make for a dry, safe boat. The construction is rugged, and intended to "take it." The self-bailing motor well prevents any sudden wave or backwash from entering the boat.

All lumber used should be first-grade white oak, dark red Philippine mahogany, or Sitka spruce. All plywood must be intended for marine or exterior use. All joints throughout the construction should be glued with rescorcinol or urea-resin glue. All fastenings should be bronze, hot-dipped galvanized, or brass.

BUILDING INSTRUCTIONS

FRAMES: The frames are fabricated from 1-inch material: oak, mahogany, or spruce. The bottom and side frame members are joined with a ⅜-inch plywood gusset on either side of the frames. The bottom frame members at No. 1, No. 2, and No. 3 are in single width from chine to chine. The frame at No. 4 has the two half frame members joined together by a floor timber of the same material as the frame. The plywood gussets are assembled to the frames with glue, and nailed with annular thread type nails. The floor timber on No. 4 is assembled with a minimum of five 1½-inch No. 8 screws per member. The notches for the various members may be cut after frame assembly.

TRANSOM: The ¾-inch plywood transom is framed with 1-inch oak, mahogany, or spruce. All notches must be cut into the framing members before assembly to the plywood transom. In assembly, fasten the frame to the transom with 1½-inch No. 8 screws, spaced approximately 6 inches apart.

STEM: The stem is built up from two laminations of ¾-inch thick exterior plywood. In assembly, coat the mating surfaces liberally with glue, and fasten together with 1½-inch No. 8 screws, spaced a maximum of 6 inches apart.

BREASTHOOK AND CHINE BLOCKING: These members are built up from two layers of ¾-inch exterior plywood. The breasthook is used between the sheer clamps, and the chine blocking between the chines at the stem junction.

TRANSOM KNEE: The transom knee is fabricated from three laminations of ¾-inch plywood. In assembly, the knee bolts to the keel and transom with 5/16-inch carriage bolts.

BUILDING FORM: Details for the building form are given in the plans. Basically, the form consists of two longitudinal setup members that are level, both lengthwise and athwartships. These are supported on legs, the whole being anchored to the floor. The frames are

436

BOATING

STEM, breasthook and chine block assembly is mounted to No. 4 frame. Note bolting.

PLUMB each frame on leveled building form, then brace to form to prevent movement.

CHINE members are fastened at stem, sprung about hull. Chine angles across blocking.

BEVEL chine with wood rasp at each frame for easy fairing. Follow contour of frame.

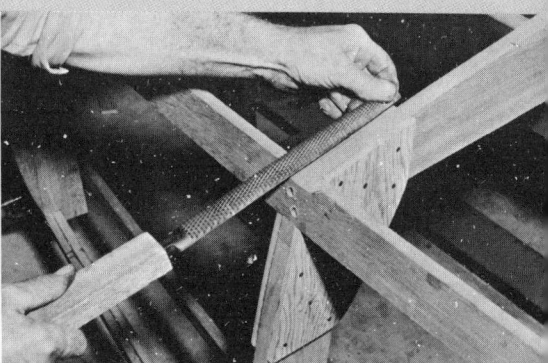

mounted bottom side up on the form, spaced per the dimensions shown, and accurately centered with a chalk line. The transom may be located by the use of the knee bolted to the keel. The height of the breasthook-stem assembly is carefully blocked to the dimension noted.

KEEL: The keel is a 1x4-inch member of oak, mahogany or spruce, laminated on the inside with ⅜-inch plywood. The keel is fitted into notches at the frame and transom, and fastened to them with 2-inch No. 10 screws.

CHINE LOG: The junction of the side planking and bottom planking is called the chine point, and the backing member is the chine log. This member is full length 1x2-inch oak or spruce. Fit into the frame notches, coat with glue, and fasten with 2-inch No. 10 screws.

SHEER CLAMP: The junction for the side planking and decking is the sheer, and the backing member is called the sheer clamp. Sheer clamps are built up from two laminations of ⅝x1¼-inch mahogany or spruce. The first layer is sprung around the hull, followed by the second layer, liberally coating the initial one with glue.

FAIRING: All of the members; sheer clamp, chine, keel, stem, and transom must be beveled or faired to allow the planking to lay flat on all areas. Care should be taken in the after section of the hull to assure that the running lines are true and straight. While fairing, always stand back from the hull and sight across the lines, to eliminate any humps or bumps in the fairing process.

BOTTOM BATTENS: The bottom 1x2-inch oak or mahogany battens are notched into each frame and the transom. They are located as noted per the drawings, and anchored in place with 2-inch No. 10 screws.

LIMBERS: Limber holes, to allow all bilge water to drain aft, should be notched on the outboard side of all longitudinals.

SIDE PLANKING: The ¼-inch side planking should be in full length. Shorter panels can be used, butt joined per the details. Lean the plywood panel against the side of the hull, and scribe around its extremities. Remove the panel and cut roughly to shape with a fine-tooth saw. The portion that will butt join with the bottom planking from approximately frame No. 4

437

BILL OF MATERIALS

OAK, MAHOGANY OR SPRUCE
  Frames, transom—40 random bd. ft., 1" stock
  Keel—1 piece 1"x4"x13'
  Battens—2 pieces 1"x2"x12'
          2 pieces 1"x2"x10'
  Chine log—2 pieces 1"x2"x18'
  Sheer clamp—4 pieces 5/8"x1¼"x18'
  Intermediate deck beam—1 piece 1"x4"x5'
  Deck battens—2 pieces 1"x2"x5'
  Strongback—1 piece 1"x3"x6'
  Motor well longitudinals—2 pieces 1"x4"x3½'
  Aft well deck beam—1 piece 1"x6"x3'
  Blocking, cleats—as required
  Floorboard battens—2 pieces 1"x2"x9'

D. F. PLYWOOD AB, EXT.
  Frame gussets, keel laminations—1 piece 3/8"x4'x8'
  Transom, stem, chine blocking, breasthook—1 piece 3/4"x4'x8'
  Floorboards, seats—3 pieces 3/8"x4'x9'
  Seat brackets—1 piece 3/4"x4'x6'

MAHOGANY FACED PLYWOOD EXT. AA
  Decking—2 pieces 1/4"x4'x8'

D. F. PLYWOOD AA MARINE
  Planking, side—2 pieces 1/4"x3'x18'
  Planking, bottom—2 pieces 3/8"x3'x16'

MAHOGANY
  Carlings—2 pieces 1/2"x4"x9'
  Dash—1 piece 1"x7"x6'
  Lower bumper rail—2 pieces 1"x4"x7'

MISCELLANEOUS
  Motor well brace—1 piece D. F. 2"x4"x3'
  Motor well plywood—cut from scraps of planking

FASTENINGS
  Screws: flat head, wood, bronze or hot dipped galvanized.
  3/4"   # 8—3 gross
  1"   # 8—4 gross
  1¼"   # 8—1 gross
  1½"   # 8—1 gross
  2"   #10—1 gross
  3"   #14—3 dozen
  Carriage bolts: complete w. nuts, washers, bronze or hot dipped galvanized.
  5/16"x4" —4 required
  5/16"x7" —2 required
  1/4"x2¼"—2 required
  Nails: annular ring type. bronze or monel 1" —2 lbs. 1¼"—1 lb.
  Glue: plastic resin type Weldwood or comparable volume Rescorinol type—10 lbs.

---

forward, must be fitted along the chine. The balance may be left long for subsequent trimming. Fasten the planking to all members, per the directions given in the fastening schedule.

BOTTOM PLANKING: The planking for the bottom is optionally ¼-inch or 3/8-inch plywood. For the rougher usage, the 3/8 inch in full length is recommended. Fit the bottom planking carefully along the part that will butt join with the side planking. Aft of this point, the bottom planking will lap the side planking to be planed off after installation. Fasten per the fastening schedule.

OUTER KEEL: The outer keel of 1-inch oak, mahogany or spruce is fastened over the joint of the bottom planking.

FIBERGLASSING: The fiberglassing of any fir plywood hull is a distinct advantage to prevent checking so common with fir plywood. A complete fiberglassing kit can be obtained from Glen L for covering the bottom only or for covering the bottom, sides, and transom. These kits provide complete material for the job including brushes, squeegee, acetone, resin, cloth, etc.

SPRAY RAIL: The 1x1¼-inch spray rail covers the junction of the side and bottom planking, and is fastened with 2-inch No. 10 screws, spaced 12 inches apart.

INTERMEDIATE DECK BEAM: The intermediate deck beam is installed as shown in the drawings, cut from 1-inch mahogany to the same crown as frame No.

FASTEN panel by clamping along chine at transom. Attach along chine line first.

BOTTOM panel clamped along centerline of stem. Attach forward from transition point.

BOATING

PLAN SET AND FULL SIZE PATTERNS are available for building this boat at a cost of $18.25. FRAME KITS which include the above are $96.00 (plus shipping costs). Illustrated Malahini plans sell for $9.25. Send all orders to Glen L. Marine Designs, 9152 E. Rosecrans, Bellflower, California. Specify plan FB-MALAHINI in whatever form.

TRANSOM

TRANSOM IS CUT FROM 3/4" PLYWOOD- FRAMED WITH 1" OAK OR MAHOGANY

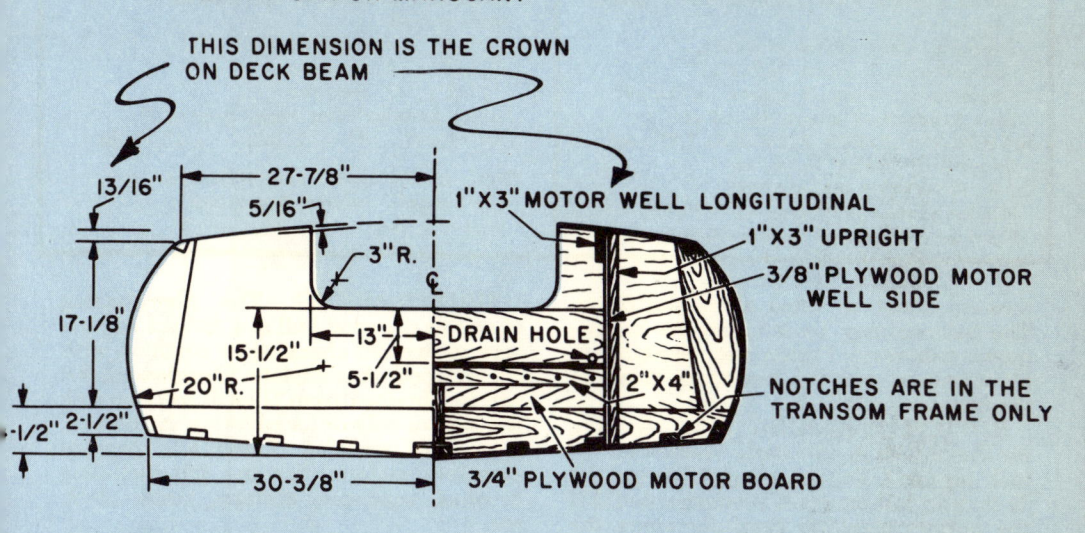

THIS DIMENSION IS THE CROWN ON DECK BEAM

13/16"
27-7/8"
5/16"
3" R.
1"X 3" MOTOR WELL LONGITUDINAL
1"X3" UPRIGHT
3/8" PLYWOOD MOTOR WELL SIDE
17-1/8"
15-1/2"
13"
5-1/2"
20" R.
2"X 4"
DRAIN HOLE
NOTCHES ARE IN THE TRANSOM FRAME ONLY
1/2" 2-1/2"
30-3/8"
3/4" PLYWOOD MOTOR BOARD

FRAME NO. 1

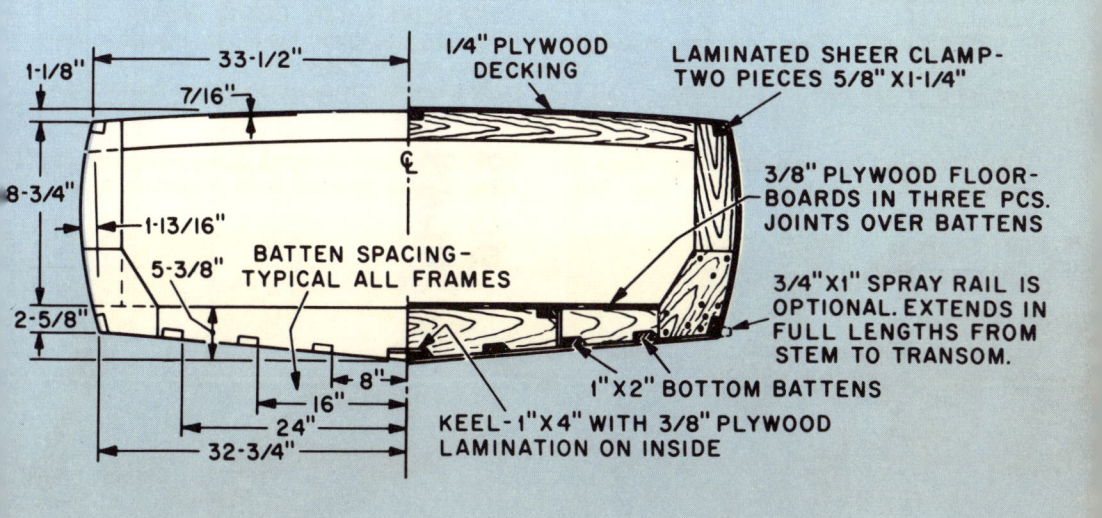

1-1/8"
33-1/2"
7/16"
1/4" PLYWOOD DECKING
LAMINATED SHEER CLAMP- TWO PIECES 5/8" X 1-1/4"
8-3/4"
1-13/16"
5-3/8"
3/8" PLYWOOD FLOOR- BOARDS IN THREE PCS. JOINTS OVER BATTENS
BATTEN SPACING- TYPICAL ALL FRAMES
3/4"X1" SPRAY RAIL IS OPTIONAL. EXTENDS IN FULL LENGTHS FROM STEM TO TRANSOM.
2-5/8"
8"
16"
1"X2" BOTTOM BATTENS
24"
32-3/4"
KEEL-1"X4" WITH 3/8" PLYWOOD LAMINATION ON INSIDE

439

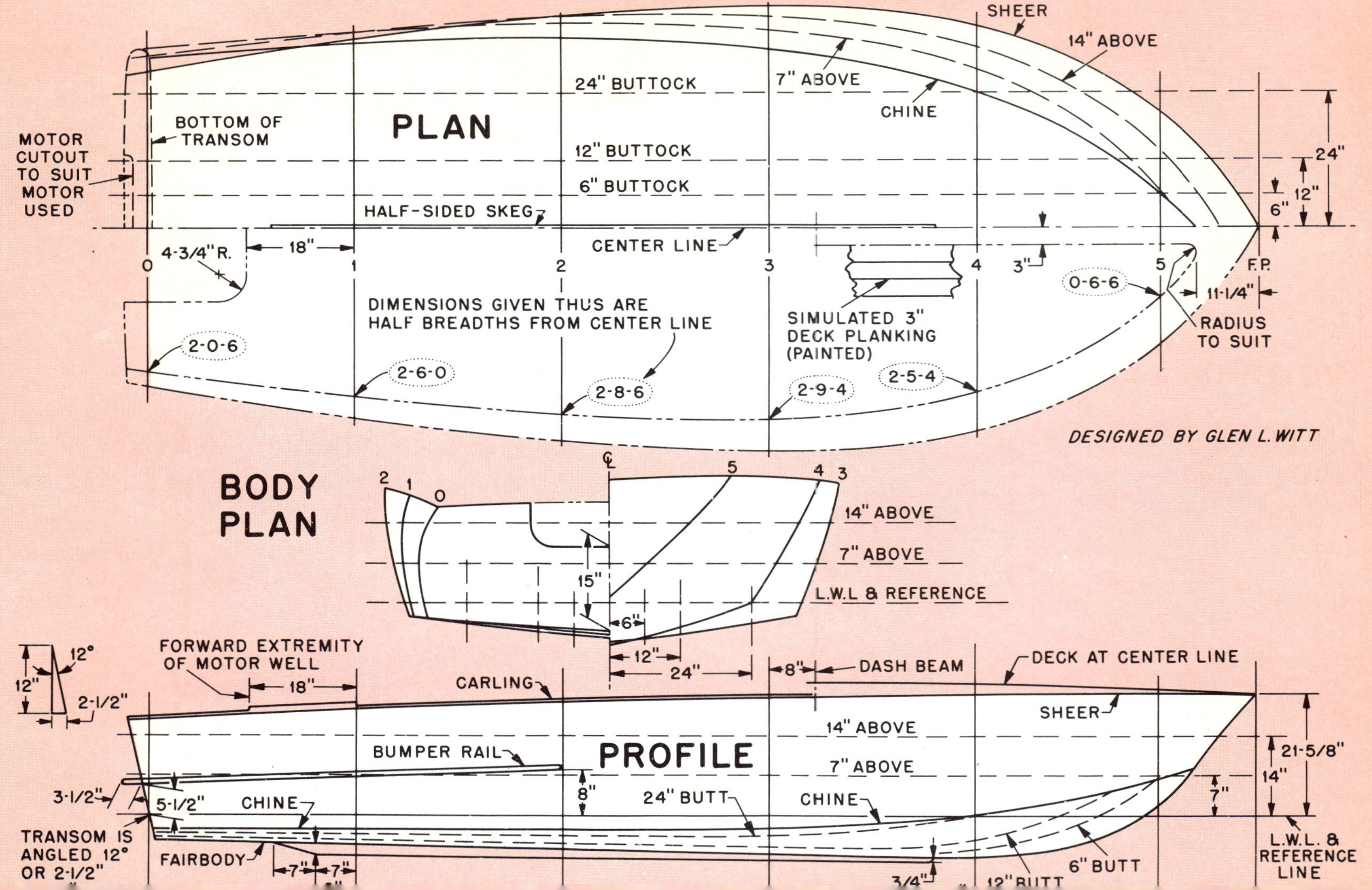
SHEER
14" ABOVE
7" ABOVE
CHINE
24" BUTTOCK
12" BUTTOCK
6" BUTTOCK
PLAN
BOTTOM OF TRANSOM
MOTOR CUTOUT TO SUIT MOTOR USED
HALF-SIDED SKEG
CENTER LINE
4-3/4" R.
18"
0
1
2
3
4
5
F.P.
24"
12"
6"
3"
11-1/4"
0-6-6
RADIUS TO SUIT
DIMENSIONS GIVEN THUS ARE HALF BREADTHS FROM CENTER LINE
SIMULATED 3" DECK PLANKING (PAINTED)
2-0-6
2-6-0
2-8-6
2-9-4
2-5-4
DESIGNED BY GLEN L. WITT
BODY PLAN
14" ABOVE
7" ABOVE
L.W.L & REFERENCE
15"
6"
12"
24"
8"
DASH BEAM
DECK AT CENTER LINE
FORWARD EXTREMITY OF MOTOR WELL
CARLING
12°
12"
2-1/2"
SHEER
PROFILE
BUMPER RAIL
21-5/8"
14"
7"
3-1/2"
5-1/2"
CHINE
24" BUTT
TRANSOM IS ANGLED 12° OR 2-1/2"
FAIRBODY
3/4"
12" BUTT
6" BUTT
L.W.L. & REFERENCE LINE

DECK FRAMING

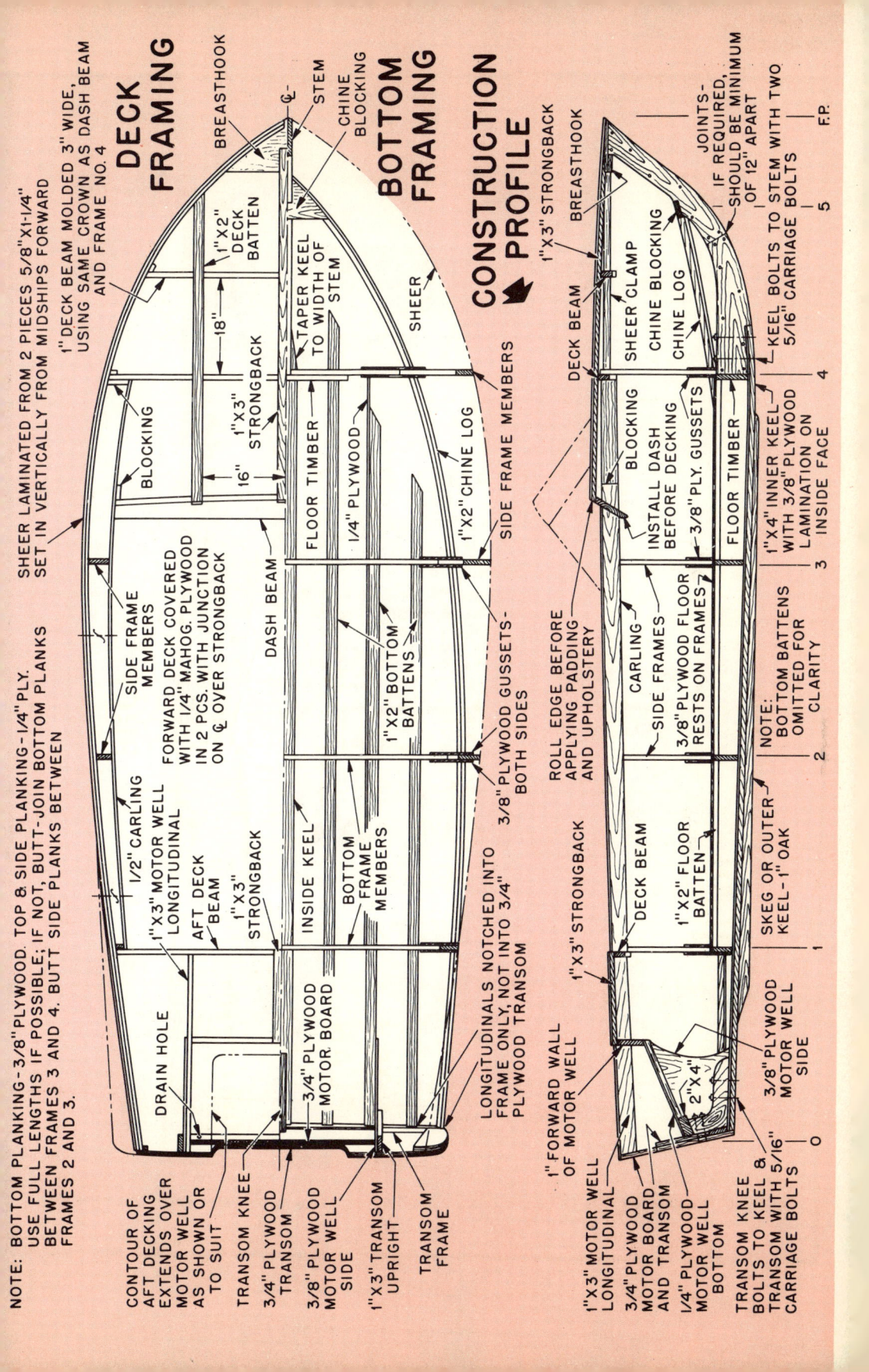

BOTTOM FRAMING

CONSTRUCTION PROFILE

FRAME NO. 2

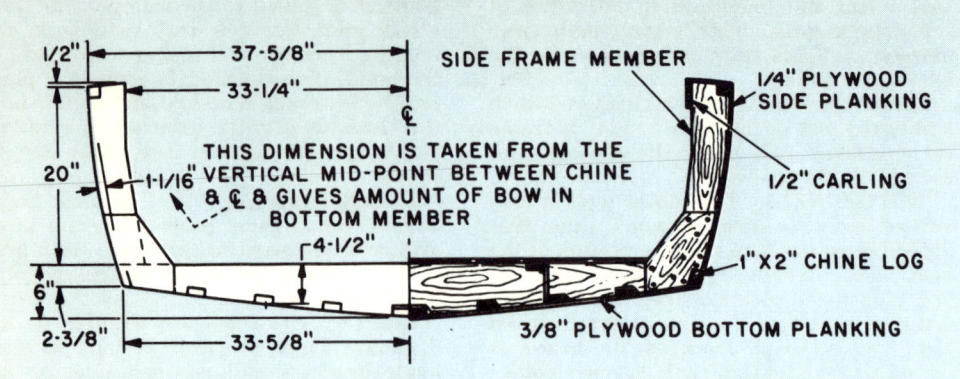

- 1/2"
- 37-5/8"
- 33-1/4"
- SIDE FRAME MEMBER
- 1/4" PLYWOOD SIDE PLANKING
- 20"
- 1-1/16"
- THIS DIMENSION IS TAKEN FROM THE VERTICAL MID-POINT BETWEEN CHINE ₵ & ₵ & GIVES AMOUNT OF BOW IN BOTTOM MEMBER
- 1/2" CARLING
- 4-1/2"
- 1"X2" CHINE LOG
- 6"
- 2-3/8"
- 33-5/8"
- 3/8" PLYWOOD BOTTOM PLANKING

FRAME NO. 3

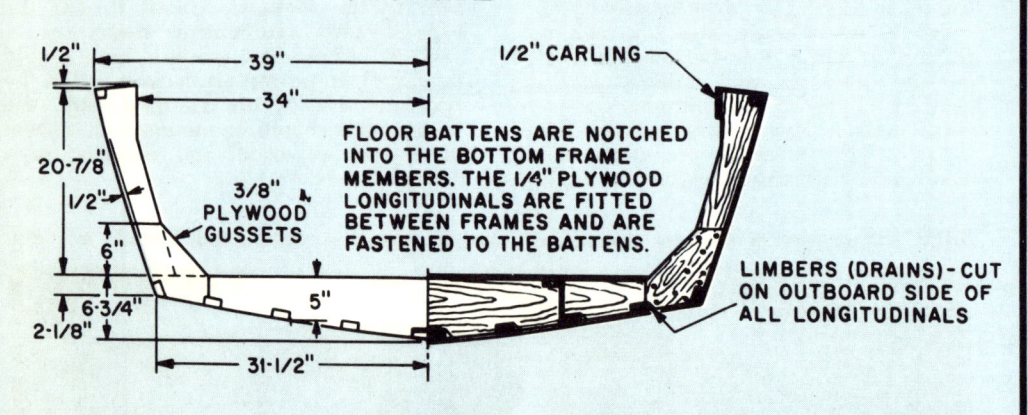

- 1/2"
- 39"
- 34"
- 1/2" CARLING
- 20-7/8"
- 1/2"
- 3/8" PLYWOOD GUSSETS
- FLOOR BATTENS ARE NOTCHED INTO THE BOTTOM FRAME MEMBERS. THE 1/4" PLYWOOD LONGITUDINALS ARE FITTED BETWEEN FRAMES AND ARE FASTENED TO THE BATTENS.
- 6"
- 5"
- 6-3/4"
- 2-1/8"
- 31-1/2"
- LIMBERS (DRAINS) - CUT ON OUTBOARD SIDE OF ALL LONGITUDINALS

FRAME NO. 4

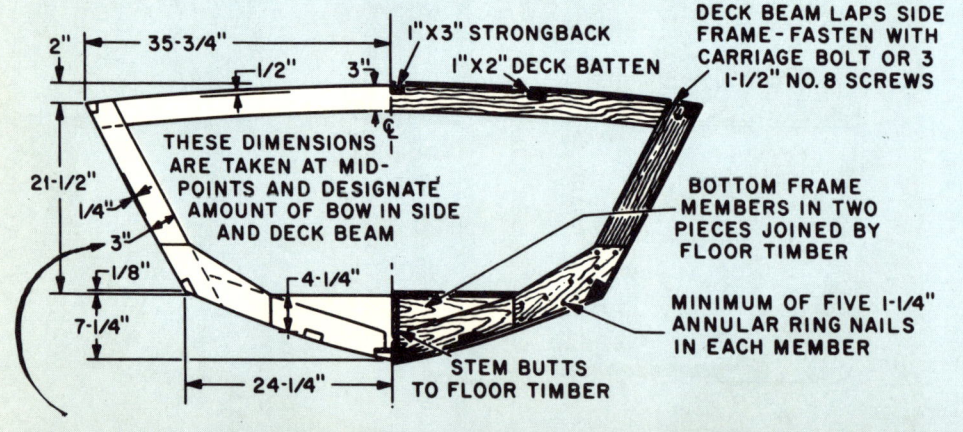

- 2"
- 35-3/4"
- 1/2"
- 3"
- 1"X3" STRONGBACK
- 1"X2" DECK BATTEN
- DECK BEAM LAPS SIDE FRAME - FASTEN WITH CARRIAGE BOLT OR 3 1-1/2" NO. 8 SCREWS
- 21-1/2"
- 1/4"
- 3"
- THESE DIMENSIONS ARE TAKEN AT MID-POINTS AND DESIGNATE AMOUNT OF BOW IN SIDE AND DECK BEAM
- BOTTOM FRAME MEMBERS IN TWO PIECES JOINED BY FLOOR TIMBER
- 1/8"
- 4-1/4"
- 7-1/4"
- 24-1/4"
- STEM BUTTS TO FLOOR TIMBER
- MINIMUM OF FIVE 1-1/4" ANNULAR RING NAILS IN EACH MEMBER

MINIMUM OF 3" WIDTH ON BOTH - SIDES & BOTTOM MEMBERS AND DECK BEAMS - (TYPICAL OF ALL FRAMES)

4. Fasten to the blocking on the sheer, as indicated.

CARLING: The carling is the member that forms the longitudinal extremity of the cockpit area. This 1-inch mahogany member extends from the transom to the No. 4 deck beam.

DASH BEAM: The dash beam of 1-inch mahogany, cut at the same crown as frame No. 4, is fastened between the carlings with 2-inch No. 10 screws.

MOTOR WELL: The motor well is fabricated from ⅜-inch plywood sides that extend from the batten at the bottom of the boat to the decking longitudinal member, and is fastened to a 1x3-inch transom upright, as indicated. On top of the transom knee, a 2x4-inch Douglas fir brace is bolted to the transom with ¼-inch bolts.

STRONGBACK: The 1x3-inch strongback is located on the centerline of the boat, and is notched into each of the frames in each of the deck beams.

DECK BATTENS: The 1x2-inch mahogany or spruce deck battens are located per the drawings, and notched into the beams similarly to the strongback.

DECKING: The decking must be faired to allow the decking to mate to all members. Forward decking is ¼-inch mahogany-faced plywood. The decking should extend along the side decks as far as possible, from a 4x8-inch panel. At this point, it is joined to the side decking with a butt joint. Use a ⅜-inch butt block, extending 3 inches to 4 inches to the side of the joint. The decking is nailed in place per the fastening schedule. Before it is laid, the decking may be grooved to simulate planking with a power saw, table saw, or router.

FLOORBOARDS: The ⅜-inch floorboards are in three parts. They are fitted around the frames to provide a flush area in the cockpit, resting on battens notched into the frames.

SEATS: The seats are detailed in the drawings. These consist of ¾-inch plywood angle-brackets with ⅜-inch sides or ½-inch sides and bottoms.

STEERING AND CONTROLS: The steering and remote controls should be sent to the forward cockpit to suit the type of motor and controls used.

GAS TANK: The gasoline tank should be stored under the aft deck area. On the opposite side of the gasoline tank, the battery box should be mounted on a sheet of ⅜-inch plywood, and enclosed in a fiberglass box. •

BASIC framework of decking completed. Carling members, strongback battens in place.

BOATING

BARNABY

by Henry Clark

Build this 16-foot cabin cruiser for under $300

THIS is it! For less than $300—$233 to be exact--I built this 16-foot cabin cruiser. Framing lumber for the hull costs $43; plywood planking $80; miscellaneous wood, screws and paint $64; control hardware $46; total cost for the hull, $233. Roomy but trailable; it's small enough to keep our lot uncluttered. It carries a slew of camping gear, plus my wife, three kids —and a dog! Yet it planes easily, just like a runabout. Good stability, sturdy oak framing, 3/8-inch plywood hull and mahogany trim for that "cruiser" look. The cabin sleeps two adults plus a child.

The wheel and controls in the cabin are for use in wet weather. They are coupled to the helm in the open cockpit for stand-up or sit-down steering. Portholes for Junior to watch the splash, a memory every boy should have—wide gunwales for walking—grab rails on the roof—windows that open for ventilation —an upper windshield to keep the wind off the skipper—fuel tanks under seats, which are hinged—seat back that lowers, for motor attention—a self-bailing water well to keep out following seas—a high freeboard to keep out spray. Barnaby's got 'em all!

I built her in three months' "spare" time, from Labor Day to Christmas. Barnaby is a project for workshoppers with a *few* power tools and a penchant to get into something big like a boat. I don't need to take a poll to know how many of you guys have been confounded by construction curves, bludgeoned by blueprints, outwitted by offsets, lashed by loft lines and intimidated by terminology that was designed more to confine you to lacquering loveseats than to launch you on boat-building.

Check the bevel of the chines and keelson with a fairing stick so that the planking will lie flush.

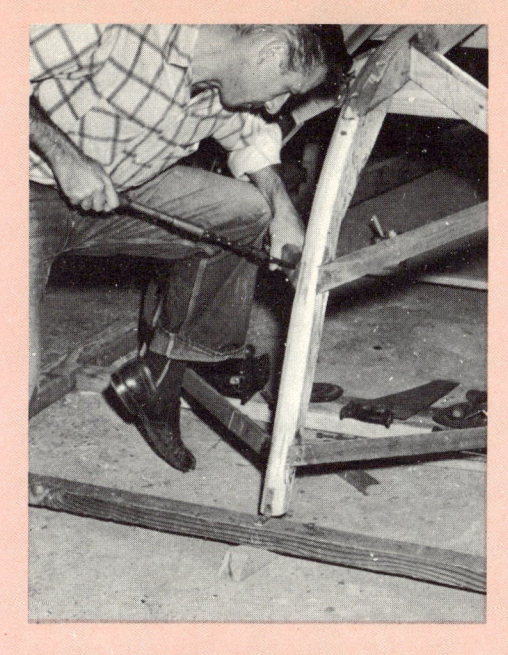

Pressure is exerted with the knee to bend the chines in for fastening them securely.

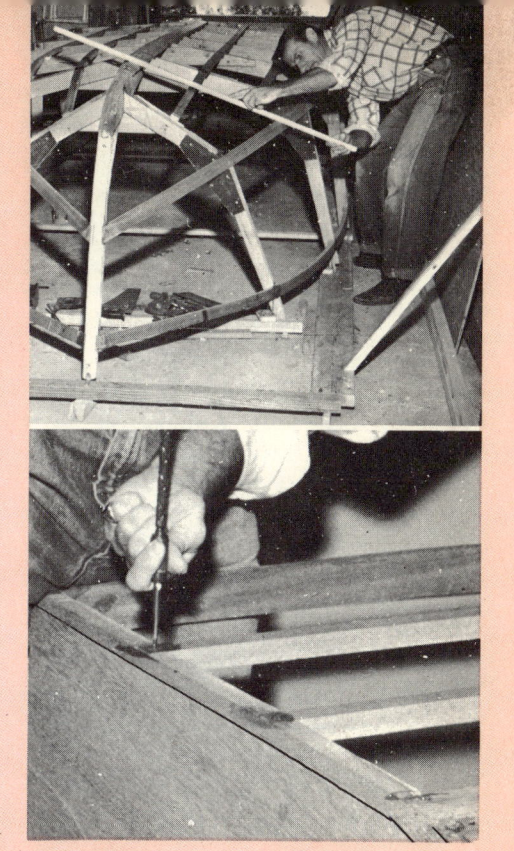

Stringers go into notches at bottom of the transom frame, as shown. Glue and screws hold them.

PLANKING FOR THE SIDES, BOTTOM AND DECK IS CUT FROM PLYWOOD PANELS.

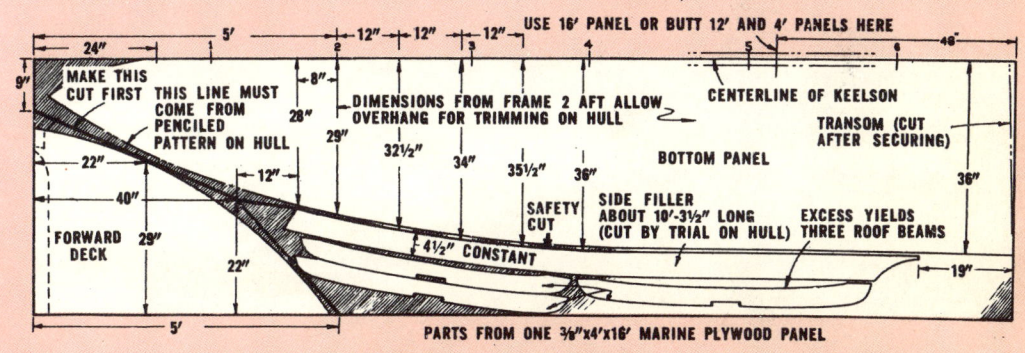

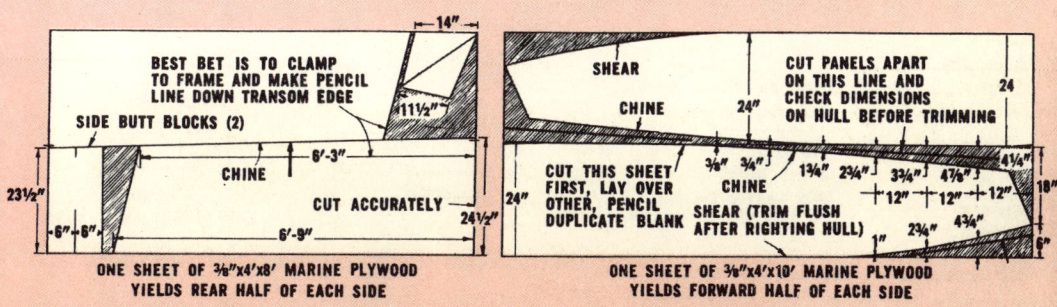

USE 16' PANEL OR BUTT 12' AND 4' PANELS HERE

MAKE THIS CUT FIRST
THIS LINE MUST COME FROM PENCILED PATTERN ON HULL
DIMENSIONS FROM FRAME 2 AFT ALLOW OVERHANG FOR TRIMMING ON HULL
CENTERLINE OF KEELSON
TRANSOM (CUT AFTER SECURING)
BOTTOM PANEL
SAFETY CUT
SIDE FILLER ABOUT 10'-3½" LONG (CUT BY TRIAL ON HULL)
EXCESS YIELDS THREE ROOF BEAMS
FORWARD DECK
4½" CONSTANT

PARTS FROM ONE ⅜"x4'x16' MARINE PLYWOOD PANEL

BEST BET IS TO CLAMP TO FRAME AND MAKE PENCIL LINE DOWN TRANSOM EDGE
SIDE BUTT BLOCKS (2)
CHINE
CUT ACCURATELY

ONE SHEET OF ⅜"x4'x8' MARINE PLYWOOD YIELDS REAR HALF OF EACH SIDE

SHEAR
CHINE
CUT PANELS APART ON THIS LINE AND CHECK DIMENSIONS ON HULL BEFORE TRIMMING
CUT THIS SHEET FIRST, LAY OVER OTHER, PENCIL DUPLICATE BLANK
CHINE
SHEAR (TRIM FLUSH AFTER RIGHTING HULL)

ONE SHEET OF ⅜"x4'x10' MARINE PLYWOOD YIELDS FORWARD HALF OF EACH SIDE

445

BOATING

But don't be afraid of this boat. It looks like work, and it is, but you will be amazed at how quickly it progresses.

My advice for starting is this. Study the six frame, or rib, drawings given here. Then order the lumber for them cut to the lengths specified and assemble them into frames with Weldwood glue, screws and bolts. When you have completed the six simple rib frames, you are looking at your actual boat coming to life.

To work from these pages, lay out the frame lines full-size on large Kraft paper. Bisect the paper with a center line. Draw each outline in a different color crayon to avoid confusion. Starting at the bottom of the sheet, lay each frame a few inches above the last. The dimensions will keep you out of trouble, plus the fact that all frames are cut on straight lines. This is a planing hull with shallow V bottom. The flat bottom makes it safe with any load and certainly makes it extremely easy to secure the bottom plywood panels. It may pound

FASTENING AT STEM AND TRANSOM. BEVELING OF CHINE AND FITTING OF SIDES.

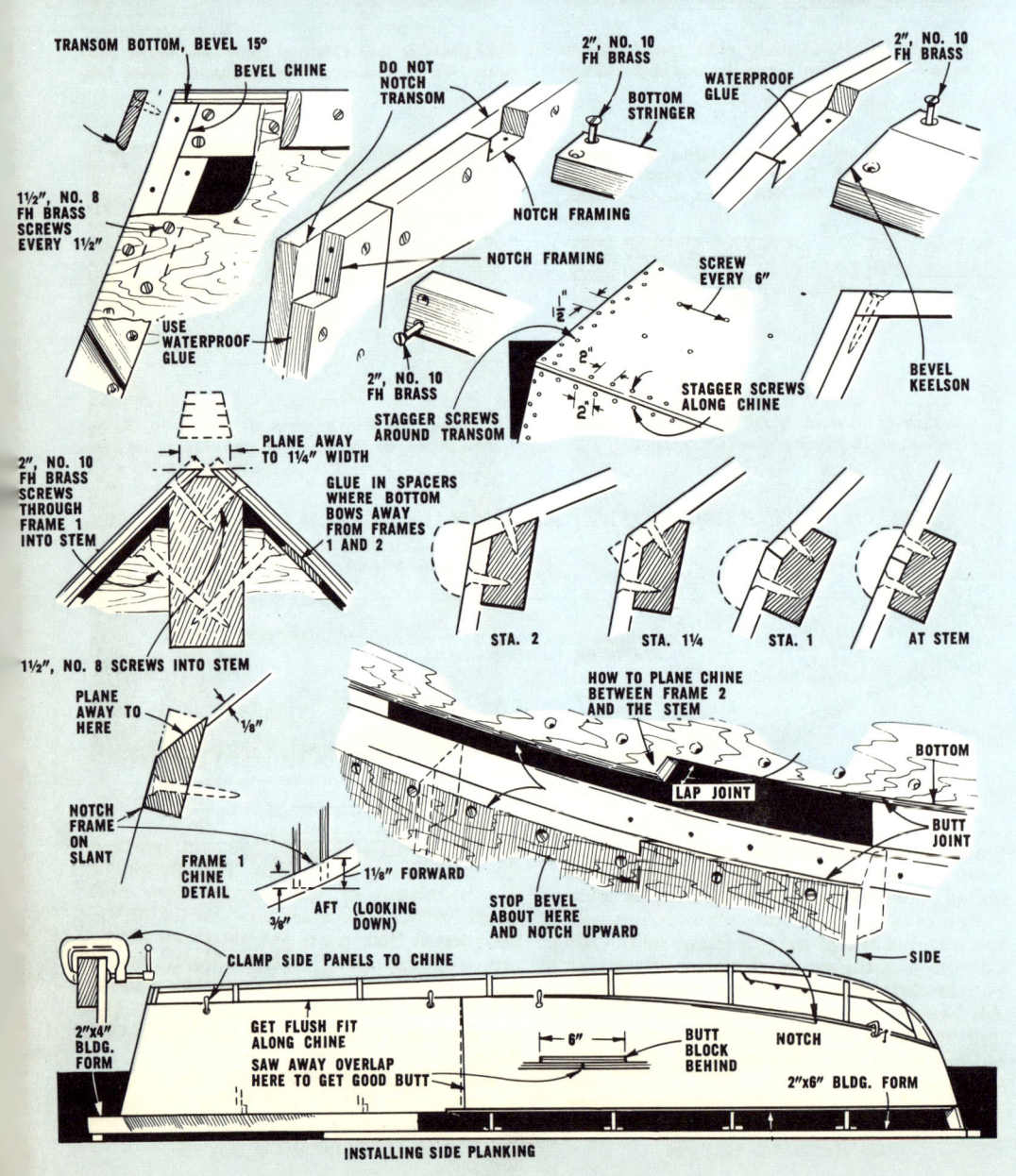

Photo here shows outlining side panel against chine and sheer of hull frame for accurate cutting.

Side panel is then clamped on to bore screw pilot holes. It's then removed for a careful gluing job.

The aft end of the bottom planking is fastened after forward end is secured in place. Crosspieces stay in until the hull is turned over, right.

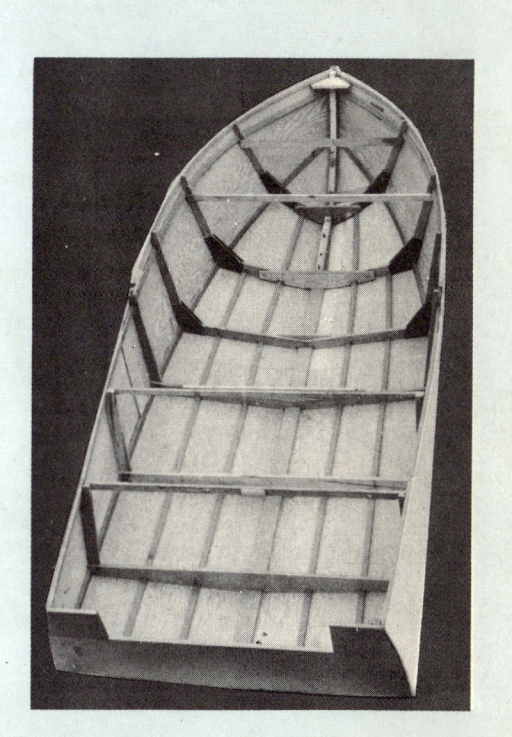

going over small chops. Adding a slight bow to each frame bottom member will soften whatever pound might annoy you.

Photos show how the plywood gussets are screwed and glued to a frame joint. Oak battens join the transom upper and lower panels and form the motor clamp board. All battens are pre-notched before gluing and screwing to the transom inner face. Do not notch the transom panel itself. See drawing.

With all frame ribs now complete, along with transom and stem, you can now cut the inner keel, or keelson. The keelson is the backbone of the upside-down hull frame, which you must now set up on the floor jig. A floor jig is not necessary if you are working on a wooden floor. But a home-built boat is always a garage project, it seems, so you need the jig shown in the drawing, as you must build the hull upside down.

While the hull is still on the jig, prepare to attach the spray rails along the chine.

447

BOATING

The cabin roof is ½-inch plywood which can be bent very easily. A layer of fiberglass covers it.

These do two things. They divert spray from lapping up along the hull and they seal the open joint where the sides and bottom panels meet. These can be oak, as they bump the docks, but mahogany works so much easier and is almost as hard. Before securing the rails, sand the chine edge smooth. Use glue and screws to attach the spray rails. Foot pressure helps, as shown in photo.

At this point you can start enjoying life by knocking out the jig blocks and lifting up the bow, on props, to have a look at the inside of your new pride and joy. This is really a big moment and gives you a chance to inspect joints for later attention. When you recover from this pleasure, you can lower it again and face the last "bottom" task. That consists of brushing on two coats of Firzite, sanding these when dry, and brushing on at least two coats of a fine exterior enamel of your own color choice. White Firzite was chosen because it covers the plywood grain very well and

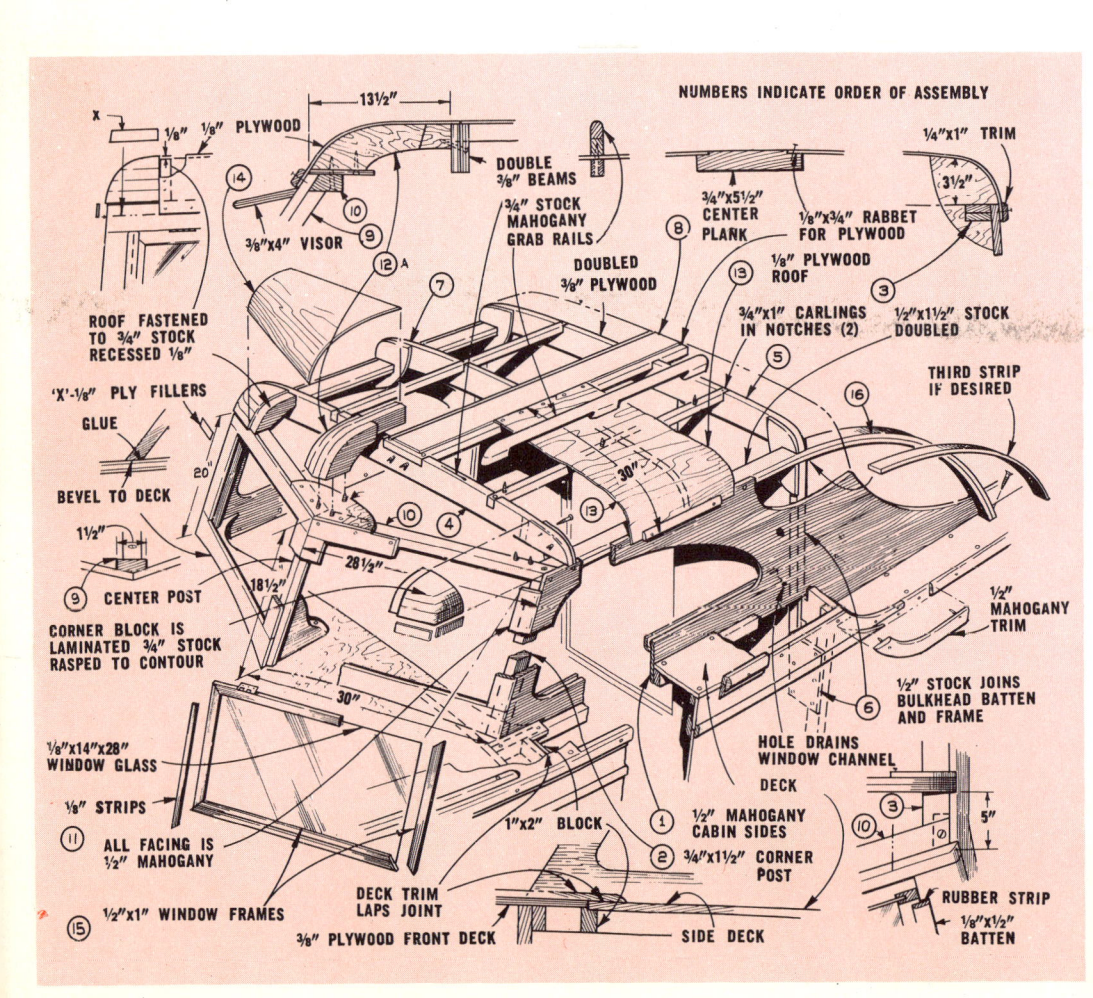

448

is the best base color for the white enamel that will cover the finished sides.

With the hull propped up, you can now insert the top short sheer rail and lay in the four-inch side filler panel. Reasons for this filler are worth noting. It gives you a stepped-up deck, for seaworthiness, and more room for the two bunks. Also, it gives the cabin windshield a lower profile. Best of all, it permits the use of 24-inch side panels, eliminating the need of cutting 28-inch panels out of 48-inch stock.

Before doing any "topside" work, cradle the hull securely. Oak knees joining the sheer rail to transom batten are placed only after you know the hull is resting true. Bevel ends to suit and screw through the sheer rail and through the transom batten with two-inch No. 10 screws, two per joint. Now you can put a motor on the transom. The notch was first designed to take two 15-hp motors but two mahogany wings now close it in for use with one 35-hp Bigtwin Evinrude.

Diagram across the page shows cabin construction. The circled numbers indicate sequence of building.

Sliding door is installed to save space. Opening is 18 inches wide and is framed with ¾x1½-inch stock. Door panel has cleat on the inside top which slides between a pair of cleats nailed to the roof beam. The retaining panel is being nailed in place in the photograph shown below.

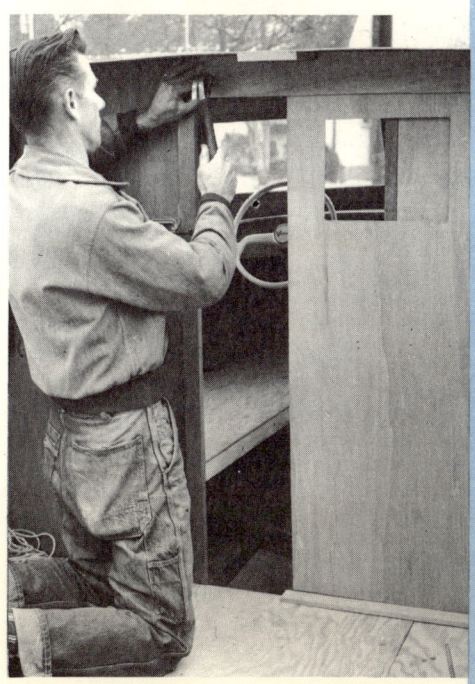

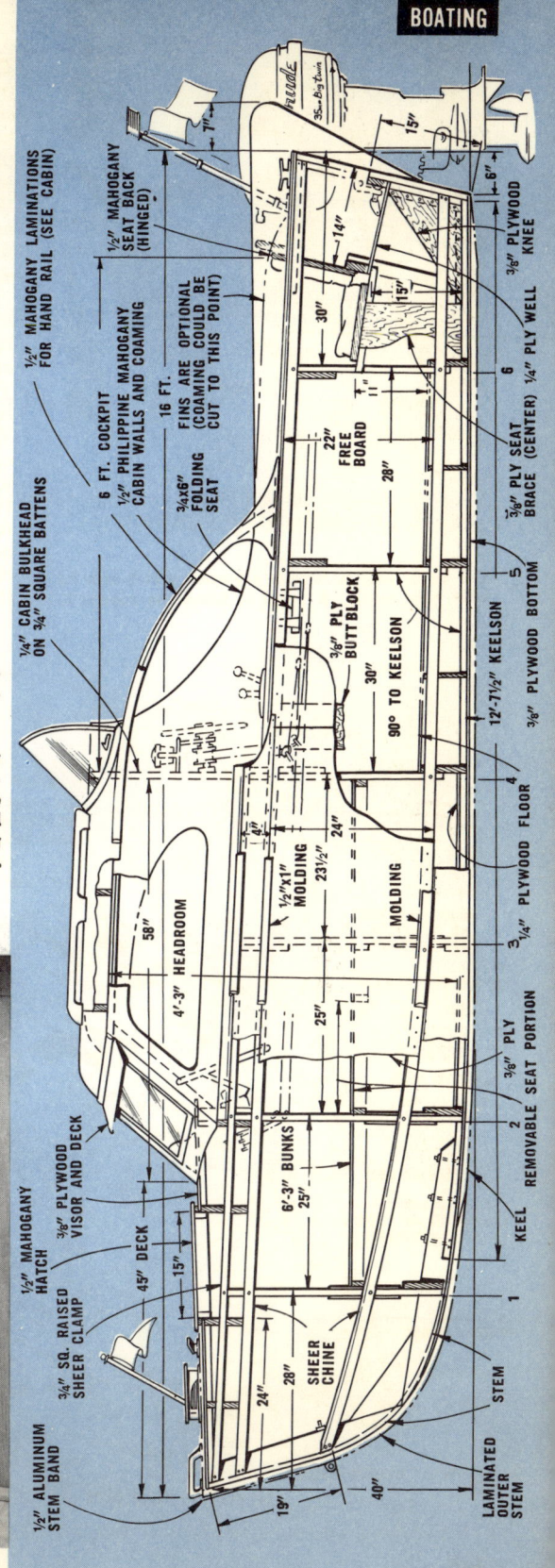

BOATING

449

BOATING

The photograph here shows a happy crew preparing for lunch in the ship's cockpit.

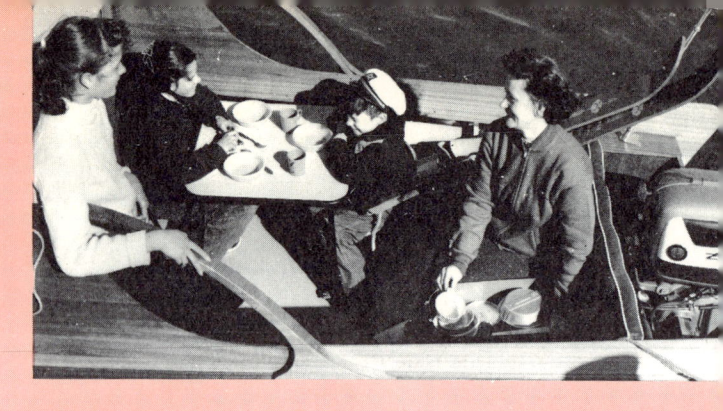

Diagram across the page shows exploded view of entire boat. Side planking is composed of three pieces.

Diagram below shows that the building form is made level and rigid, and the framing is erected upon it.

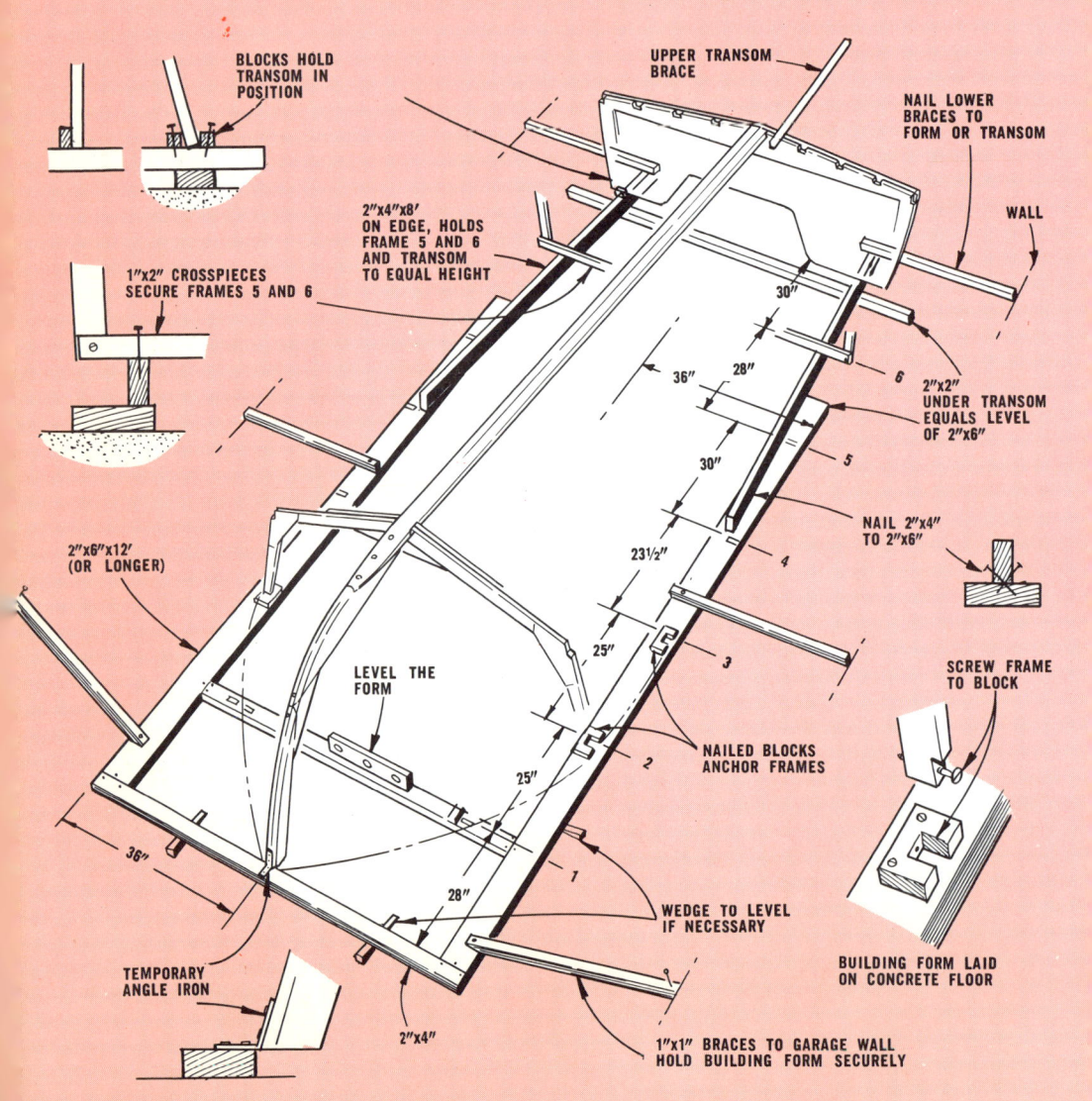

BLOCKS HOLD TRANSOM IN POSITION

UPPER TRANSOM BRACE

NAIL LOWER BRACES TO FORM OR TRANSOM

1"x2" CROSSPIECES SECURE FRAMES 5 AND 6

2"x4"x8' ON EDGE, HOLDS FRAME 5 AND 6 AND TRANSOM TO EQUAL HEIGHT

WALL

2"x2" UNDER TRANSOM EQUALS LEVEL OF 2"x6"

NAIL 2"x4" TO 2"x6"

2"x6"x12' (OR LONGER)

SCREW FRAME TO BLOCK

LEVEL THE FORM

NAILED BLOCKS ANCHOR FRAMES

WEDGE TO LEVEL IF NECESSARY

BUILDING FORM LAID ON CONCRETE FLOOR

TEMPORARY ANGLE IRON

2"x4"

1"x1" BRACES TO GARAGE WALL HOLD BUILDING FORM SECURELY

BOATING

You will stand a lot on the deck, so screw and glue all joints tightly. The beam exposed to the cabin, or the "dash panel," should be mahogany. The deck is cut out of the bottom panel blank as shown in the drawing. Saw this out and repeat for the other half of the deck. Pencil the hatch opening under the deck panel and cut. Use a fairing stick to see that the deck panel will touch each beam in a smooth curve. Use half-inch Philippine mahogany for decking. This stock is duty-free and is quite low in price. It is used extensively on this little cruiser for a big cruiser look. Four of these planks form the side decks, as in drawing.

Before starting the cabin, trim away about three inches of front deck hanging over the dash panel into a sweeping curve to where the cabin side will meet it. Cut the cabin sides out of mahogany blanks and glue the upper and lower halves together. The cockpit floor is quarter-inch plywood, cut as shown in the drawing. If you're a

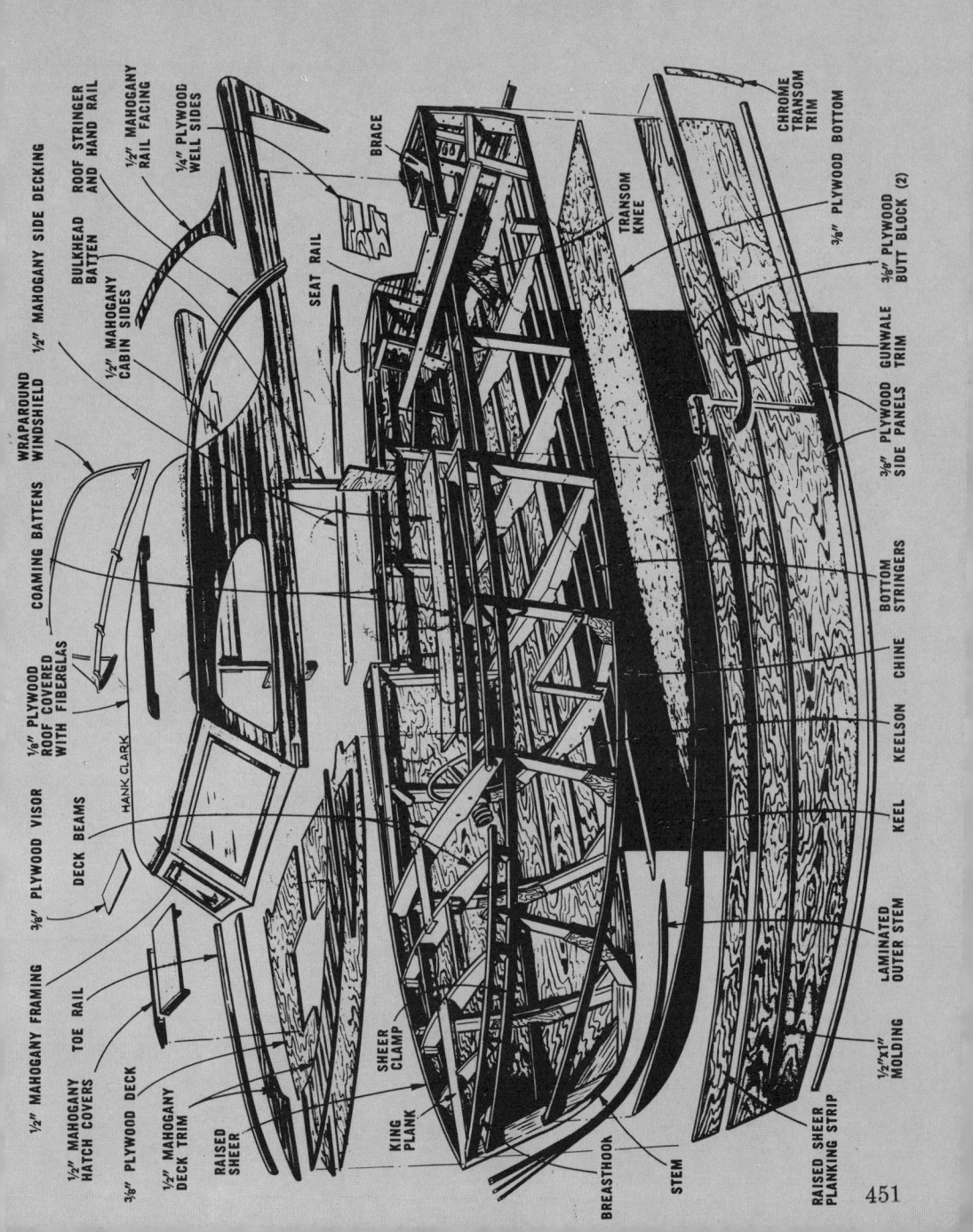

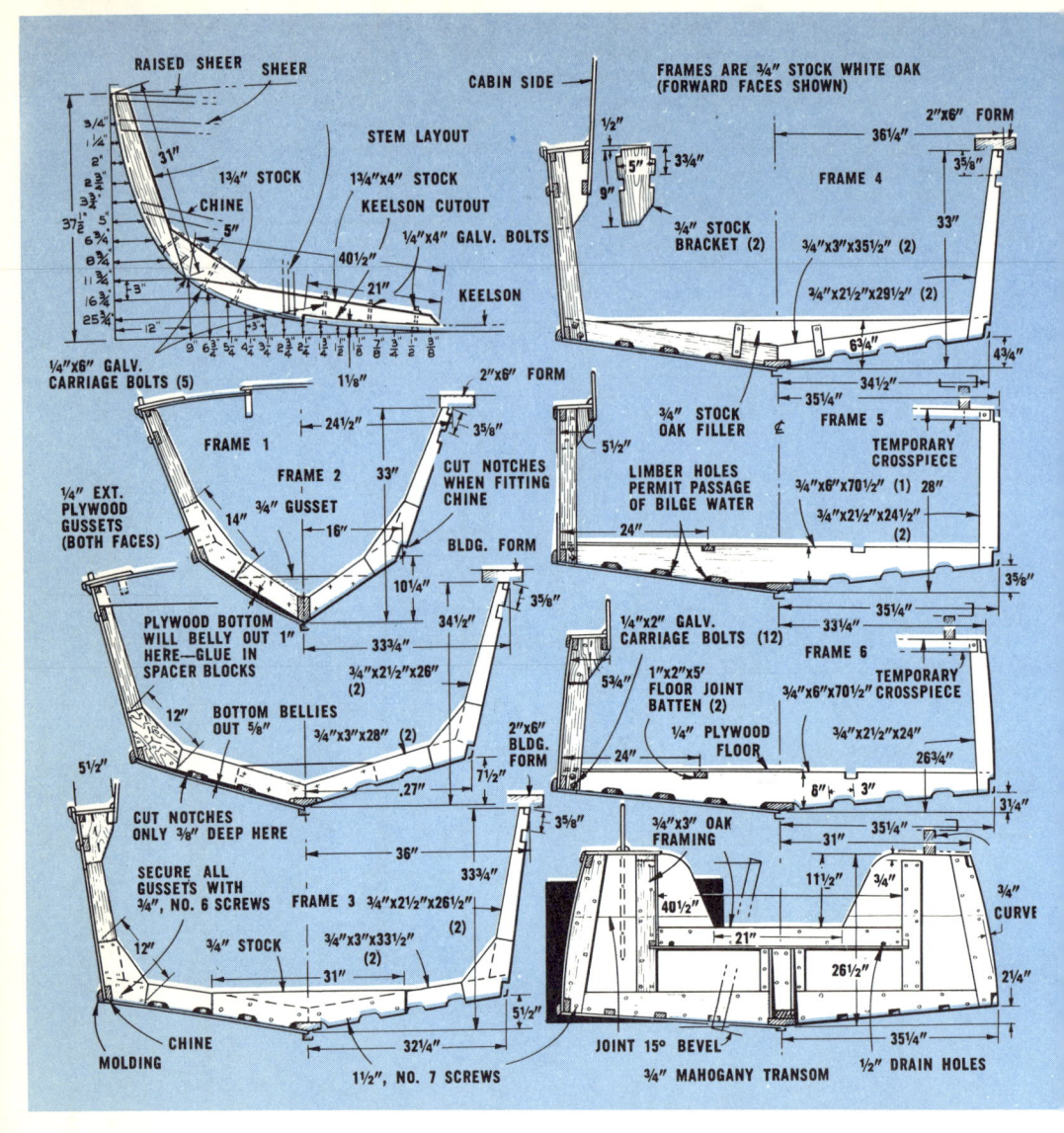

BOATING

452

BOATING

Diagram across the page gives further building details. Frames, stem and transom are built first, then erected on building form.

Diagram at the right is a plan view of hull framing. Note immediate floor beams and battens which will support the cockpit floor.

Photo below, across the page, shows the launching of the completed cruiser.

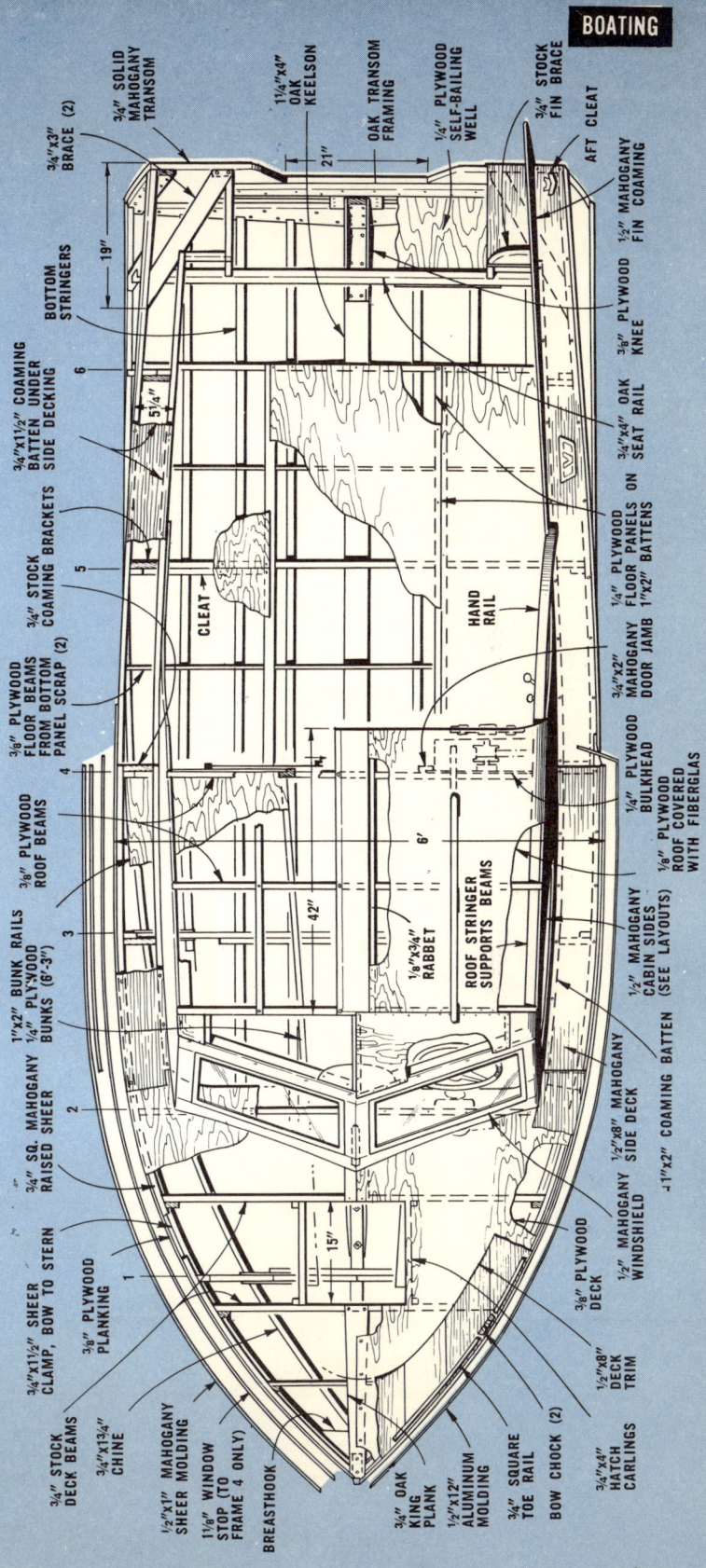

Labels (clockwise from upper left):
- 3/4" SOLID MAHOGANY TRANSOM
- 3/4"x3" BRACE (2)
- 1 1/4"x4" OAK KEELSON
- OAK TRANSOM FRAMING
- 1/4" PLYWOOD SELF-BAILING WELL
- 3/4" STOCK FIN BRACE
- AFT CLEAT
- 1/2" PLYWOOD FIN COAMING
- 3/8" PLYWOOD KNEE
- 3/4"x4" OAK SEAT RAIL
- 1/4" PLYWOOD FLOOR PANELS ON 1"x2" BATTENS
- 3/8"x2" MAHOGANY DOOR JAMB
- 1/4" PLYWOOD BULKHEAD
- 1/8" PLYWOOD ROOF COVERED WITH FIBERGLAS
- 1/2" MAHOGANY CABIN SIDES (SEE LAYOUTS)
- 1/8"x3/4" RABBET
- ROOF STRINGER SUPPORTS BEAMS
- 1"x2" COAMING BATTEN
- 1/2"x8" MAHOGANY SIDE DECK
- 1/2"x8" MAHOGANY WINDSHIELD
- 3/16" PLYWOOD DECK
- 1/2"x8" DECK TRIM
- BOW CHOCK (2)
- 3/4"x4" HATCH CARLINGS
- 3/4" SQUARE TOE RAIL
- 1/2"x12" ALUMINUM MOLDING
- 3/4" OAK KING PLANK
- BREASTHOOK
- 1 1/8" WINDOW STOP (TO FRAME 4 ONLY)
- 1/2"x1" MAHOGANY SHEER MOLDING
- 3/4"x1 3/4" CHINE
- 3/4" STOCK DECK BEAMS
- 3/4"x1 1/2" SHEER CLAMP, BOW TO STERN
- 3/8" PLYWOOD PLANKING
- 3/4" SQ. MAHOGANY RAISED SHEER
- 1"x2" BUNK RAILS
- 1/4" PLYWOOD BUNKS (6'-3")
- 3/8" PLYWOOD ROOF BEAMS
- 3/8" PLYWOOD FLOOR BEAMS FROM BOTTOM PANEL SCRAP
- 3/4" STOCK COAMING BRACKETS
- 3/4"x1 1/2" COAMING BATTEN UNDER SIDE DECKING
- BOTTOM STRINGERS
- CLEAT
- HAND RAIL

453

BOATING

heavyweight use ⅜-inch plywood instead.

The top plate, which bends down aft to become a railing, is responsible for the straight run. The cabin cutaway drawing shows the general order of assembly. Strength is gained by doubling the roof side plate and extending it to bend down to the aft deck as a handrail. This bend also takes some muscle work. Cut all window frames and sash from scrap mahogany.

From here on the task is one of finishing. A smart move now is to use a good wood preservative. It's insurance against fungus that forms when water soaks, then dries out in the keel when you have the boat covered. Actually, this little hull is completely accessible and you can easily reach every damp spot with a sponge. Our boat is always in the yard under cover, or in the garage in really bad weather, not soaking at some berth.

Our plans for the boat this summer call for a polyethyelene cover over the cockpit with air mattresses on the floor for men folks. The gals can have the cabin. Cabin has no head but disposable units are available now. Cooking is done on a cylinder gas unit mounted on a hinged shelf in the cockpit. Nooks and corners for gear are everywhere in this short 16-footer, the real deal being the cabin.

All mahogany was spar-varnished with about six coats. Hull received three coats of white outdoor enamel. Do not paint your bottom color up along the chine to

Barnaby is easy to handle as this female skipper finds out. Boat moves easily through the water, looks like a million.

Proof of the boat's attractive appearance are these two photos. Paint boat whatever colors appeal to you. Two-tone jobs are always interesting.

Maneuverability is another feature of this boat. You'll have no trouble docking her and she's easy to climb around.

LARGE SCALE PLANS
and full-size rib drawings are available for building boat. They are $7.50. Order from Henry Clark, 36 Highwood Drive, Dumont, New Jersey. Specify Plan FB-Barnaby.

stem. This is a runabout technique. For your "cruiser" look, break it off over the chine and keep it level with water line, or a few inches above. Use masking tape. All deck hardware as well as running lights, are from the fashionable new Vollrath Viking line. We carry this baby on a Pacemaker 900 trailer, with Fulton winch, two-way ratchet. This rig has a tilt feature which helps you load or unload the boat.

All in all, Barnaby is a snappy little job that gave us loads of pleasure last year. We're all pepped up looking forward to another summer of boating. No more traffic jams, cops, flies, gasoline fumes and traffic lights. We're really starting to live—and you, too, can live it up by starting to build Barnaby. •

BILL OF MATERIALS

Size	Use	Amount
MAHOGANY		
¾"x2"x18'	Chines	2
¾"x1¼"x12'	Bottom Stringers	4
¾"x1¼"x9'	Bottom Stringers	2
¾"x18"x6'	Transom	1
¾"x10"x4'	Transom	1
¾"x1½"x18'	Normal Sheer Clamps	2
¾"x¾"x10'	Raised Sheer Clamps	2
1"x7"x6'	Cabin Dash Panel	1
½"x8"x9'	Side Decking	3
½"x8"x6'	Side Decking	2
½"x12"x8'	Cabin Walls and Fins	4
½"x12"x10'	Cabin Walls and Fins	1
½"x12"x6'	Cabin Walls and Fins	1
½"x12"x48"	Hatch Cover	1
¾"x2"x48"	Door Jambs	2
¾"x¾"x36"	Grab Rails	2
½"x12"x5'	Seat Back	1
½"x1¼"x8'	Gunwale Trim (Aft of Sta. 4)	2
½"x1"x10'	Gunwale Trim	2
½"x12'	Quarter-Round Cabin-to-Deck Molding	2
WHITE OAK		
1"x4"x6'	Rear Seat Rail	1
¾"x2½"x24'	Frame Sides	1
¾":3"x20'	Frame Bottoms	1
¾"x6"x18'	Frame Bottoms	1
¾"x3"x9'	Transom Framing	1
1"x1¼"x18'	Keel	1
1⅛"x4"x13'	Keelson	1
2"x4"x74"	Stem	1
2"x5"x18'	Stem	1
¾"x6"x7'	Gussets (Frames 1, 2, 3)	1
EXTERIOR FIR PLYWOOD		
¼"x4'x8'	Floor, Bunks	2
⅜"x4'x16'	Bottom and Deck Planking	2
⅜"x4'x8'	Rear Sections of Side Planking	1
⅜"x4'x10'	Front Sections of Side Planking	1
¼"x30"x30"	Gussets (Frames 1, 2, 3)	1
⅛"x32"x6'—6"	Cabin Roof (Ext. Flush Door Stock)	2
SPRUCE OR FIR		
¾"x6"x4'	Center Roof Plank	1
¾"x12"x64'	Rear Seat	1
1"x2"x24'	Bunk Frames	1
1"x2"x6'	Floor Battens	2
½"x1"x12'	Side Molding	2
1"x6"x9'	Deck Beams	1
1"x3"x6'	Hatch Carlings	1

455

BOATING

CANVASBACK

by S. Calhoun Smith

Build this kayak with hand tools and C-clamps

THIS kayak is the answer for young people who want to build an inexpensive boat for summer fun. We turned out several Canvasbacks at exactly $21.81 apiece—and each took only a week of spare time. A shop full of power tools isn't necessary, either. Ours consisted of a power jig saw and a quarter-inch electric hand drill. But all the work can be done with ordinary hand tools and a few C clamps.

Canvasback will carry one adult but it's handiest when paddled by a youngster. The boat is stable in the water and, even though it can be turned over, it won't sink. It's also light enough to be carried with ease. Building is so simple that the "jig" consists of only two blocks and a few bricks.

Apart from the exterior plywood, boat grade spruce is the best lumber to use for Canvasback. The next choice would be a good grade of fir. If you cannot obtain either of these, top-grade white pine can be purchased at most lumberyards. You can get 12-foot lengths of 1x4 or 1x6 (actual thickness about ¾ inch) and have them planed to ⅝-inch thickness and ripped into the three required widths.

Canvasback can be built on any flat surface. Begin by cutting the stem, stern and frames from exterior plywood as detailed in the drawing shown here. To simplify matters later on, you can also mark the fastening points for the stringers on each frame. Next cut the keelson to the exact length. You're then ready for the three steps shown in the construction drawings. Step 1 consists of gluing and screwing the stem and stern to the keelson, marking the frame locations and putting one-inch blocks under the stem and stern. In step

BOATING

COCKPIT COAMING 2¾"x35" (2 REQ'D.)

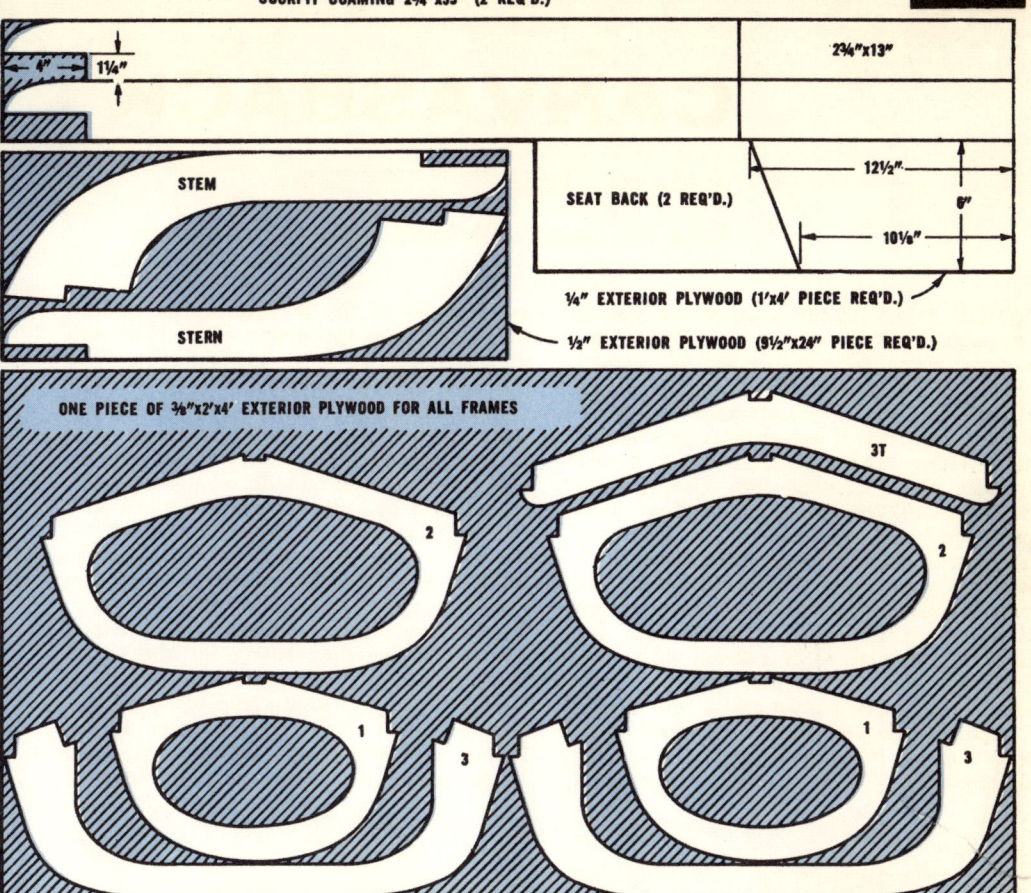

4" 1¼" 2¾"x13"

STEM

SEAT BACK (2 REQ'D.) 12½" 6" 10⅛"

STERN

¼" EXTERIOR PLYWOOD (1'x4' PIECE REQ'D.)
½" EXTERIOR PLYWOOD (9½"x24" PIECE REQ'D.)

ONE PIECE OF ⅜"x2'x4' EXTERIOR PLYWOOD FOR ALL FRAMES

3T
2 2
1 3 1 3

2, you add the frames, making sure they're vertical and square with the keelson. Then you nail temporary spreaders across the open tops of the two center frames. Step 3 calls for the addition of about four bricks at the center to hold the curve of the keelson. Then you add the sheer clamps which are exactly 12 feet long.

Before attempting to fasten the sheer clamps, look at the plan drawing for the measurements which give the frame locations on the sheer. Mark each sheer clamp at the center and then mark the frame locations on either side of the center mark. Next temporarily screw the sheer clamps to the No. 3 frames and bend them in so that you can mark their ends for beveling where they meet the stem and stern. Be sure the No. 1 and No. 2 frames are located properly when you do this or the sheer clamps will not curve correctly. After marking, remove the sheer clamps, cut the bevels with a saw and sand them smooth. Then install the sheer clamps permanently with glue and screws. Proceed from the center frames toward the

All edges of the completed boat frame must be planed and sanded smooth so that the canvas cover will not wear at any spots. This is important.

457

EACH SQUARE EQUALS 1"

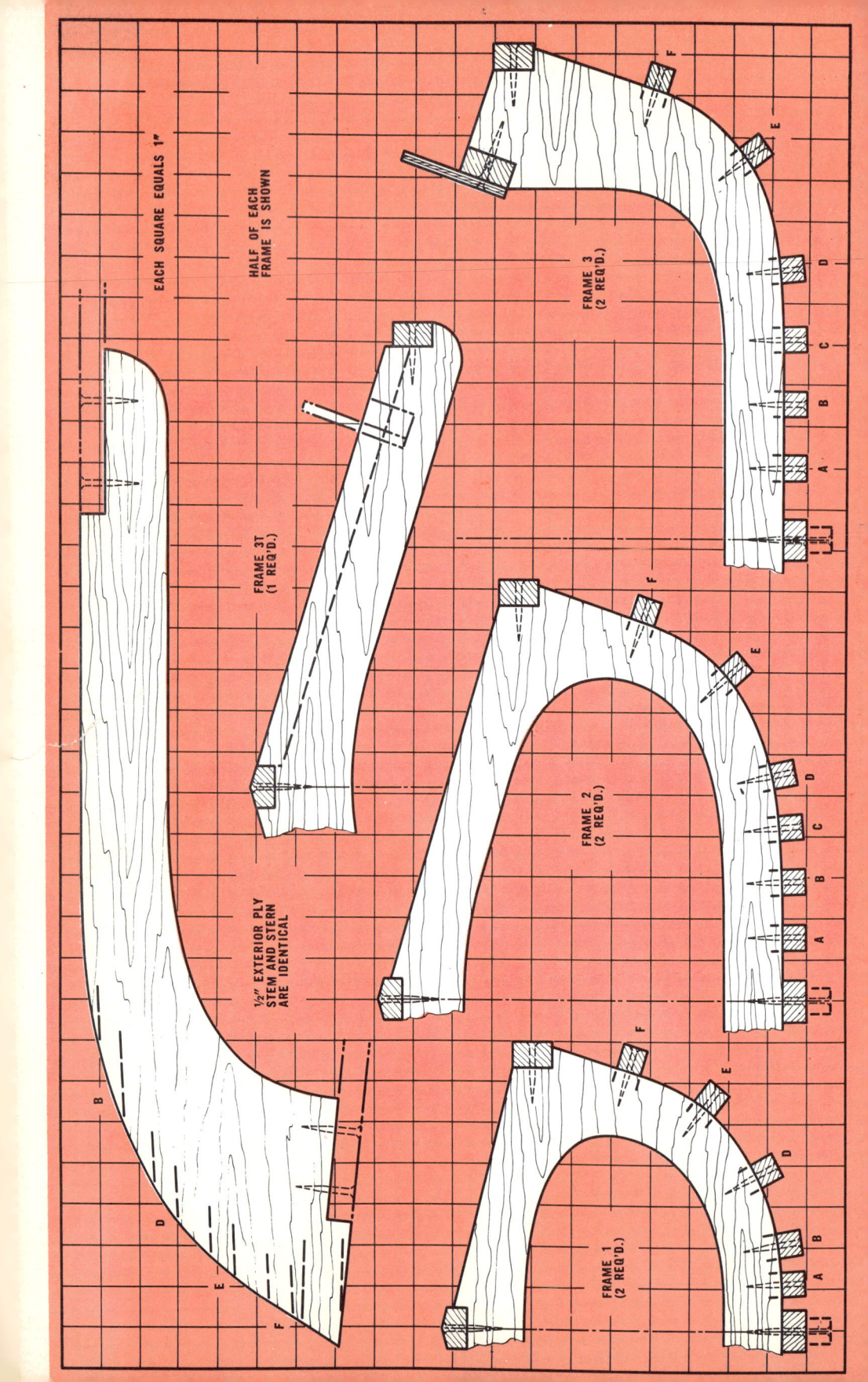

HALF OF EACH FRAME IS SHOWN

FRAME 3
(2 REQ'D.)

FRAME 3T
(1 REQ'D.)

½" EXTERIOR PLY STEM AND STERN ARE IDENTICAL

FRAME 2
(2 REQ'D.)

FRAME 1
(2 REQ'D.)

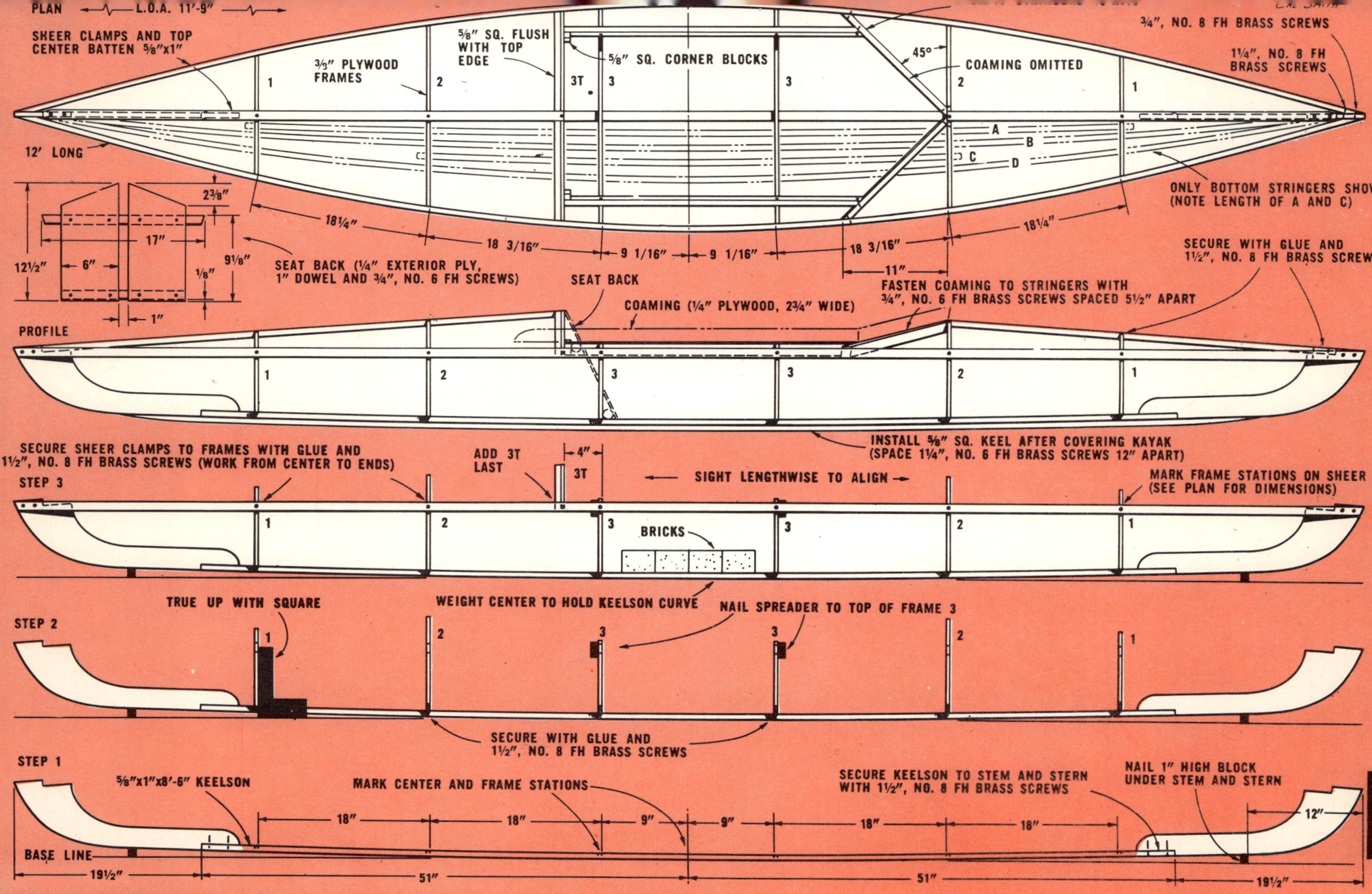
PLAN
L.O.A. 11'-9"
SHEER CLAMPS AND TOP CENTER BATTEN 5/8"x1"
3/8" PLYWOOD FRAMES
5/8" SQ. FLUSH WITH TOP EDGE
5/8" SQ. CORNER BLOCKS
45°
COAMING OMITTED
3/4", NO. 8 FH BRASS SCREWS
1 1/4", NO. 8 FH BRASS SCREWS
12' LONG
A
B
C
D
ONLY BOTTOM STRINGERS SHOWN (NOTE LENGTH OF A AND C)
18 1/4"
18 3/16"
9 1/16"
9 1/16"
18 3/16"
18 1/4"
11"
2 3/8"
17"
12 1/2"
6"
9 1/8"
1/8"
1"
SEAT BACK (1/4" EXTERIOR PLY, 1" DOWEL AND 3/4", NO. 6 FH SCREWS)
SEAT BACK
SECURE WITH GLUE AND 1 1/2", NO. 8 FH BRASS SCREWS
FASTEN COAMING TO STRINGERS WITH 3/4", NO. 6 FH BRASS SCREWS SPACED 5 1/2" APART
COAMING (1/4" PLYWOOD, 2 3/4" WIDE)
PROFILE
INSTALL 5/8" SQ. KEEL AFTER COVERING KAYAK (SPACE 1 1/4", NO. 6 FH BRASS SCREWS 12" APART)
SECURE SHEER CLAMPS TO FRAMES WITH GLUE AND 1 1/2", NO. 8 FH BRASS SCREWS (WORK FROM CENTER TO ENDS)
ADD 3T LAST
4"
3T
SIGHT LENGTHWISE TO ALIGN
MARK FRAME STATIONS ON SHEER (SEE PLAN FOR DIMENSIONS)
STEP 3
BRICKS
TRUE UP WITH SQUARE
WEIGHT CENTER TO HOLD KEELSON CURVE
NAIL SPREADER TO TOP OF FRAME 3
STEP 2
SECURE WITH GLUE AND 1 1/2", NO. 8 FH BRASS SCREWS
STEP 1
5/8"x1"x8'-6" KEELSON
MARK CENTER AND FRAME STATIONS
SECURE KEELSON TO STEM AND STERN WITH 1 1/2", NO. 8 FH BRASS SCREWS
NAIL 1" HIGH BLOCK UNDER STEM AND STERN
18"
18"
9"
9"
18"
18"
12"
BASE LINE
19 1/2"
51"
51"
19 1/2"

BOATING

BILL OF MATERIALS

SPRUCE, FIR OR WHITE PINE

Bottom stringers and keel	13—5/8"x5/8"x12'
Sheer clamps, keelson and top center battens	4—5/8"x1"x12'
Cockpit stringers	1—5/8"x1 1/4"x8'

EXTERIOR FIR PLYWOOD

Frames	1—3/8"x2'x4'
Stem and stern	1—1/2"x19"x24"
Cockpit coaming and seat back	1—1/4"x12"x48"

FLATHEAD BRASS WOOD SCREWS

Stem, stern, frames to keelson and sheer clamps, top center battens to frames, cockpit stringers	41—1 1/2", No. 8
Stringers to stem and stern	20—1 1/4", No. 8
Stringers to stem and stern	20—3/4", No. 8
Stringers to frames	68—1 1/2", No. 6
Keel	12—1 1/4", No. 6
Cockpit coaming and seat back	24—3/4", No. 6

MISCELLANEOUS

Copper tacks	2 boxes—7/16", No.
Waterproof glue	3 1/2 ounces
10-ounce canvas	4 yards—4' width
Ambroid cement	large tube
Spar varnish	1 pint
Outside enamel	2 quarts
Clear dope (optional)	1 gallon

ends, fastening on alternate sides to prevent twisting of the hull frame. Drill pilot holes for the screws and clamp the plywood when boring to prevent splitting.

When the sheer clamps are fastened, deck frame No. 3T is installed. Glue and nail a 5/8-inch square strip flush with the top edge of this member before fastening it between the sheer clamps. You will note a difference between the first three photos and the plans in regard to the location of frame 3T. Originally, this member was attached directly to frame No. 3. However, it was later moved four inches aft for better back slant and body weight locations; so, follow the plans when you install it.

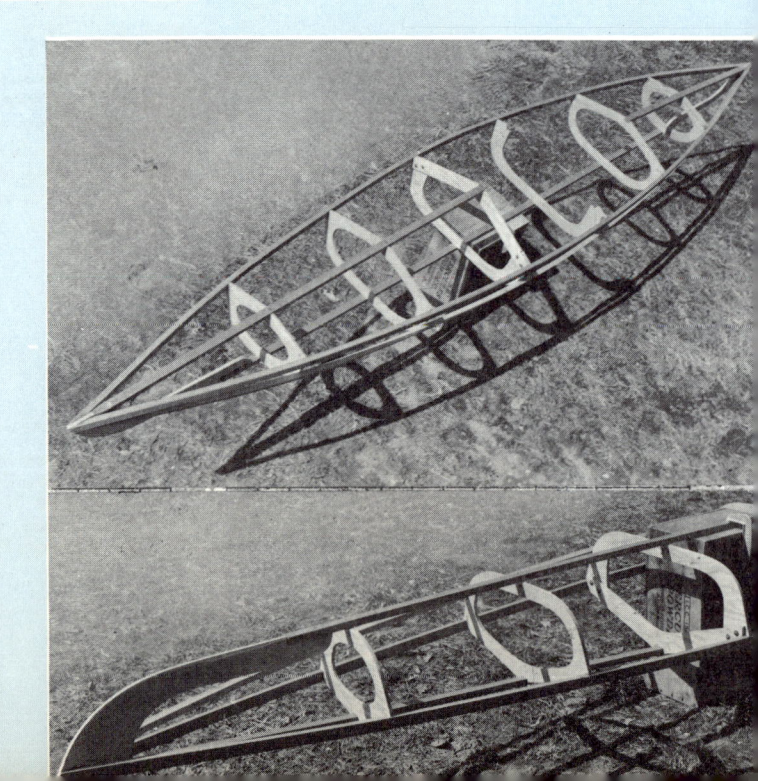

The top center battens go in next and then the stringers. The fastening points for the stringers are shown on the frame drawings. Attach stringer B first and then fasten its duplicate on the other side of the keelson. Then do D, E and F. This method prevents any twist in the hull frame that might occur if all the stringers were fastened on one side first. Note that stringers A and C, which go in last, do not extend the full length of the hull; all the others do. Naturally, the ends which butt against the stem and stern must be beveled and the ends of A and C should be rounded off. Sand all the sharp edges smooth so that the canvas will lie against a smooth surface. The cockpit stringers are installed last to complete the hull frame. Fit these by the cut-and-try method and then secure them with glue and screws.

The frame is now ready for covering. Take care to sand it smooth and then apply at least two coats of spar varnish, allowing each to dry thoroughly. We use 10-ounce canvas but a 12- or 14-ounce weight could be used. A four-yard length, four feet wide, is enough to cover the bottom in one piece. The decks can be covered with leftover pieces.

Attaching the canvas is a two-man operation; one pulls and the other tacks. Begin by marking a centerline lengthwise on the canvas. Start tacking at the center of the keelson, stretching the canvas and spacing the tacks about six inches apart. Work as far as the start of the stem and stern curve. Then go back to the center and stretch and tack for about a foot along one sheer clamp, spacing the tacks about three inches apart. Then go to the other side and do the same. Next add tacks in between so that the spacing is reduced to one inch. Proceed in this manner along the sheer, working toward both ends alternately. In this way, wrinkles are minimized and worked out toward the ends.

When tacking is completed along the keelson and sheer, cut the canvas along the centerline over the curve of the stem and stern. Working at the stem first, apply a liberal amount of Ambroid cement and then pull the canvas around from one side and tack it on the other. Then apply more cement, pull the canvas around from the other side and tack it so that it overlaps. Last, give the joint a coat of cement on the outside. The same procedure is used at the stern.

Excess canvas is trimmed off about ¾ inch in from the sheer clamps and used to cover the decks. Begin at the rear, tacking the straight edge of one of the rough excess triangles along the top center batten. Space the tacks two inches apart. Then pull down and tack to the outside of the sheer clamp. Next put cement along the top center and overlap with another piece of canvas, tacking every inch. Then tack it along the sheer. Finish the rear deck by tacking over frame 3T. The sides are then covered to the junction of the side and forward cockpit stringers. Then the forward deck is covered in the same manner as the rear. Apply cement at all joints and overlap the canvas before tacking. Last, trim the edges neatly, apply cement and smooth them down.

To shrink the canvas tight, it is wetted thoroughly. Further shrinking can be accomplished by applying two coats of clear dope, but this is not absolutely necessary. Three coats of outside enamel completely seal and finish the canvas. Then, after painting, the keel is installed. The cockpit coaming, which goes on last, is given two coats of spar varnish before fastening. The seat back drawing is self-explanatory.

While a double paddle can be made, we suggest buying one. Should the cover ever be torn, a canvas patch can be applied with Ambroid cement. Happy boating! •

Two people have to apply canvas, one stretching, the other tacking. Copper tacks, one inch apart, hold the canvas in place, as photo above shows.

LARGE SCALE PLANS

of the frame, stem and stern members will greatly simplify construction. For these plans send $2 to Mechanix Illustrated Plans Service, Fawcett Bldg., Greenwich, Conn. Specify Plan No. B-238, Canvasback.

BOATING

FROSTFISH

By Cal Smith

For top speed thrills on ice build this 16½ footer.

IF you've never experienced the sensation of flashing over the ice at 40 mph, you're really missing a thrill. Building Frostfish will put you into this exhilarating winter sport and you can do it for $100—less if you already own a sailing paddleboard, dinghy or canoe.

Frostfish was designed to be quickly and easily built. Ordinary lumber and construction grade steel are used throughout and hardware store fittings are specified rather than more expensive marine hardware. The sail and spars are adapted from the Alcort Sailfish but lateen or Gunter canoe rigs and dinghy spars and sails of 40 to 65 square feet can be used.

Completely portable, Frostfish can be taken apart or assembled in a few minutes. The body weighs 65 lbs., the runner plank is 40 lbs. and the rig is 15 lbs.—any of which can be handled by one adult. The total 120-lb. weight is easily carried on top of a car or station wagon.

This is a fun craft, easy to sail and highly maneuverable. Carrying one adult or two youngsters, she'll do 35 to 40 mph in 20 to 25 mph winds. And she's safe. With the low lateen rig, she stays down on the ice where she belongs.

Construction is reduced to the barest essentials. The body is built of 2x4's joined in an acute isosceles triangle with plywood and 1x4 crosspieces. The runner plank is a 2x8 and the runners are built of steel angle, 2x4 fir or pine and 1x4 oak. Careful selection at the lumberyard will enable you to find good clear fir or pine. Although fancy woodworking isn't involved, a circular saw and a jig or band saw will speed up building. A drill press should be used for drilling the metal parts.

Begin with the body. The sides are at a 5° angle with the centerline, so power tools can be preset at this angle. After beveling the ends, lay the sides on sawhorses and nail a piece of scrap 1x2 across

BODY SIDES are 2x4's joined in a triangle shape with plywood and a 1x4 crosspiece.

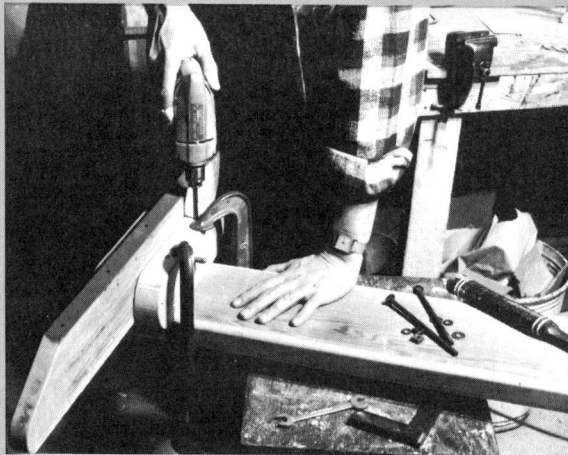

RUNNER CHOCKS are carefully aligned and clamped for boring holes in runner.

BOATING

RUNNERS are made from 1/2x1-in. steel angle, then bolted completely through 5/8-in. oak. Large scale plans show details of different types.

BOATING

STEERING RUNNER. Steel straps serve as bearing plates for bolts used in assembly.

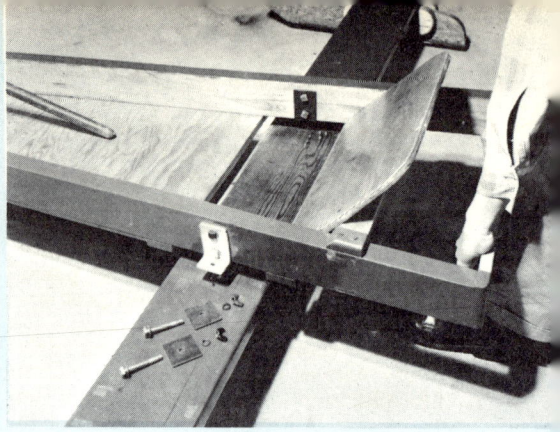

LOWERING the body of the ice boat onto the runner plank. Bolts go through angles.

STEPPING THE MAST. Each stay connects to eyebolt, one forward and two on runner plank.

the front end to join them temporarily. Then glue and screw the 1x4 crosspiece in place at the rear end. Next cut out the half-inch plywood crosspieces for the front section and screw the bottom ones in place. The bottom piece of the ¾-inch plywood mast step is then bored with a ¾-inch dia. hole for the steering post and fastened in place. The half-inch plywood floor is put on later since it must be fitted to meet the runner plank cleat.

Now turn the body over and install the plywood and 1x4 crosspieces. Before screwing down the front piece, put an eyebolt in place for the forestay. Then cut the lower mast step of ¾-inch plywood to fit the foot of the mast. This piece should fit snugly inside the 2x4's behind 1x4 crosspiece and should be glued and screwed to the bottom ¾-inch plywood panel. The 2¼-inch mast step hole should be located a quarter-inch forward of the hole in the top panel to give a 3° rake to the mast. Bore the top mast step panel for the mast and steering post and screw it in place, shifting it to align the mast and post accurately.

With the crosspieces in place, the body is turned bottom up to mark the position of the runner plank. Carefully align the plank so that it will be at right angles to the centerline. The best way to do this is to measure the diagonal from the ends of the runner plank to the front of the body. The diagonal dimensions must be equal. When the plank alignment is set, attach 1x2 cleats across the bottom of the body fore and aft of the runner plank, fitting them snugly against the runner plank edges. The half-inch plywood floor can now be screwed and glued to the bottoms of the 2x4's.

Turn the body over again to add the seat back. Bevel the edge of a 1x2 at 45° to form the seat back cleat. Screw it in place and then attach the other cleats below. This completes the woodwork on the body. Go over the whole structure with sandpaper, rounding off all edges.

The runner plank can be tackled next. If you wish to go to the extra trouble, you can make up a laminated, arched runner plank that will make the boat ride easier on rough ice. Use two layers of 1x8-in. boat grade spruce, glued while clamped in the arched position. Set up two sawhorses under each end of the plank with a scrap

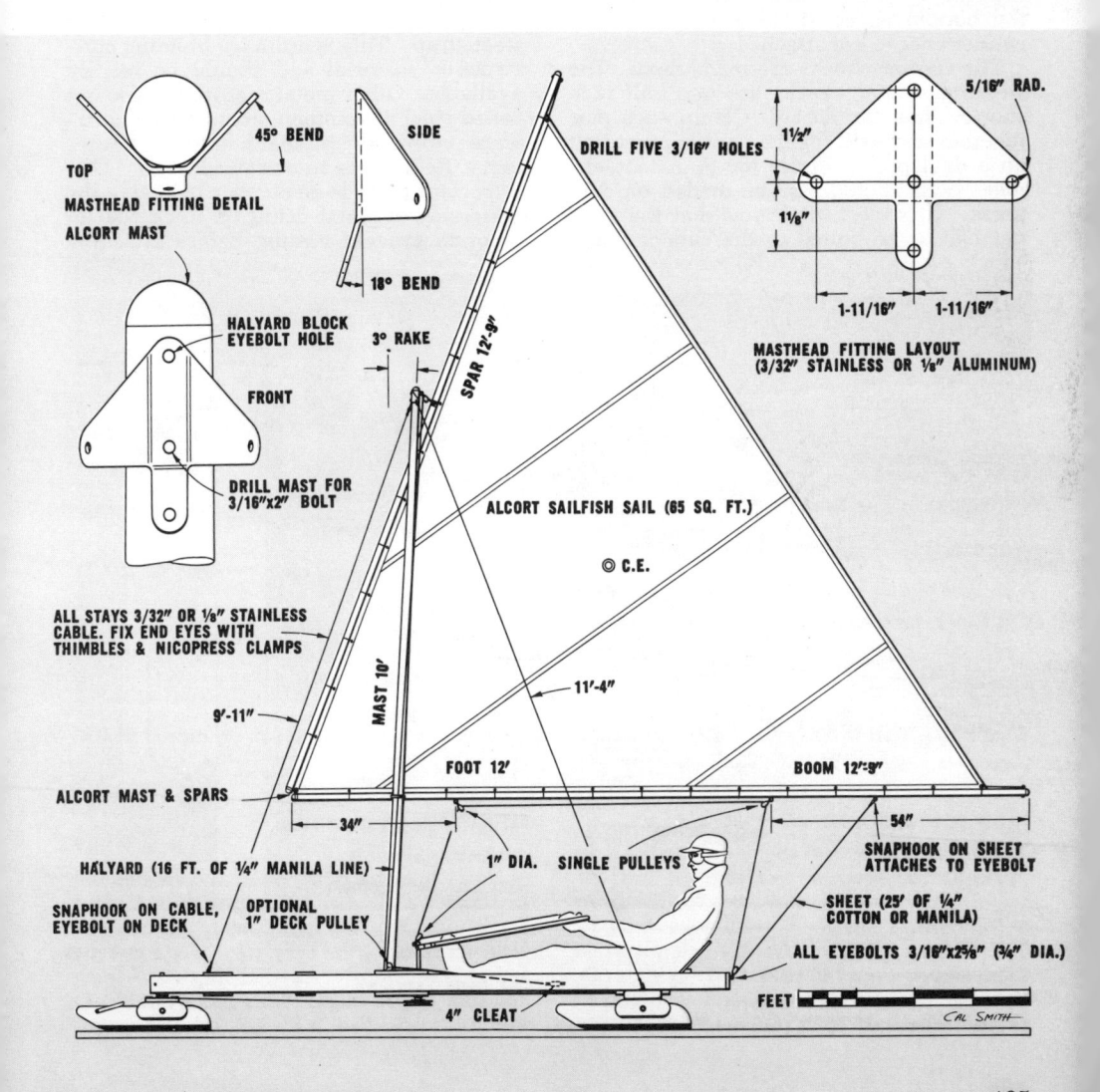

465

BOATING

length of 2x4 between the ceiling and the plank center to bow down the center a half inch more than desired. Use waterproof glue and clamp the lamination at the center. Also clamp both sides every eight inches. You will need at least two dozen clamps.

The simple runner plank used on the original Frostfish is an eight-foot length of 2x8 pine. We sorted through a considerable stack of lumber to find a knot-free piece. We selected one that was warped close to the desired arch. The plank should be carefully marked at the center and ends trimmed square. The edges are planed and sanded one quarter round except along the top edges touching the cleats under the body and on the bottom edges at the ends where the runner chocks are attached.

The runner chocks are made next. The steering runner chocks are one half inch shorter than the others. Clamp each pair together and drill for the runner pivot bolt on a drill press. Holes for $\frac{5}{16}$-in. attachment bolts should also be drilled on drill press. It is most important that the runner chocks be bolted to the runner plank at right angles so that the runners are exactly parallel. Any toe-in or out of the main runners will only create unnecessary drag. A trick to help maintain chock alignment is to cut a ⅛-inch groove the width of chock into the bottom of the runner plank so that chock is set into the runner plank. Bolt the chocks in place on the plank, putting ⅛x2-inch strap bearing plates (C) on top of the plank to prevent crushing the wood when the bolts are tightened down.

The steering chock should be made next. Cut a groove for plate B in the chock tops. This plate serves as a bearing surface for the upright pivot (king) bolt. The large-scale plans contain detailed drawing of fittings such as plates B and C. Most of these fittings are cut from ⅛x2-inch hot rolled steel strap. This is ordinary building construction material and should be readily available. Other metal required is also hot rolled steel of common sizes. Some hardware stores or builder's supply houses carry Redi-Rods in required sizes. One important point to remember is to give the underside of metal fittings a thick coat of paint to prevent rusting before attaching

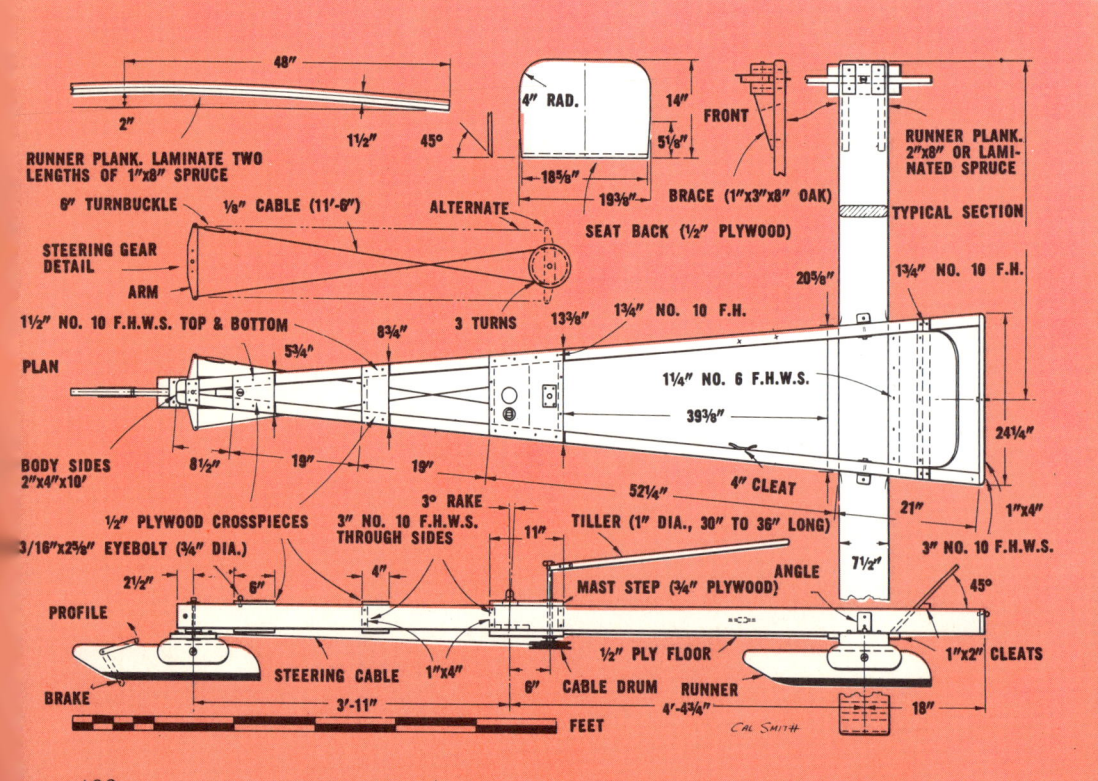

BOATING

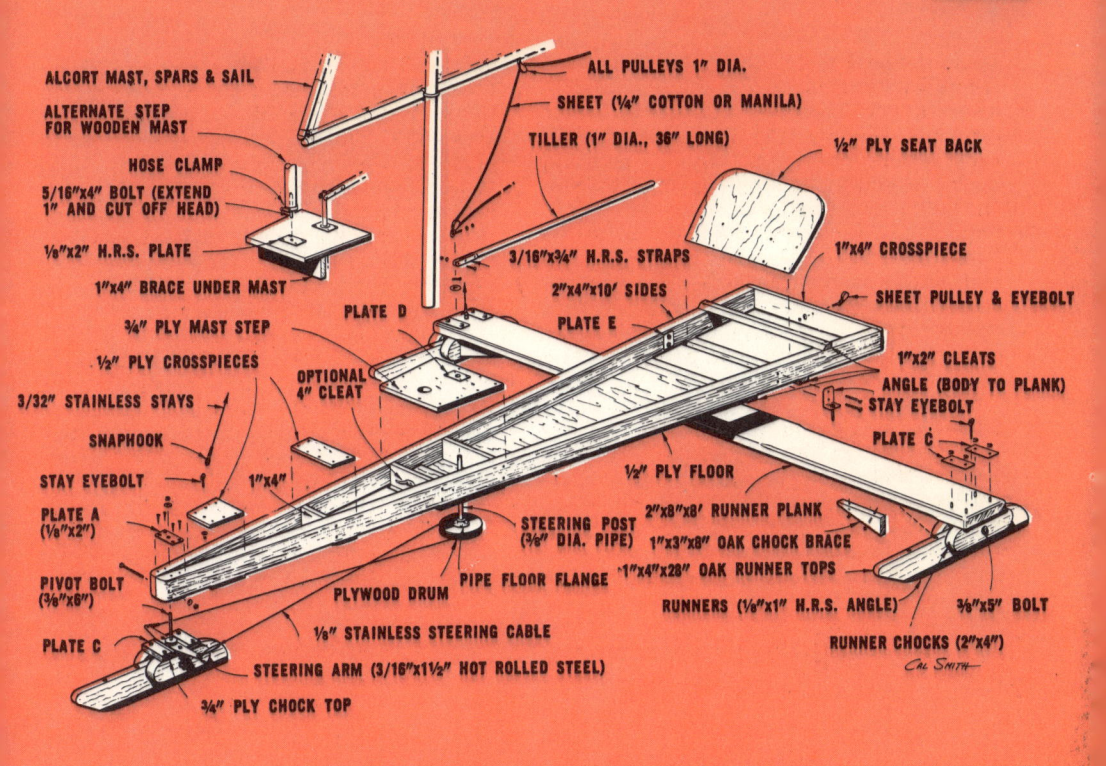

Diagram labels:
- ALCORT MAST, SPARS & SAIL
- ALTERNATE STEP FOR WOODEN MAST
- HOSE CLAMP
- 5/16"x4" BOLT (EXTEND 1" AND CUT OFF HEAD)
- 1/8"x2" H.R.S. PLATE
- 1"x4" BRACE UNDER MAST
- 3/4" PLY MAST STEP
- 1/2" PLY CROSSPIECES
- 3/32" STAINLESS STAYS
- SNAPHOOK
- STAY EYEBOLT
- PLATE A (1/8"x2")
- PIVOT BOLT (3/8"x6")
- PLATE C
- ALL PULLEYS 1" DIA.
- SHEET (1/4" COTTON OR MANILA)
- TILLER (1" DIA., 36" LONG)
- 3/16"x3/4" H.R.S. STRAPS
- 2"x4"x10' SIDES
- PLATE D
- OPTIONAL 4" CLEAT
- 1"x4"
- PLATE E
- 1/2" PLY FLOOR
- 2"x8"x8' RUNNER PLANK
- STEERING POST (3/8" DIA. PIPE)
- 1"x3"x8" OAK CHOCK BRACE
- 1"x4"x28" OAK RUNNER TOPS
- PIPE FLOOR FLANGE
- PLYWOOD DRUM
- 1/8" STAINLESS STEERING CABLE
- STEERING ARM (3/16"x1 1/2" HOT ROLLED STEEL)
- 3/4" PLY CHOCK TOP
- 1/2" PLY SEAT BACK
- 1"x4" CROSSPIECE
- SHEET PULLEY & EYEBOLT
- 1"x2" CLEATS
- ANGLE (BODY TO PLANK)
- STAY EYEBOLT
- PLATE C
- RUNNERS (1/8"x1" H.R.S. ANGLE)
- 3/8"x5" BOLT
- RUNNER CHOCKS (2"x4")
- CAL SMITH

them permanently in place with screws.

The runners come next. These are very important parts of any ice boat so extra care is required. Cut the oak tops to shape and sand them in smooth. Then drill for the pivot bolt on a drill press. The runners used on Frostfish consist of $\frac{1}{8}$x1-inch hot rolled steel angle bolted flat to the bottom of the oak top. The lower edge of the angle is ground to a 45° V. This edge is also ground with a crown of about $\frac{1}{16}$ inch running fore and aft. Grinding is easier after the angle is bolted to the oak. Drill bolt holes in the angle first and use them as a guide to drill holes in the oak.

Runners should be maintained as sharp as possible by grinding and filing. The hot rolled steel will not hold an edge as long as harder steels, so when your Frostfish starts to sideslip, quit sailing and break out the file. Runners can be hardened (not tempered) or a bead of tool steel can be welded onto the running edge and ground to a V shape. This latter trick, done by a competent welder, will reduce the need for frequent sharpening.

The entire boat should be painted before attaching the fittings. Prime the wood and paint or varnish it as desired. Two or three coats of good grade enamel should be sufficient unless the boat must be left out in the weather for long periods. Then at least four coats of enamel will be necessary.

Starting at the bow, screw the two plates (A) to the body top and bottom. Then screw on the two plates (D) for the steering post. Put the body in place on the runner plank, centering it exactly, and bolt it through the angles on the sides.

The steering gear shown gives automobile-type steering. That is, move the tiller left and the boat turns left and vice versa. You may wish to hook up the tiller boat-fashion so that moving the tiller to the left

---

LARGE-SCALE PLANS

include complete details of all structural members and fittings, a bill of materials and suggestions for adapting other sail rigs. To order a set, send $5.00 to MI Plans Service, Fawcett Bldg., Fawcett Place, Greenwich, Conn. Specify Plan B-239, Frostfish.

BOATING

steers the boat to the right. This is the traditional arrangement and should be followed if you expect to sail against other ice boats. Simply lead the cables directly back around the drum without crossing them. If you do not wish to build a drum and cable steering gear, you can bolt a duplicate of the front steering arm to the flange on the steering post and connect the ends with auto-type tie rods. The steering cable or rods should be provided with a tightening device. Any slippage of the cable around the drum can be reduced by taking up on a turnbuckle.

Now for the go-power. We picked the lateen rig because of its simplicity and low cost. Although the Alcort Sailfish rig is not strictly an ice boat sail, it pushes Frostfish along at a good clip. It will not stand up in 40-50 mph gusts because it is not as rugged as regular ice boat sails, so exercise some caution in strong winter winds. Other sails and rigs of similar area can also be used on Frostfish. Old Town makes lateen canoe rigs of 40, 45, 55 and 65 square feet area and Grumman can supply a lateen rig of 45 square feet and a Gunter rig of 65 square feet. Dinghy sails and spars could also be adapted. Whichever rig you use, be sure to locate it correctly on the boat. Take the trouble to work out the center of effort for your particular sail as shown in the drawing in the large-scale plans. This will insure good balance and trim.

You'll like Frostfish. We've certainly enjoyed the original. There's nothing quite like zipping over the ice, and when a good gust hits you—wow! That acceleration really racks you back in the seat. If you can get your friends interested, build two or three boats and enjoy some racing. Competition adds even more zest and you'll find yourself glad to be out when a winter wind is blowing. •

FROSTFISH is quickly set up once you reach the lake, and she will give many speed thrills.

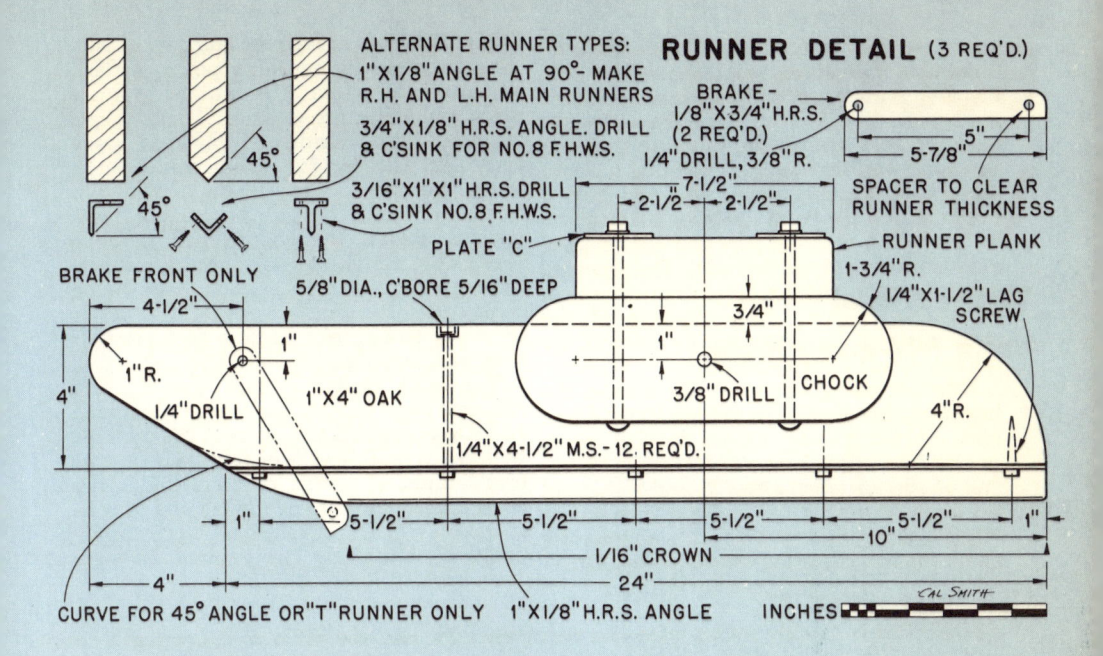

BOATING

RUNNER DETAIL (3 REQ'D.)

ALTERNATE RUNNER TYPES:
1"X1/8" ANGLE AT 90°- MAKE R.H. AND L.H. MAIN RUNNERS
3/4"X1/8" H.R.S. ANGLE. DRILL & C'SINK FOR NO. 8 F.H.W.S.
3/16"X1"X1" H.R.S. DRILL & C'SINK NO. 8 F.H.W.S.

BRAKE- 1/8"X 3/4" H.R.S. (2 REQ'D.) 1/4" DRILL, 3/8" R.

SPACER TO CLEAR RUNNER THICKNESS

PLATE "C"
RUNNER PLANK
1-3/4" R.
1/4"X1-1/2" LAG SCREW

45°
45°
BRAKE FRONT ONLY
4-1/2"
1" R.
4"
1/4" DRILL
1" X 4" OAK
5/8" DIA., C'BORE 5/16" DEEP
7-1/2"
2-1/2" | 2-1/2"
3/4"
1"
3/8" DRILL
CHOCK
4" R.
1/4"X 4-1/2" M.S.- 12 REQ'D.
1"
5-1/2"
5-1/2"
5-1/2"
5-1/2"
1"
10"
1/16" CROWN
24"
CURVE FOR 45° ANGLE OR "T" RUNNER ONLY
1"X1/8" H.R.S. ANGLE
INCHES

CAL SMITH

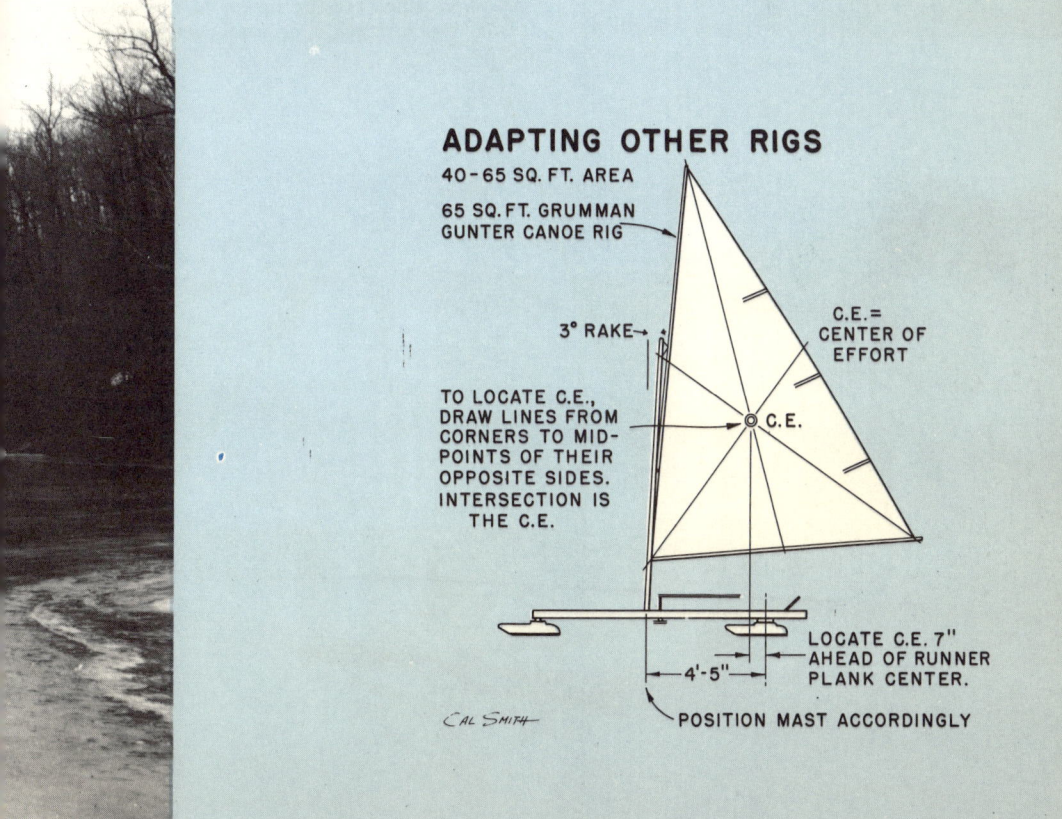

ADAPTING OTHER RIGS

40-65 SQ. FT. AREA
65 SQ. FT. GRUMMAN GUNTER CANOE RIG
3° RAKE
C.E.= CENTER OF EFFORT
TO LOCATE C.E., DRAW LINES FROM CORNERS TO MID-POINTS OF THEIR OPPOSITE SIDES. INTERSECTION IS THE C.E.
C.E.
4'-5"
LOCATE C.E. 7" AHEAD OF RUNNER PLANK CENTER.
POSITION MAST ACCORDINGLY

CAL SMITH

469

BOOKCASES

Bookcase With Table

This sectional series has a fold-away table.

THREE coats of lacquer and two of wax give these living room pieces a dark but attractive gloss. The walnut grain is wavy and quite pronounced. Three sheets of cedar-filled, hardwood plywood were carefully chosen for their appearance. Since the sheets were to be turned into furniture which would be visible from various angles, the walnut had to be a reasonable match not only between sheets but between both sides of each sheet. Being cedar-filled the sheets were lighter, easier to work, and fifteen cents a foot cheaper than ordinary five ply hardwood plywood.

The wall against which the finished cabinets were to stand is fourteen feet long and it was decided to construct the cabinets with an overall length of ten feet. A ten-foot cabinet, of course, presents difficulties from a viewpoint of portability and of construction. These difficulties were eliminated by designing the cabinet in three

When in use, the table is supported by a folding leg. End table is hinged vertically.

All three units can be varied in size to suit room measurements or wall arrangement.

BOOKCASES

sections; two of them four feet in length. This design made it possible to utilize more fully a standard sheet of plywood which is either 4x8 or 4x6 feet. The height of the pieces, being less than 3 feet, also made it possible to economize on wood.

The center cabinet was designed to function in several interesting ways. It breaks up what would otherwise be a monotonous ten-foot row of books and forms a center point of attraction which the books now enhance. It also provides a convenient storage space for liquors and a chess set. Most important, of course, is that the door of this cabinet functions as a table in the raised position. This is achieved with a piano hinge and a folding walnut leg which disappears inside the cabinet when the door is closed. In the raised position the table can be used to serve food buffet style or beverages. It may be used too for chess, cards and other games.

Again in order to avoid monotony the right-hand section of the cabinet was planned to include a large walnut arm that swings upward on a piano hinge to allow access to the books beneath. In the lowered position this arm serves as an end table for an adjacent and comfortable upholstered chair. The arm is large enough to hold a lamp, books, tobacco, flower vase, and ash trays all within easy reach. The top shelf of this section was also cut short to provide a space for those few extra large books which will not fit into even the largest lower shelf of any bookcase.

The three shelves of both long sections vary in height, of course, to allow for an organized arrangement of books according to their size. The top shelf is only 8 inches in height, the middle shelf 9 inches, and the bottom one a generous 11 inches.

The entire cabinet was fastened together with simple butt joints, utilizing a white

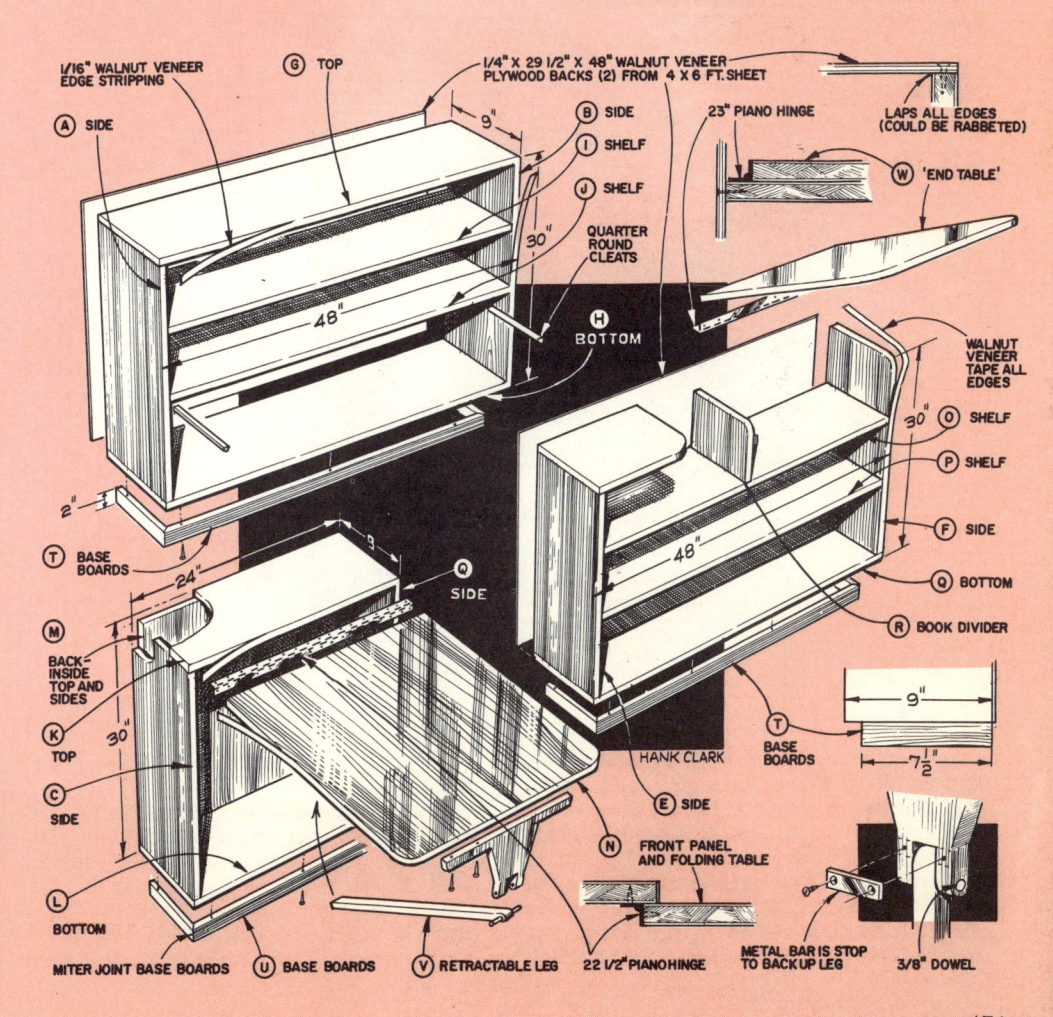

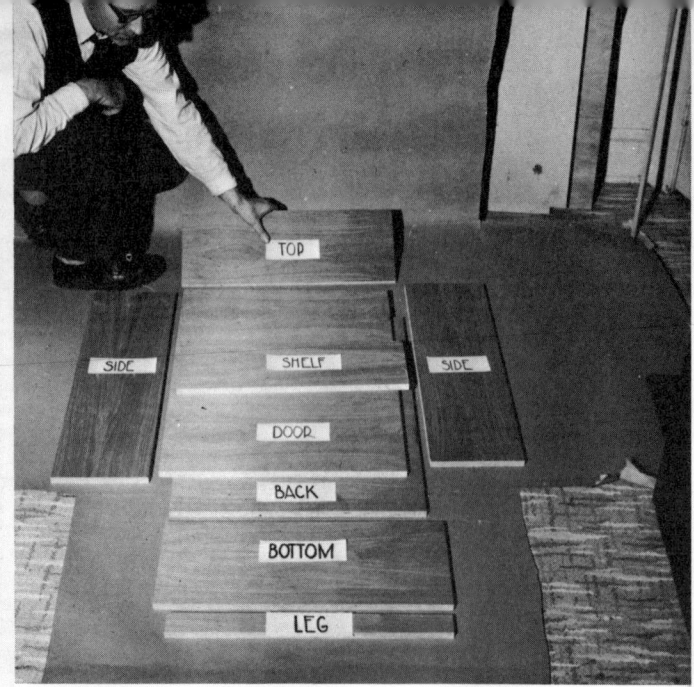

Careful planning is necessary for adjacent panels to match in grain direction and texture.

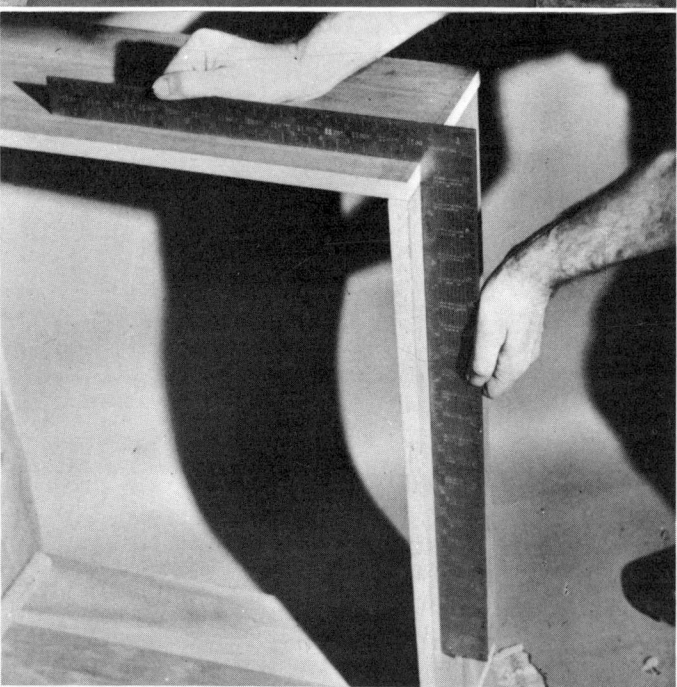

Before glue sets, check all angles for squareness, then clamp in both directions securely.

polyvinyl glue, finishing nails puttied over, and corner blocks of quarter round molding. The edges of the plywood were taped with walnut wood tape anchored in place with contact cement.

Chrome hardware was utilized in hinges, handles and catches. The folding leg moves on a three-eighth-inch maple dowel rod and is held rigid in the extended position by a half-inch band of steel on the inside of the leg.

Walnut legs two inches in width support the three sections of the cabinet and provide foot-room underneath the bottom shelf. These are held in place with glue, screws, and corner blocks. This is the only place in the cabinet at which butt joints were not used. The corners of the legs were

BOOKCASES

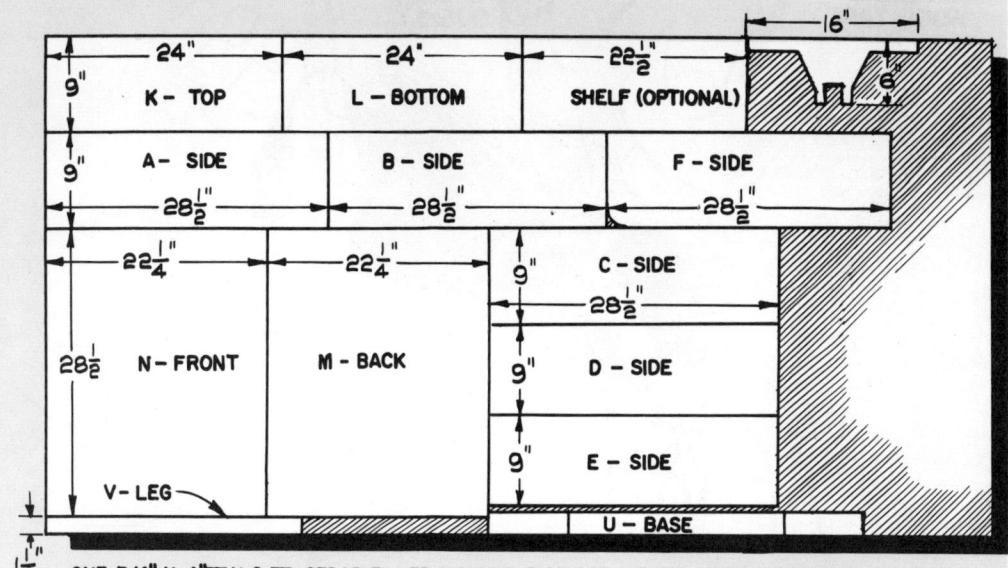

ONE 3/4" X 4 FT. X 8 FT. CEDAR FILLED WALNUT PLYWOOD YIELDS CENTER CABINET AND SIDES

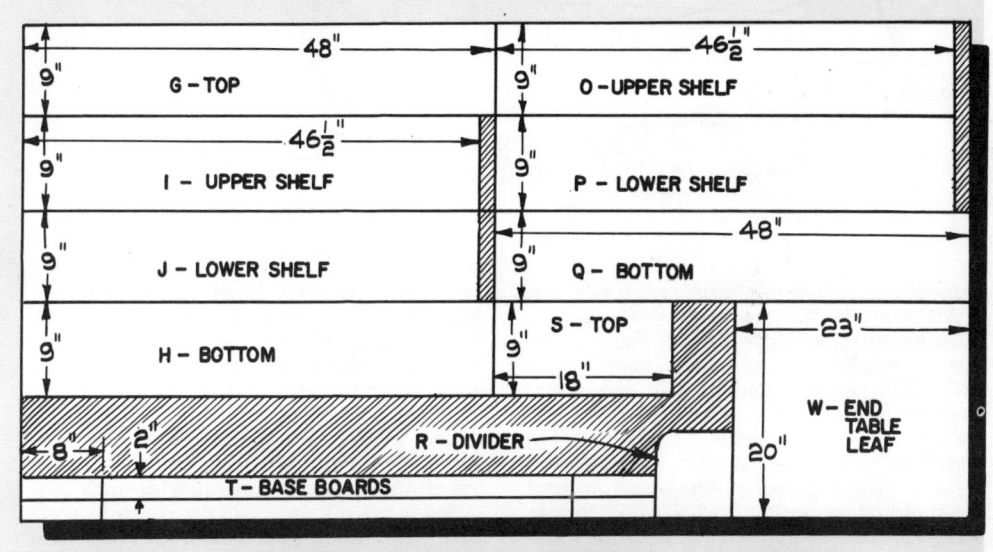

ONE 3/4" X 4 FT. X 8 FT. SIMILAR, YIELDS ALL SHELVES FOR TWO FLANK CABINETS

mitered, glued and screwed to the bottom.

Begin to make this cabinet by laying out all of the pieces on the plywood sheets with the grain of each piece running in the proper direction. Lay out the center cabinet first so that the large door which is the most prominent piece in the finished cabinet will be cut from the most beautiful part of the sheet. Remember that each piece will be ⅛ inch less in width than the finished piece. This is an allowance for the taped edges which will be added later. Each tape will utilize almost $\frac{1}{16}$ inch of space.

When cutting these pieces on a table saw set the blade a mere eighth of an inch above the surface of the wood and feed the wood slowly to secure a smooth, unsplintered edge. Use a sharp combination blade, or a

473

BOOKCASES

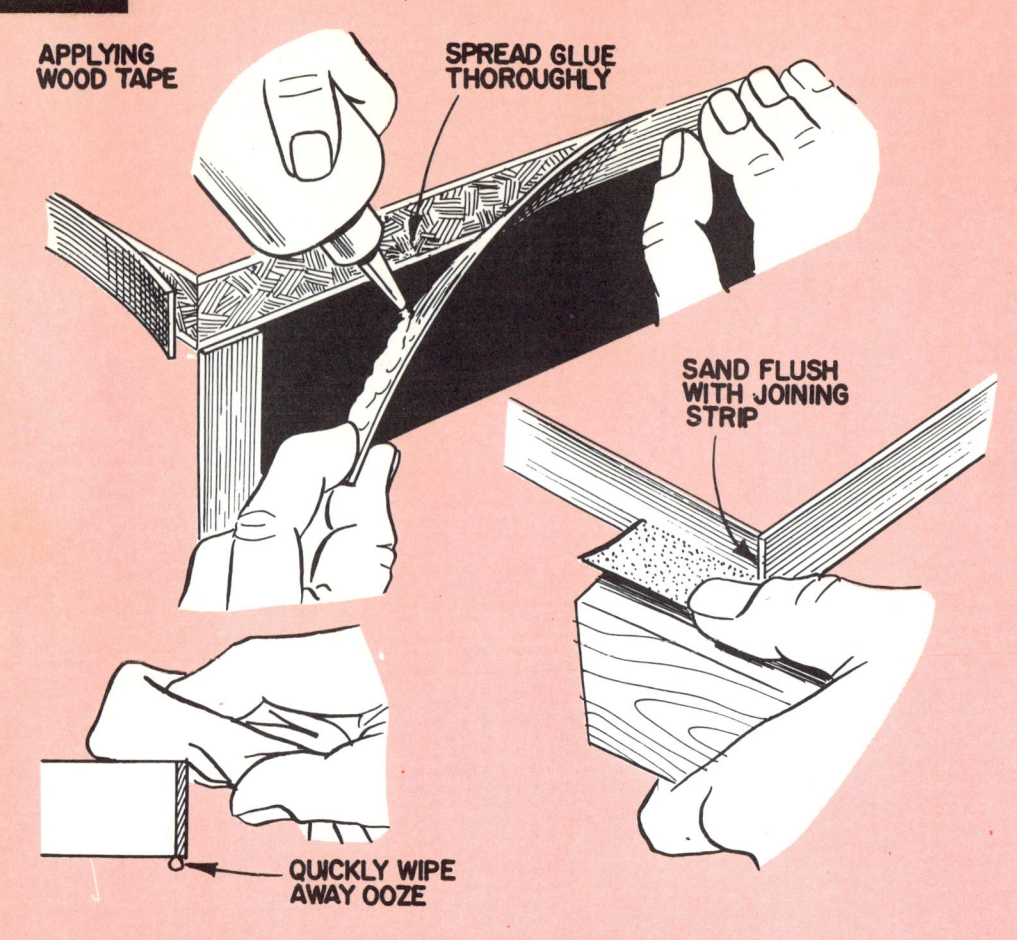

APPLYING WOOD TAPE

SPREAD GLUE THOROUGHLY

SAND FLUSH WITH JOINING STRIP

QUICKLY WIPE AWAY OOZE

a special plywood one with fine teeth. set.

After all of the pieces for one section have been cut to size, assemble them in the proper relationship to check the fit, size and grain. Mark them in this assembled position for easy final assembly.

Now cut the quarter round molding which is to be used to add strength and rigidity at the corner joints. Mark around the molding on both pieces of wood so that the glue can be applied neatly. Start the finishing nails into the molding at this point and then apply the glue. Keep a clean rag handy to wipe away any excess glue as hardened glue is difficult to remove. As soon as the four pieces of the center cabinet frame are assembled, place the cabinet back in position inside the frame. Then anchor it to the frame with glue and finishing nails.

Check the cabinet with a large framing square immediately before the glue sets. Small adjustments may be made at this point to achieve a square cabinet. It is important that this cabinet be accurately squared so that the large door which must be added later will fit exactly inside the front edge of the frame. Then, if the large door is sawed carefully, its edges will not have to be planed and its rectangular shape will not be destroyed.

The folding leg of the center door may be made next. After it has been drawn carefully on the three-quarter-inch plywood cut it out on a jig saw, if one is available, or a band saw. Cut both sections of the leg from a matching portion of the plywood so the final assembly will be uniform in appearance. Round off all of the leg corners with a file. The hole for the dowel rod may be drilled next. This can be done accurately and easily by clamping the two pieces together and drilling both at the same time. Do not drill completely through the top piece as a spot of glue in this hole will serve to grip the dowel and hold it in position permanently.

Tape the edges of the leg assembly next. Be sure there is enough space for the tape

BOOKCASES

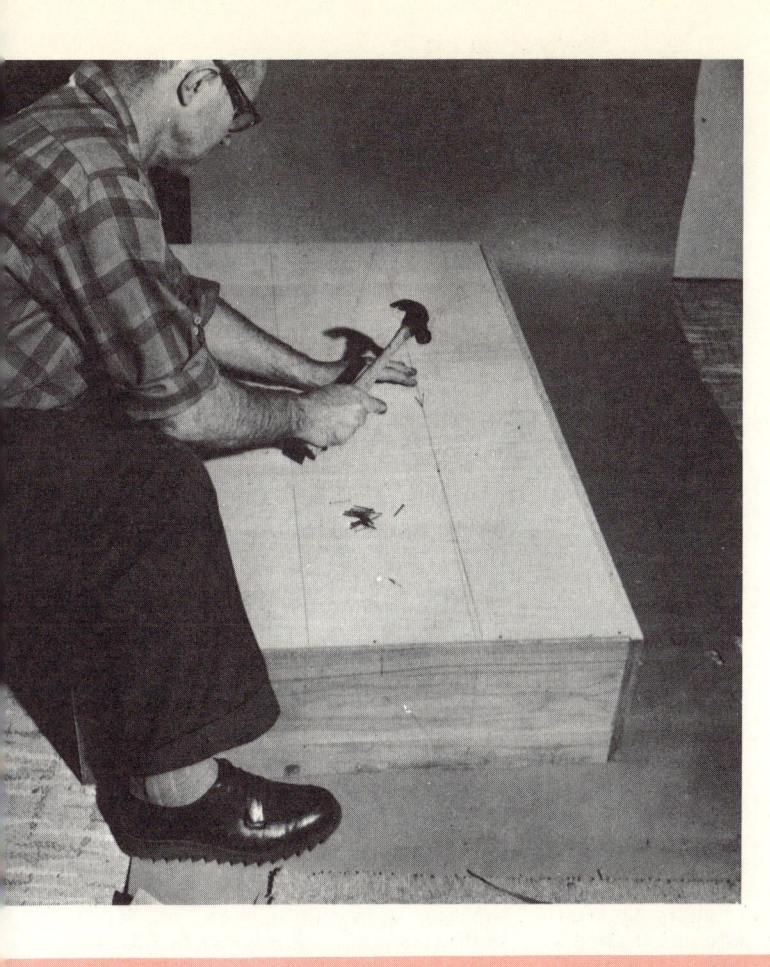

Backing panel can be nailed or screwed to all edges and shelves for stiffness and rigidity.

so the two pieces will not bind when assembled. Also remember that space must be provided for the two or three coats of lacquer and wax which must be applied before the leg is finally assembled.

The entire leg assembly is locked to the under side of the door with glue, screws, and corner block. Use flat headed wood screws and countersink the heads so deep that they cannot be seen. These need not be covered over as the holes always face the floor or are out of sight inside the cabinet.

Turn the cabinet over to install the piano hinge. Attach the hinge to the door first and then, after positioning the door carefully in the opening, mark, drill, and screw the remaining hinge leaf to the cabinet. Proceed by tightening three screws first and closing the door to check for fit. If the fit is not a good one move two of the screws and check again. When an accurate fit has been secured install the remainder of the screws. Make sure the screws are of the proper size to fit the countersunk holes of the piano hinge. If the screw heads are too large the hinge will not close properly. If a 1¼-inch hinge is used, the screws should not be larger than a No. 4.

The piano hinge which connects the folding arm or end table to the right-hand section of the cabinet is installed in the same manner as the hinge on the center section. This hinge and arm may be installed before the small partition or shelf divider is added. This procedure will permit you to secure the proper clearance between the partition and the folding arm easily. Add the small top shelf to this section last and anchor it to the cabinet back and side with reinforcing corner blocks of quarter round molding. Use glue and finishing nails.

After all of the shelves are in position add the back panels. These back panels are of ¼-inch walnut plywood and should fit inside the ends and top shelf. After glue has been applied to the edges of the boards and the cabinet has been turned over lay

BOOKCASES

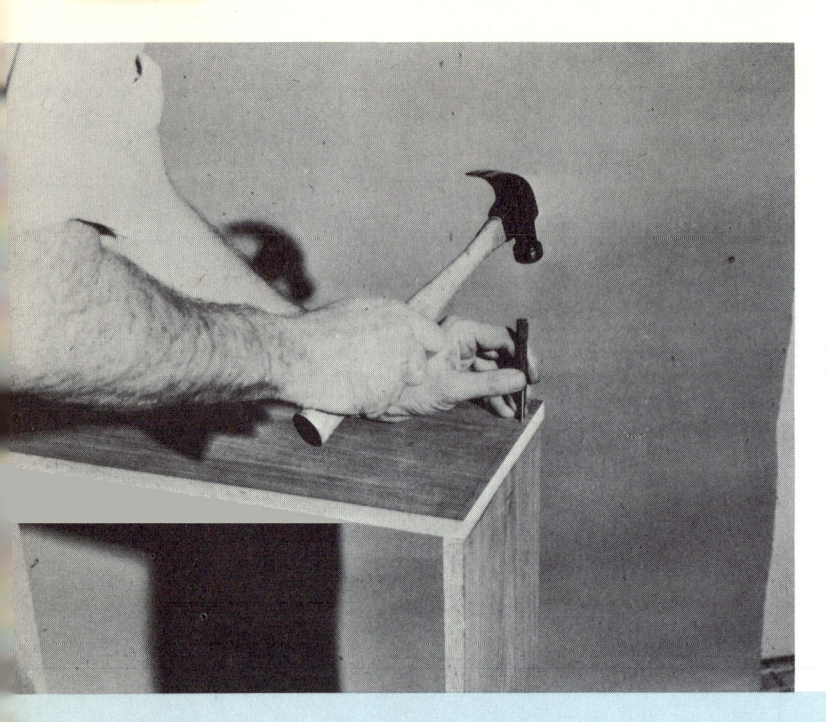

Carefully set all nails and putty with wood dough tinted to match the finished panels.

the back in position and nail it into place with 1-inch common wire nails. Draw guide lines for these nails with a straightedge. Common nails, having a definite head, develop greater holding power and will not be visible. The glue, of course, will add even greater strength and rigidity. Quarter round molding may be added next on the inside of the cabinet between the under side of the shelves and the cabinet back. The quarter round molding used for this purpose may be covered with walnut wood tape or stained before being installed. This will make them not merely functional but an attractive part of the cabinet. Install these molding pieces neatly as far as the glue is concerned because this excess glue must be removed before the finish is applied. If the glue is not removed the finishing material whether lacquer or varnish will not penetrate through the glue and will leave a whitish area and thus spoil the appearance of the cabinet.

Now go over the entire cabinet with a nail set and drive all visible nail heads below the surface of the wood. Fill the resulting holes with colored putty or walnut dust and glue.

The next step, of course, is the addition of the legs. The cabinet must be turned over for this job. Cut the legs to the proper length and miter the corners. Now counterbore the holes for the screw heads so that the heads will be set deeply into the wood and off the floor. Mark the position of the legs carefully on the bottom of the lower shelf and, at the same time, the location of the screw holes in the shelf. Drill pilot holes in both the legs and the lower shelf juncture. Apply the glue to both legs and shelf before placing the legs in the proper location. After checking for correct alignment insert the screws and tighten them carefully. Lastly, add a long corner block to the inside back of the legs for additional strength. Do this with glue and finishing nails. Sand the corners (the mitered joints) before the glue has dried. Do this lightly and the joint will be practically invisible to the human eye. Also remember to turn the cabinet right side up before the glue has set in order to allow the leg joint to set with the full weight of the cabinet on it.

Use some very fine or 00 steel wool to prepare the cabinet for finishing materials. If necessary use some fine sandpaper to remove all glue spots particularly at the edges where the contact cement may be visible on the tape. After steel wooling, since walnut is hard wood, the wood may be dampened slightly to raise all loose fibers, and steel wooled again.

The first coat of lacquer (or varnish) may be applied liberally and quickly. Be sure to cover the entire cabinet inside and out in order to seal the wood and to pre-

BOOKCASES

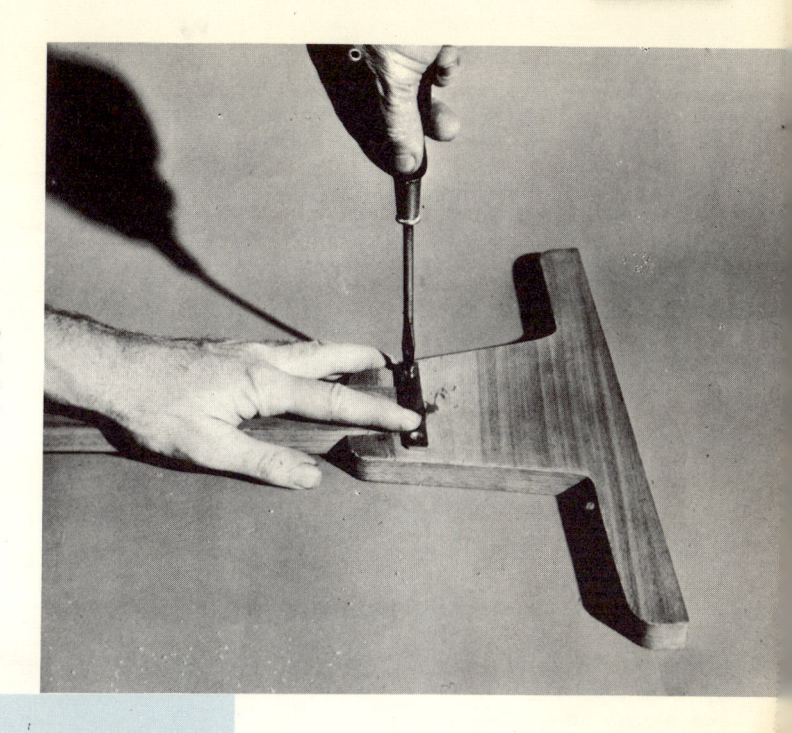

Table leg has back-up bar of metal to keep leg vertical in use. Hinge is a ⅜" dowel.

Last step is to mount base boards with counter-bored screws from the bottom up.

vent moisture content changes. This coat must be sanded or steel wooled thoroughly until all runs and rough spots are removed. Much of this coat will not be visible after the application of steel wool. Apply the second coat carefully, avoiding runs and drops. After this second coat has dried thoroughly steel wool it lightly or as much as necessary. When applying the third coat be sure to avoid scrubbing motion with the brush. Stroke the brush in one direction and allow the lacquer to flow evenly onto the wood. If enough lacquer is flowed onto the wood, brush marks will be minimized and a smooth glossy fiinish will result. Of course, all finishing should be applied in as dust free a room as possible.

After the third coat has been applied and allowed to harden completely it should be steel wooled lightly to remove any dust bumps or lingering runs. Wipe the steel wool dust off the wood with a soft dust cloth before applying the wax.

Use a good paste wax and apply it liberally on the first coat. After this coat has dried, rub it hard with a soft cloth and apply another but lighter coat of wax. Polishing or rubbing this coat is the last step in the finishing of the cabinet.

If the table top is to be used for alcoholic beverages, a plastic such as Micarta might be considered. • *By Bill Moore*

BOOKCASES

Modular Bookcase

It's lightweight and sturdy, is made from wood and wrought iron.

by Robert Lasson
and Martin Shaff

ATTRACTIVE unit of ½-inch square wrought iron and wooden shelves is 36 inches long. As case becomes full, other matching units can be made to same specifications.

THE design of this light-looking but extremely sturdy bookcase was planned so that subsequent units could be built to match. It's exactly 36 inches long, 29 inches in overall height, and 9⅝ inches deep—just the right depth to accommodate standard 10-inch lumber very snugly. Not a single nail or screw is used to attach the shelves to the frame. The top and bottom shelves rest both on their respective shelf supports and also on the cross supports. The top shelf is further retained by a small enclosure of its own, which forms an attractive touch. The middle shelf rests only on the two shelf supports at either end, but is firmly kept in place by the weight of books.

Built-in "book ends" have been incorporated into the design, too. These are merely lengths of wrought iron placed at the indicated intervals above shelf levels.

The lower shelf holds somewhat larger books than the upper one; actual placement of shelves may, of course, be juggled to suit your own needs.

If you have mostly small cloth or paper-bound books, you can probably get away with 8-inch lumber for your shelves. In this case, simply make the frame to match. In fact, it's wise to get your lumber first in any case, since widths differ slightly from mill to mill. Let the width of your lumber determine the depth of your frame.

The ½-inch wrought-iron frame was made to specifications by a local welding shop at low cost. If you have your own welding rig, so much the better. First make the two end assemblies, which will resemble two ladders with the first two rungs 1 inch apart, and the remaining ones at larger intervals (see illustration). Weld all shelf supports and "book ends." Then simply connect the two "ladders" with two pairs of cross supports at top and bottom. These are easiest to attach by welding, of course.

BOOKCASES

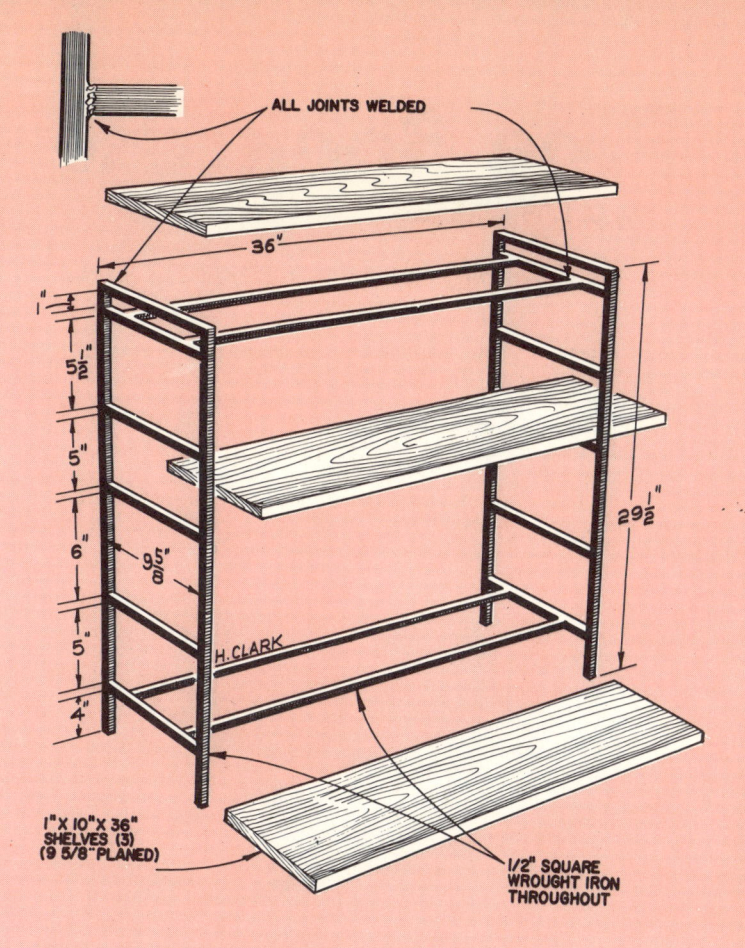

DIAGRAM here gives all necessary dimensions and construction details. Study carefully before doing job.

END VIEW shows top and bottom shelves are supported by cross supports. Middle shelf rests on the regular cross members of end assemblies, as shown.

However, if you are the roving kind who's on the move frequently, the cross supports may be drilled and tapped, and then machine-screwed in place. In this way, your bookcase can be disassembled and put into a very small package. However, chances are that a machine-screwed bookcase will not be as sturdy as an all-welded one—and it will be more expensive to make.

After all welds are made, file all the joints to remove excess metal and apply a coat of dull black paint. Install the shelves, and that's all there is to it. Used here was a mahogany shelf on top and two pine ones below for a contrasting effect.

The shelves were finished with three coats of linseed oil, which was steel-wooled between coats and then waxed. Rubber tips may be placed under the four legs, if desired. And when this bookcase gets filled up—just build another one to match. •

BOOKCASES

Knotty Pine Bookcase

by C. L. Widdicombe

Beautiful wood and simple construction produce this attractive model

THIS bookcase makes up very attractively in knotty pine although the rich depth of red cedar is not to be discounted when choice of materials is made. In selecting wood for the project make certain that the knots are sound and hard, and have no black rings around them. Knots of this type, although protected to some measure by finish, do tend to loosen and might fall out. This is an important fact to remember.

For the most part, this bookcase can be constructed with hammer and saw, although power tools do speed the job and ensure a better quality in the finished project. For the craftsman who does not possess a power saw, almost any builders' supply house has a mill and for a small fee will cut the components to size. •

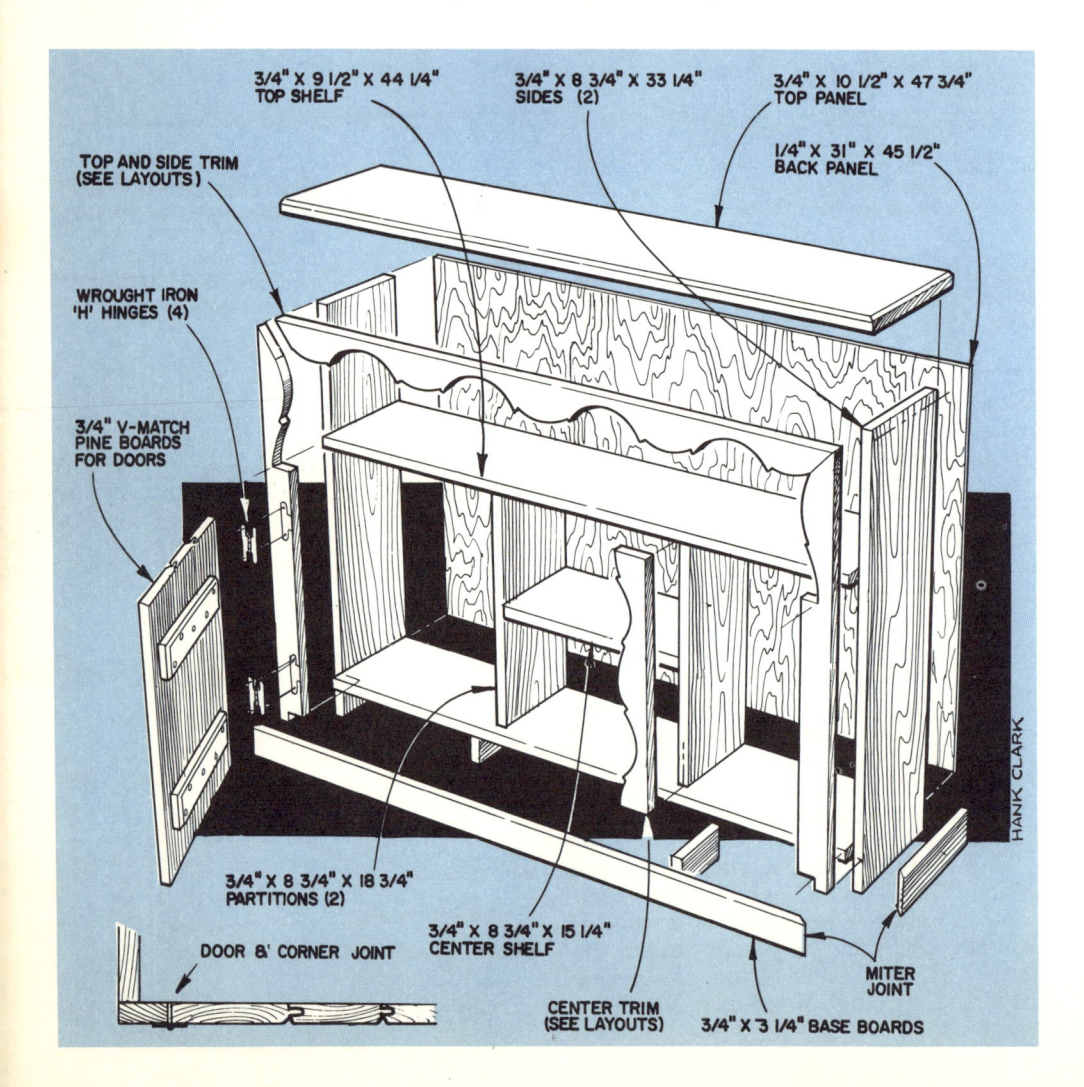

Labels on diagram:
- 3/4" X 9 1/2" X 44 1/4" TOP SHELF
- 3/4" X 8 3/4" X 33 1/4" SIDES (2)
- 3/4" X 10 1/2" X 47 3/4" TOP PANEL
- 1/4" X 31" X 45 1/2" BACK PANEL
- TOP AND SIDE TRIM (SEE LAYOUTS)
- WROUGHT IRON 'H' HINGES (4)
- 3/4" V-MATCH PINE BOARDS FOR DOORS
- 3/4" X 8 3/4" X 18 3/4" PARTITIONS (2)
- 3/4" X 8 3/4" X 15 1/4" CENTER SHELF
- DOOR & CORNER JOINT
- CENTER TRIM (SEE LAYOUTS)
- 3/4" X 3 1/4" BASE BOARDS
- MITER JOINT
- HANK CLARK

Planing a bevel on top of bookcase is one of the final jobs in turning out this handsome knotty pine bookcase. As photos and diagrams show, construction is simple. Finish with clear lacquer, shellac, varnish.

Photo at right shows workman laying out pattern for scroll, then transferring it to wood. Diagram below shows dimensions and design of scroll work.

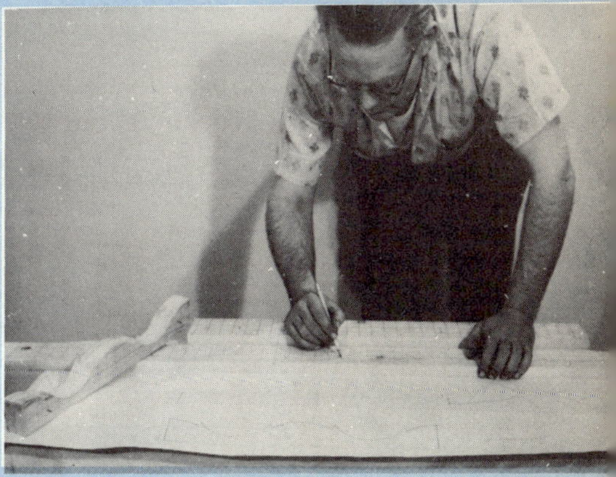

MATERIALS NEEDED

¾-inch KNOTTY PINE:

1 piece 10½ x 47¾ (Top)
2 pieces 9½ x 44¼ (Shelves)
2 pieces 8¾ x 33¼ (Sides)
2 pieces 8¾ x 18¾ (Centre Partitions)
1 piece 8¾ x 15¼ (Shelf)
1 piece 3¼ x 45 } (Approx. Length.
2 pieces 3¼ x 12 } Mitred Base Trim.)
1 piece 45¾ } (Scrolled Ornamental
2 pieces 18¾ } Trim)
2 pieces 30½ } (Width As Per Patterns)
1 piece ¼" Firply 30 x 45¼ (Back)
4 pieces Firply 2¾ x 11⅞ (Door Battens)

2 doors 1" V-match 13⅞ x 18⅝
2 pair hinges
2 knobs
2 door catches

⅜" hardwood dowels
1½" finishing nails
32 1¼" #10 round head brass screws

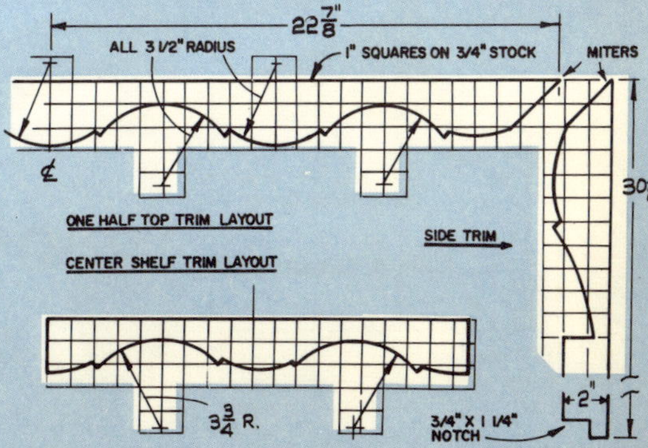
22 7/8"
ALL 3 1/2" RADIUS
1" SQUARES ON 3/4" STOCK
MITERS
℄
30 1/2"
ONE HALF TOP TRIM LAYOUT
SIDE TRIM
CENTER SHELF TRIM LAYOUT
3 3/4 R.
2"
3/4" X 1 1/4" NOTCH

BOOKCASES

To build bookcase, cut out parts to dimensions given in diagram. Then, using glue and clamps, assemble sides and bottom and center shelf. Check for squareness. Then drill holes into shelves, insert glue and ⅜-inch dowels which will serve as screws. Unit stands overnight to give glue a chance to harden securely.

The next day saw off any excess dowel, sand unit. Then assemble center section in similar manner, only this time using nails instead of dowels. The nails will not show. Check unit again for squareness. Diagram below shows dimensions for various parts and construction details.

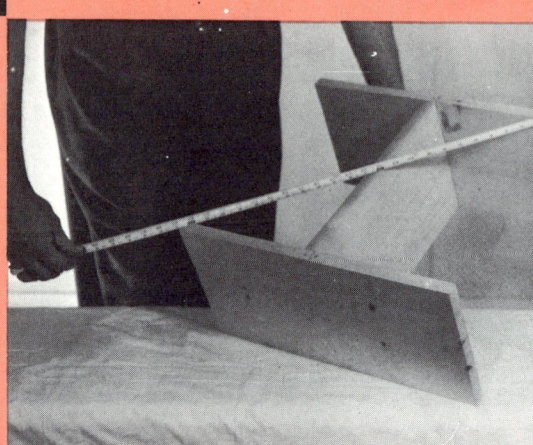

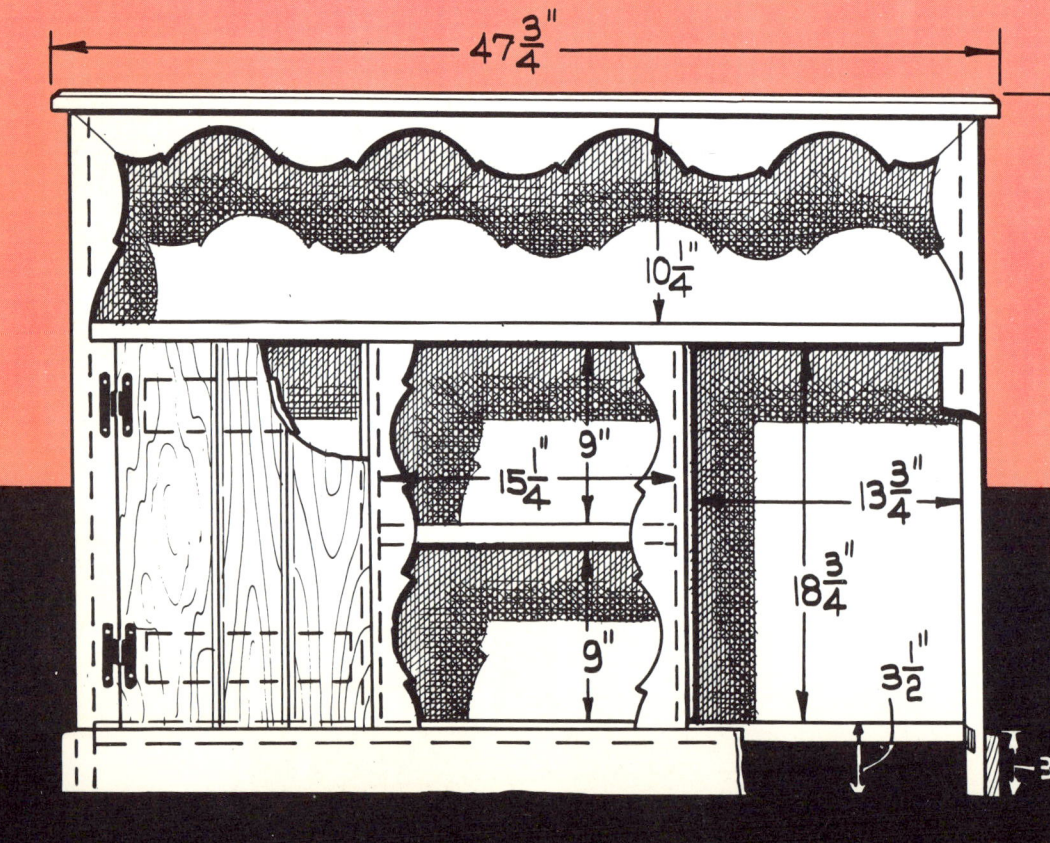

BOOKCASES

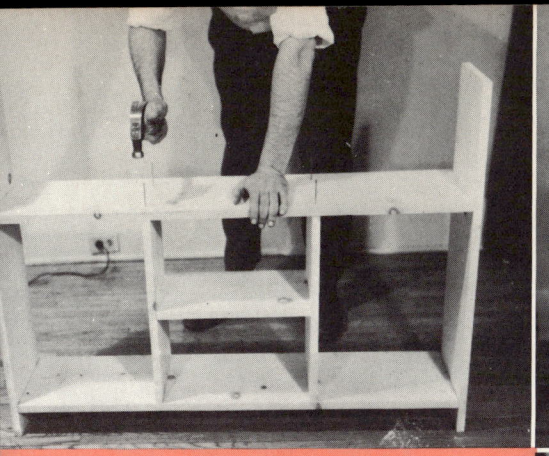

Center unit is then nailed in place, as shown. Attach the top in the same manner, and then the back panel, as shown in photographs. Drive nails beneath surface, later fill holes with wood putty.

Bookcase doors are three pieces of knotty pine V-match. Smaller 4-inch piece fits in middle, the other 6-inch pieces fit on each side. Glue between grooves of boards and clamp together. Then attach battens with glue and screws. Before attaching doors with hinges, place the base trim, as indicated in the diagram.

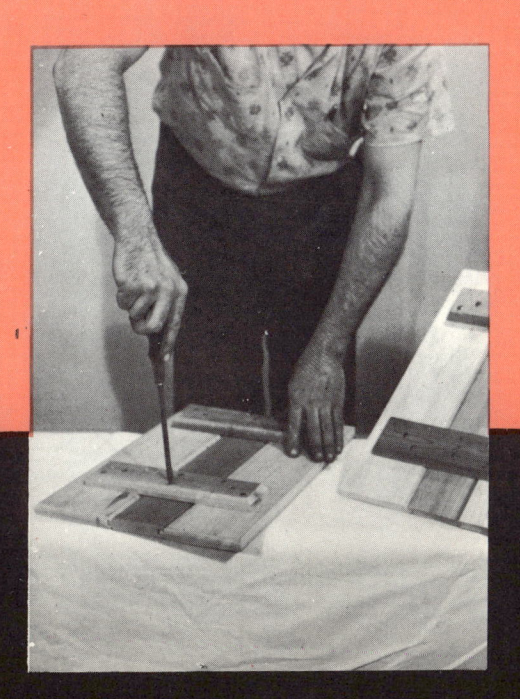

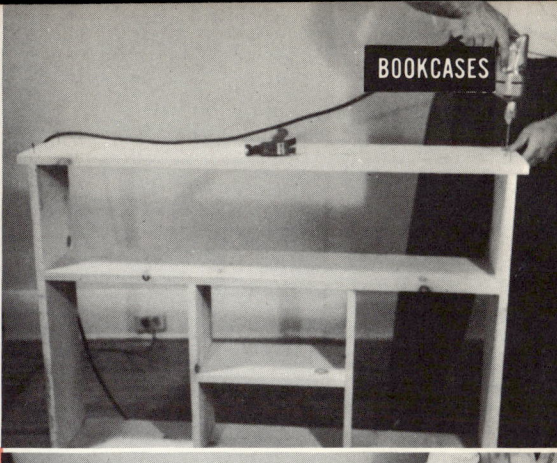

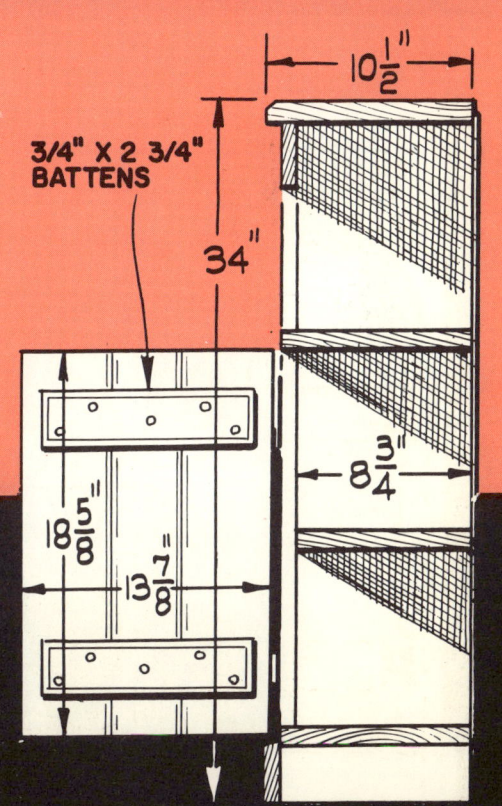

3/4" X 2 3/4" BATTENS

34"

10 1/2"

8 3/4"

18 5/8"

13 7/8"

BOOKCASES

Suspended Book Shelf

An easy-to-make project that fits any informal theme of decoration.

By Ken Whitmore

IF YOU HAVE ever been annoyed by the necessity for bookends to keep books from falling, here is an idea that might appeal to you. These rope-suspended book shelves eliminate that problem. The shelves hang at an angle, and the books remain in place without need of special holders.

Very functional and attractive, this shelf design fits well into any hard-to-use wall space and goes with any informal theme of decoration. It requires a minimum of construction, with only simple implements to put it together. The amount of materials needed can be purchased for the modest sum of approximately $7.00, and the shelves can be painted, lacquered, or left in natural wood to suit the taste. •

Shelves are made of 50" lengths of shelf pine, two 10" wide for book rests and two 12" wide for blackboards; plus rope, brackets and hooks.

BOOKCASES

Four 8x8-inch corner irons are only supporting braces for shelves, and they are attached to pine boards three inches from the outside edge.

Four equal triangular wood blocks are cut and attached to backside, two to a shelf. These keep shelf bottom from wall at desired angle.

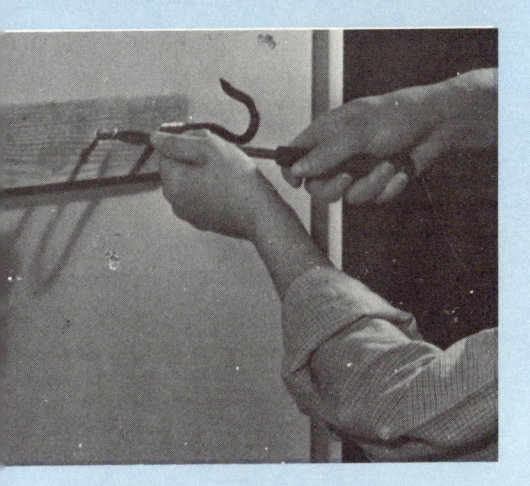

A 1x3-inch board cut the length of shelves was screwed into wall studs, then hooks were placed into supporting board three inches from edges.

A side view of the assembled shelves shows details of rope sling, knot placements, the back rests on wall and suspension from metal hooks.

Hemp rope is passed thru ½-inch holes made in both sides of bottom and back boards, and knots are tied to keep upper shelf at required level.

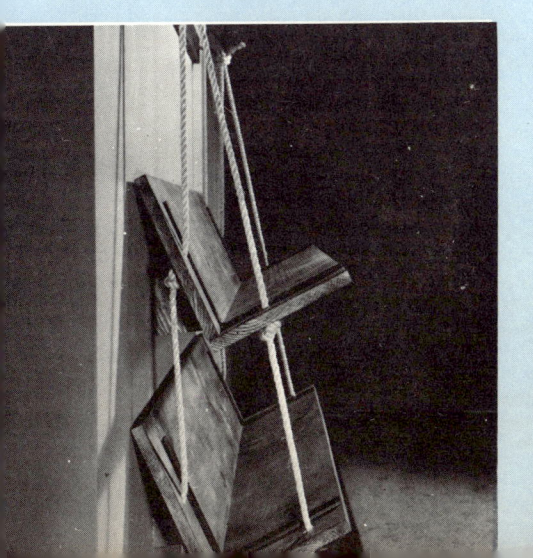

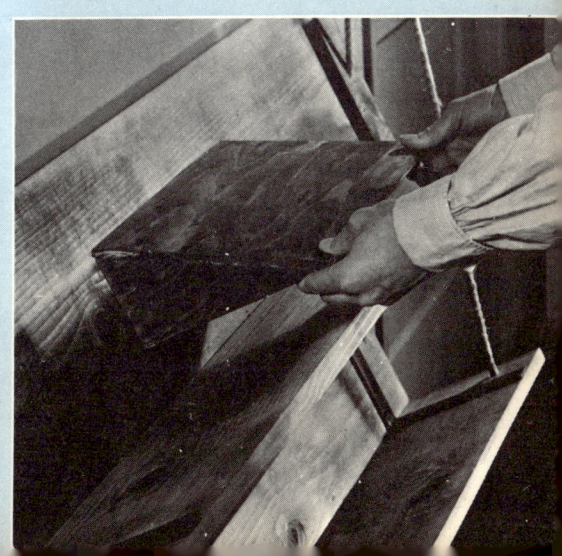

A triangular block can be constructed to fit the right angle of shelf. This makes a level top usable for a plant or decorative ornament.

BOOT BIN

WHAT'S TO BE DONE with muddy boots, drippy overshoes? A well-ventilated boot bin provides the answer. It also serves as a handy place to sit when putting overshoes on or taking them off. It's an ideal companion piece for the guest closet described on the preceding pages.

The bin has a false bottom of Peg-Board. Melting snow can drip through its holes into a shallow metal tray which slides under the bin, is removable for easy cleaning. The Peg-Board front and the hinged, slat top assure quick drying of wet things within.

A good height for the bin is 16 inches. By slanting its front inward, heel space is achieved and more comfortable sitting. A Stanley continuous hinge for the top gives sturdy support. Place the hinge at least 8 inches forward of the wall so that when the top is opened it will stay back and won't fall shut.

A 6-inch shelf, with a 1x4 gallery, 12 inches above the seat is a back rest. The narrow shelf is a handy place to put mail you want to remember to get off, or for incoming mail for distribution to other members of the family. •

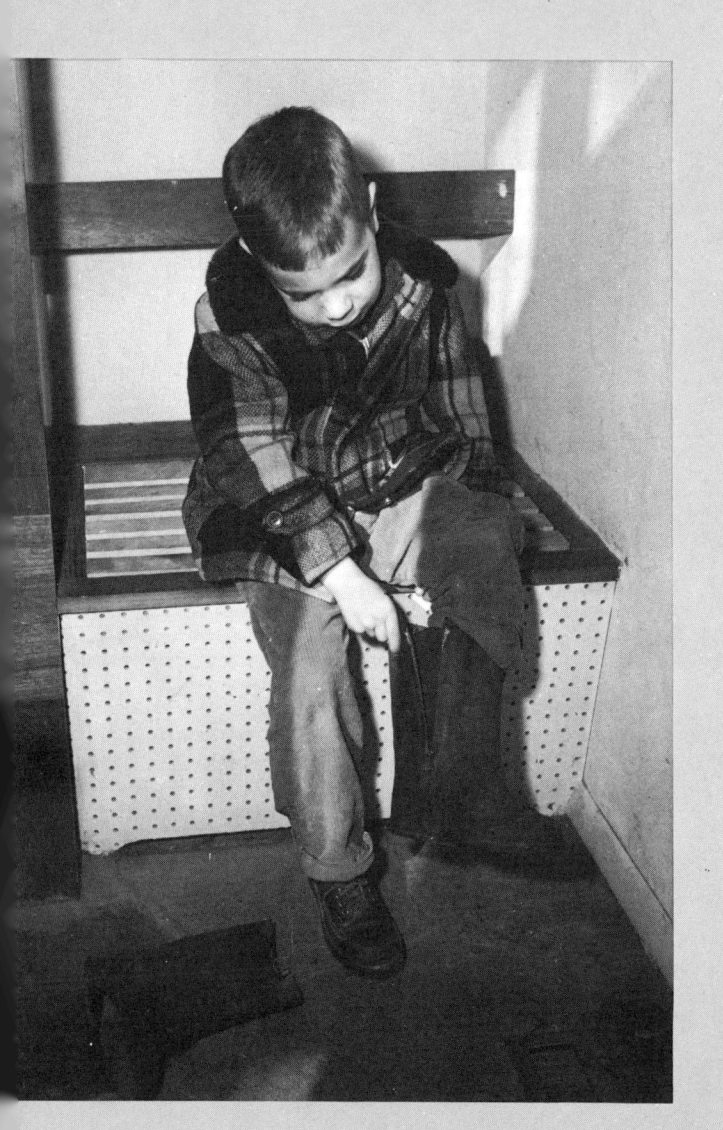

The bin framework is constructed of 1x2- and 1x3-inch pine stock.

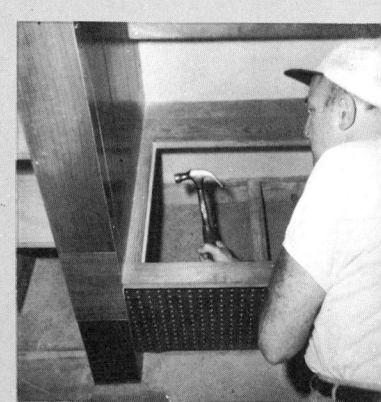

A ½-inch ledge nailed below side trim acts as stop for bin's lid.

BOOT BIN

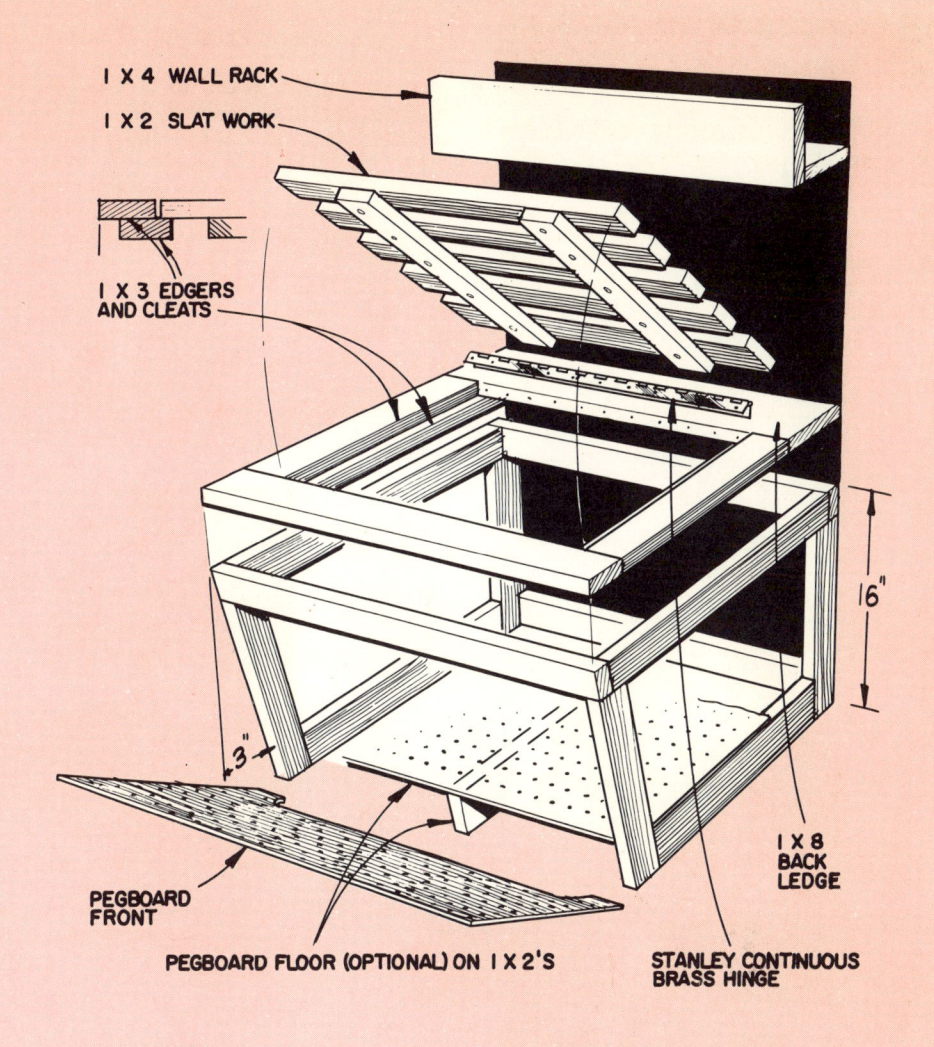

- 1 X 4 WALL RACK
- 1 X 2 SLAT WORK
- 1 X 3 EDGERS AND CLEATS
- 16"
- PEGBOARD FRONT
- PEGBOARD FLOOR (OPTIONAL) ON 1 X 2'S
- STANLEY CONTINUOUS BRASS HINGE
- 1 X 8 BACK LEDGE
- 3"

False bottom of Peg-Board is cut in two pieces for easy removal. It rests on a 1x2-inch frame.

Top, attached to frame with Stanley continuous hinge, is made of slats spaced ¾ inch apart.

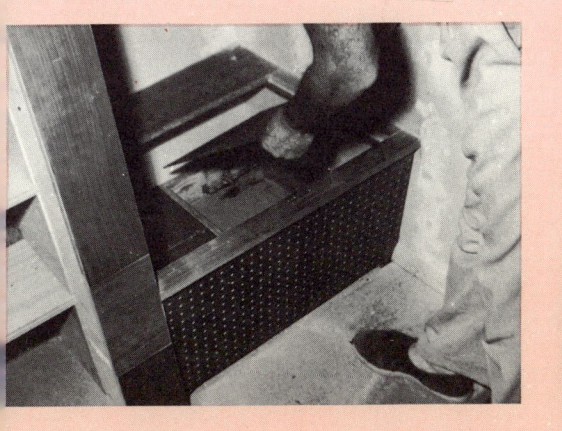

BRICK

At a corner where plumb line cannot be hung, erect and anchor a 2x4 guide to save time and assure plumb corner.

It takes practice, but knowing how to build a square corner and straight course with brick that has been properly mortared will really qualify you as a handy man.

How To Lay Brick

BRICK

Spread enough mortar on a course to lay four or five brick at a time; always carry a full trowel.

Zigzag the mortar with point of trowel to assure a good bond and make for easy adjustment of brick.

LIKE all other construction, bricklaying has its own special tricks of the trade. Square, plumb and true corners are the mark of good masonry. For this reason, the corners are always laid up first, in what is called the mason's lead. This consists of laying up several courses of brick in both directions, making sure that the corner is plumb and square.

Where there is no adjoining structure from which to hang a plumb line, a 2x4 guide can be set at the corner and firmly braced after it is plumbed. Experienced masons may scorn the use of such guides, but the handy man will find that they save time and help him to construct a plumb corner. As the courses of brick are laid, the guide should be checked to make certain that it has not been pushed accidentally out of place.

Such guides not only save time, but they allow the guide line to be stretched taut with a nail driven into the 2x4 as each stretcher course is laid. The line is strung so as to be level with the top of the bricks being laid in each course, thus providing a check on the thickness of the mortar being placed. A braided cotton cord known as a chalk line is used for this purpose because it does not stretch and sag as do ordinary cords.

Professional bricklayers who use a plumb bob and level to true their corners or leads, take extra care so that they can use these as a guide for filling in the space between. A little practice will soon train the eye to detect bricks that are out of level or out of line, and experience in handling the mortar will aid in getting it the right thickness each time.

To a certain extent, the mortar mixture also determines the thickness of the mortar between the courses. A thick or heavy mortar will tend to hold the weight of the bricks easier than a thin mortar. If thin mortar is used first and then thick mortar is mixed in the next batch, the bricks will be out of line due to the uneven thickness of mortar between them. Mortar should be of the same density and plasticity at all times.

Those who lay brick for the first time will be tempted to spread just enough mortar on the course below to fit one brick at a time. This is slow and tedious work—a faster and neater job can be done if the mortar is carried to the brick a full trowel at a time. This trowelful of mortar is strung along the course, then flattened out in an even layer with the trowel, so that four or five brick can be laid on it at one time. A zigzag line is then put into the mortar with a trowel to make it easier to position and level the brick. Each brick is buttered with mortar as it is laid, and pushed snugly against the brick preceding it.

While the brick is being lowered with its buttered end placed snug up against the preceding brick in the course, the hand holding the trowel moves to the outside of the wall, ready to pick up the mortar which is squeezed out between the joints. This mortar is then dumped back on the wall, or used to butter the end of the next brick, and so on.

Mortar which is too thick makes it necessary to chop the mortar down between the bricks with the edge of the trowel when buttering—a time-consuming process. Thin mortar will ooze out, and you will have

Photos on these two pages by Weyman Smith

489

BRICK

To build masonry lead, lay corner unit in course first, then units next to it as shown below; this is most important step in building accurate walls.

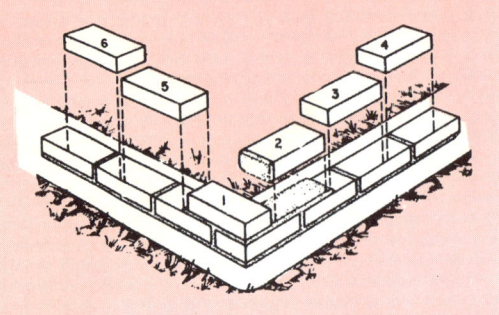

Here is what a finished lead six courses high looks like. Build same leads at other corners, fill in wall length between with use of a line.

A MASON'S LEAD

Butter end of brick as it's laid; if mortar does not stick, bricks may be too dry or mix is wrong.

While buttered brick is being placed, use trowel to pick up mortar squeezed out between the joints.

to raise a brick out of line by placing bits of brick pieces under it—which consumes even more time. Be sure mortar is right for bricklaying, and keep it right by continuing to work it on the mortarboard or in the wheelbarrow.

Old-time bricklayers laid as many as two thousand brick in a ten-hour day—but four hundred and fifty is considered a fair day's work now. Half that number will probably be a hard day's work for the handy man laying brick for the first time.

In all brick work or other masonry, except where a veneer wall is being laid outside of a frame building, the mason stands inside the wall. He keeps his scaffolding or staging always at a height that allows him to lean out over the course of outside brick, sighting down the chalk line with his eye to keep each brick true and level with the chalk line and beneath it. Even for short walls and small jobs, it pays to build a scaffolding or platform to stand on so that you can hold the same position at all times. The time it takes to build a staging is more than made up by the speed with which you can work when you're in the right position.

Once you have an idea of what your project involves, look carefully at the tools you'll need. The professional carries up to eighteen tools on his kit, but about half of these will be enough for the usual handy man's project.

First are the trowels—the bricklayer's trowel and the small pointed trowel used for finishing the mortar joints. Next, the sled-runners for compressing the mortar joints and firming the mortar against the brick in each course to make the joints watertight. Using these is important; there is a saying in the construction industry— *"a brick or masonry wall is only as tight as the mortar joints."* This means that a stream of water pouring against a brick wall is very likely to find some crevice between brick and mortar joints through which it can enter. Framework inside of many brick veneer walls has rotted due to such water or moisture entrance.

This failure of veneer brick and other walls to be completely watertight is one reason why many companies and banks nowadays refuse to make loans on houses

BRICK

Courtesy of Glen-Gery Shale Brick Corp.

Picking up mortar with trowel is a technique that takes a lot of practice, but once you get the knack of it, your job will be simplified.

Courtesy of Goldblatt Tool Co.

Not all of bricklayer's tools are needed by handy man; mason uses two trowels, sled-runners for firming joints, hammer, brush for cleaning mortar off brick, 48-inch level, 6-foot rule, chalk line, chisels, and convex jointers for compressing and firming the mortar.

BRICK

Brick-set chisel shown above is used for trimming brick to an exact line; strike firm, sharp blow.

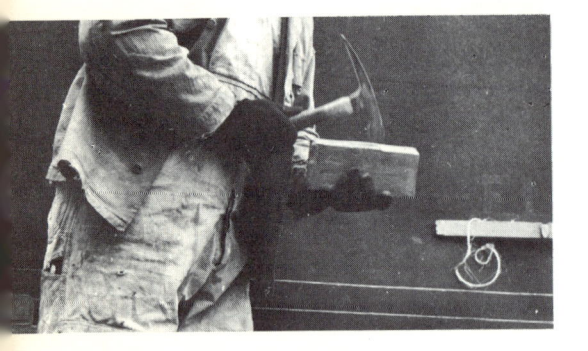

When breaking brick, hold brick in one hand and strike sharply with square head of the hammer.

Old brick give an aged, Colonial effect; mortar allowed to spot and remain on walls adds to this.

which are not equipped with gutters and downspouts to protect the walls from gushing water pouring down on them from the roof during a heavy storm. Sometimes, such water even finds its way into basements, and basements then are blamed for the poor construction of the upper walls.

After the jointing tools, there is a bricklayer's hammer, which is a must-have tool where bricks are to be cut to fit. The brick hammer has a square head and a chisel point, instead of the round head and claws of the carpenter's hammer. The square head is used to break the brick, and the chisel head to square off the roughly broken edges. Brick is broken or trimmed by holding it in one hand and striking it with the hammer in the other. Placing a brick on a board and striking it with a hammer is likely to break it into several different pieces, none of them wanted.

The brick-set chisel is used when a very careful trim is needed. The trick in using this chisel is to strike a firm, sharp blow which will be just enough to break the brick. If it does not break at the first blow, turning it over and placing the chipped line on a nail or slight elevation and then tapping the top of the brick will separate it.

The ruler and 4-foot mason's level are other needed tools. A carpenter's level is 24 inches long and consequently does not lend itself as easily to brick work. Next are the chalk line or cord, and three chisels including the 4-inch brick set, the ¾-inch and the point chisel.

A brush is included to brush the joints as the mortar sets in order to remove excess mortar from the face of the brick. In some cases, the wall is left with brushed joints. The brush is dipped in water and kept moist but not wet while it is being used. Even if all of the mortar is not cleaned off, the slight moistening which it receives will make it that much easier to remove when the brick wall is given a final acid wash at the conclusion of the work.

Brick and Mortar Patterns

Brick colors vary from cream and white to reds and browns. This color, plus the type of bond and the color of the mortar all determine the final appearance and pattern of a brick masonry wall.

In some localities it is possible to obtain used brick at a considerable savings, and architects frequently employ these to give an aged or Colonial effect to buildings. As a good burned brick will last almost forever, the homeowner can save money by using them if they are in sound condition. Unburned brick or those made for use in interiors should not be used outside because

BRICK

freezing and thawing may disintegrate them due to their absorption of moisture.

In climates where rainfall is heavy, either the "V" or round joint is preferred for brickwork. A trowel joint may tend to catch and hold water coming down the walls, so avoid joints where the mortar is not trimmed from the walls. Also, in moist climates various insects tend to make their homes under extruded mortar joints.

There are four basic types of brick bonding: the running bond, common bond, Flemish bond and English bond. Sometimes combinations of these joining methods are used.

In running bond—also called stretcher bond—the brick joints are staggered over each other by one-half their length. Common bond consists of five or six courses of running bond followed by a course of "headers," or brick which are laid at right angles to the face of the wall. This latter bond binds the front and back courses of the masonry together as a unit and also tends to prevent water which may enter outside the brick wall from running down between the outer and inner walls.

The English bond consists of alternating the header and stretcher courses as they are laid. Flemish bond is that in which header and stretcher brick alternate in the same course. Half bricks are used to make this bond and consequently more time is required.

To permit the mortar to set and harden, and to prevent cracks from forming in the wall later on, a usual practice with many architects is to allow the laying of no more than five courses of brick and a header course in one day.

Brick Veneer

Veneer is of two kinds: In one, a single brick wall is laid up outside of a frame construction. In the other, brick forms the outside wall while concrete or other blocks are used inside. These are called brick-on-frame and brick-on-masonry veneers.

In the brick-on-frame construction, the frame is usually built first, setting such framework on a foundation far enough back from the face so that there is room for a single brick wall and an air space of about 1 inch. The single brick wall is tied

BRICK BONDS

COMMON BOND
FULL HEADERS EVERY SIXTH COURSE

STRETCHER BOND
ALL STRETCHER COURSES

ENGLISH CORNER   DUTCH CORNER
ENGLISH BOND IN BRICK
ALTERNATE HEADER AND STRETCHER COURSES

Running bond consists of stretcher courses only. Flat, recessed joints like these are called raked.

BRICK

MORTAR JOINTS

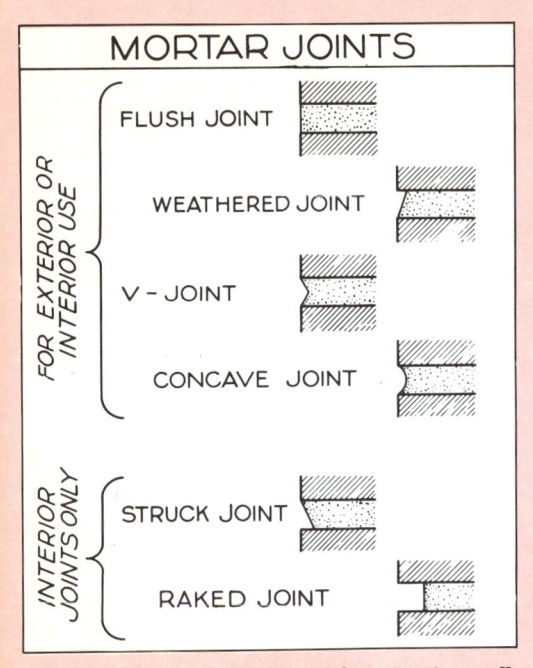

For exterior or interior use:
- FLUSH JOINT
- WEATHERED JOINT
- V-JOINT
- CONCAVE JOINT

Interior joints only:
- STRUCK JOINT
- RAKED JOINT

Bottom two joints are limited to interior walls because water could collect in shelf, cause leak.

Single-wall veneer of 4-inch brick is tied to a frame wall by metal strips laid in mortar joints.

to the frame by metal strips nailed to the frame and bent into the course of mortar as the wall is laid. A 1-inch air space between the brick and frame is necessary, not only to add to the insulating value but also to prevent any rain water that penetrates the wall from running down into the frame construction.

A recommended practice with such construction is to nail roofing paper or heavy tar paper to the outside of the frame construction before beginning to lay the brick. The slight extra cost will more than pay for itself in the extra protection it affords as a moisture barrier, especially in houses where air conditioning is being used or may be used in the future.

The brick veneer laid outside of cinder or concrete or lightweight block makes for faster and cheaper construction than the use of solid brick walls and is standard practice in nearly all modern work. Header courses of brick are laid as in the common bond type of construction, both to bind the walls together and insure against water running down inside the two masonry wall units.

Over-size Brick Work

A special brick has been developed by the clay products industry to provide a single solid wall 6 inches in thickness that is strong enough to support roof rafters, yet requires only one-wall construction. Various other types of brick also are available in certain localities, some of these 8x8 inches square and of the same thickness as common brick.

The 6-inch brick are known as SCR brick, and are cored (made with holes) so that they can be grasped readily with one hand. They weigh about twice as much as ordinary brick.

Where a solid masonry wall is used—either one-course or veneer—plans are generally made to use furring strips inside. At one time, strips of lath were laid between the courses of brick as the walls were erected and the furring strips were nailed to these. A new type of masonry nail makes this unnecessary, as do the newer lightweight blocks which allow nails to be driven into them with relative ease.

The furring strips are wood strips about 1 inch thick and 2 inches wide which are nailed to the finished wall. Tar paper or roofing paper may be tacked to the wall under the furring strips as a moisture barrier. Plaster lath is nailed over the furring strips and plaster may then be applied over this.

BRICK

Some of the new lightweight plasters made with vermiculite are themselves of such texture that they act as insulators. (An older means of insulation in some frame houses was known as "back-plastering." This consisted of nailing plaster lath between the studs in frame walls so that there would be an air space of 2 inches between them and the outside walls. Plaster was then placed over this lath, between the studs. Inside walls were then finished and plastered, so that there were two dead air spaces in the walls.)

Acid Wash for Brick Walls

After brick walls have dried and are finished, they are generally given an acid wash to remove the flaky mortar and lime left by the trowel or brush. A dilute solution of muriatic acid is used: 1 part of muriatic acid to 10 parts of water. The surface of the brick may be wet before the acid wash is applied with a strong scrubbing brush. Old clothes and gloves should be worn during this operation, because the acid is likely to splash and spatter and will burn holes in clothes as easily as it removes the lime deposits from the brick work.

Weathering will in time remove the excess mortar and lime, but the acid wash gives a wall a neat, clean and finished appearance, especially when new brick are used. •

Brick veneer bonded to a 4-inch cinder block wall makes this masonry wall 8 inches thick. Every seventh course of brick is bonded into block backing.

Most common brick types are (top) standard 2x4x8 brick, Norman, (bottom) SCR, and long, thin Roman.

BRICK

laying SCR BRICK

by **LARRY EISINGER**

MOST people planning a new home are aware of the many advantages of brick construction, but they usually make the mistake of assuming that brick is far beyond their means. This was the case years ago, but technological developments now make it possible to build a brick home at a cost nearly identical to that for a good frame dwelling.

Contrary to what many people think, there are three conventional methods of building homes with brick. First, the "brick-and-block" method calls for brick as the exterior surface with 6-, 8- or 10-inch cinder block on the inside. Both are tied together with pieces of metal imbedded in the joints while the wall is being built.

A second all-masonry method calls for the use of brick on both the inside and outside of the wall, with or without an airspace, and laid so that the wall thickness totals eight (or more) inches.

A third method, the most popular form of brick construction today, is known as the "veneer" method, where the roof of the home is held up by a conventional 2x4 wooden structure—and a single layer of brick, a veneer layer, is built up along the outside wall. Why brick veneer homes are more expensive than frame is easy to understand. The 2x4 wooden framework is first erected in exactly the same way as in building a completely frame home. Then the framing is covered with sheathing, which can be either plywood, solid wood, gypsum board or specially treated insulation board. Finally, the brick is added. Thus, you can see a great deal of material

496

BRICK

Left: Some brick must be cut and the most accurate method is with a masonry saw such as this Clipper. Right: Starting a 12-inch SCR foundation wall by laying outer course.

A single inside course bonded to the outside course with regular metal brick ties, produces a 12-inch on-grade basement wall. Right: Wall before the windows were added.

and labor goes into the wall even before the brick is added.

The technological development that now makes possible a new fourth method and a brick home at just about the same price as a good frame structure is a special size brick, considerably larger than the common brick but made of the same material. This brick, developed by the Structural Clay Products Research Foundation (and therefore labeled SCR) is wide enough so it does not require the usual 2x4 framework of brick veneer homes; the roof rests directly on top of the wall because the brick is 6 inches wide. The fact that the SCR brick is 12 inches long and $2\frac{3}{16}$ inches high makes it possible for masons to lay up to 60 percent more square footage of SCR brick than conventional bricks in the same period of time. A square foot of SCR wall requires 4½ bricks while the conventional 2x4x8 brick requires 7½ bricks per square foot.

SCR brick is also modular (6 x 12) which means it is possible to turn corners and maintain the half bond. In addition, one end of the brick has a slot to simplify mounting windows and door jambs as the wall is being built. The face is the same as a standard "Norman" brick.

The SCR brick has a few other interesting innovations. It has ten holes which are NOT present to provide an air space in the wall as most people believe. These cores are usually filled with mortar and result in a stronger bond than if the surface were flat. The holes also cut down on the weight of each brick—a very important transpor-

497

BRICK

Above: Masonry contractors moved in to do the job before the complete sub-flooring was in place. Foundation should be completely backfilled to make scaffolding easy, safe. Note how corners are built up first. Left: Close-up view showing "weep" hole and wall flashing. After the first course is above flashing, spread sand on flashing to prevent dripping masonry from adhering and clogging the weep holes. Black mortar was used.

Below: Inside view of wall showing center row of furring clips resting on brick before next course was added. Joints on inside of brick wall need not be tooled. In the background is storage shanty.

Below: Jerry Candrilli shows local union representative how to lay this labor saving brick. Large size of brick makes possible laying up to 60 percent more wall area than with regular brick.

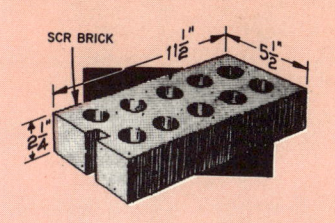

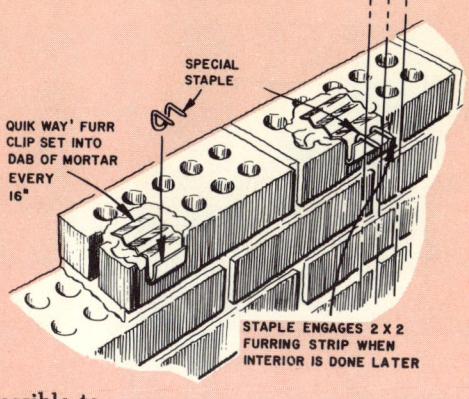

tation factor—and also make it possible to insert anchor bolts in the top of the wall to hold the roof, or head, plate secure.

An SCR brick wall is considered a solid masonry structure (because the volume of the 10 holes is less than 25 percent of the complete brick). The interior walls must be furred to house the insulation, wiring and plumbing which is accomplished with furring strips used in conjunction with clips that are set into the wall on 16-inch centers as the wall is being built. Three clips are used for each furring strip, one located about five inches from the floor, another about three feet from the floor and the top one about two feet from the ceiling. The very top of each furring strip is nailed to the head or roof plate.

You will note from the illustrations that the clips are made in such a way the wood furrings do not rest against the masonry at any point. Also, bottom of the furring strip does not rest on the floor; a piece of flashing extending completely through the brick joint is wrapped around the bottom of each furring strip. The flashing is set over the course of brick protruding above the sub-flooring (usually the fifth course) and every third brick has what is known as a "weep hole"—a hole about 3/8 inch in

Rear of brick wall at window sill height. Set windows in wall first, varying sill thickness so window does not extend above head plate. Right: Typical "story pole" and furring clip detail.

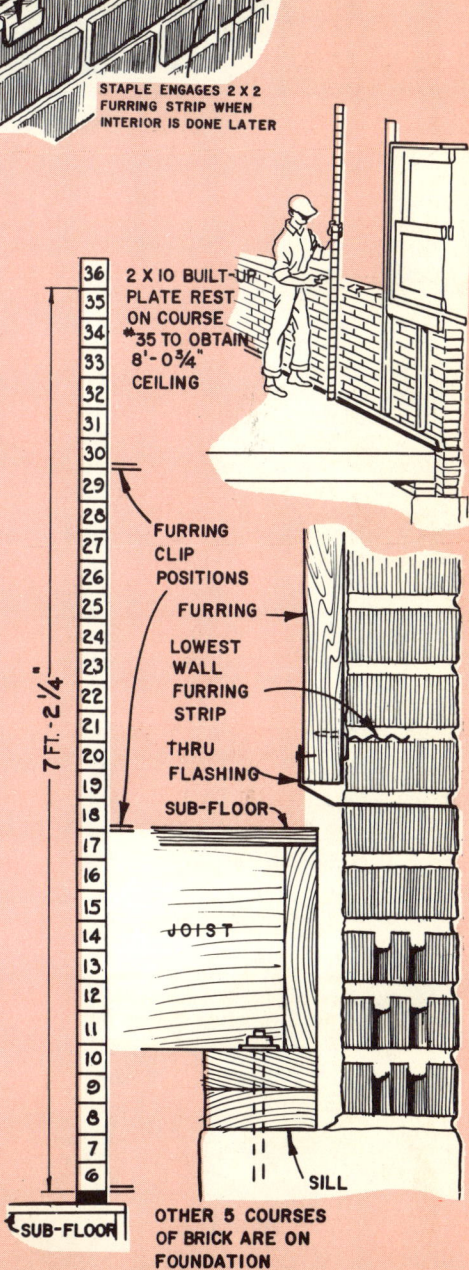

499

BRICK

Door frame is first set in place, then brick is built around frame. Note extending anchor bolts.

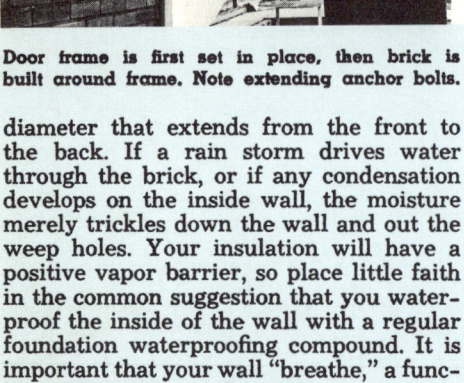

Inside view of door to screened porch. Brace the 24-inch wide pier until the roof beams are on.

diameter that extends from the front to the back. If a rain storm drives water through the brick, or if any condensation develops on the inside wall, the moisture merely trickles down the wall and out the weep holes. Your insulation will have a positive vapor barrier, so place little faith in the common suggestion that you waterproof the inside of the wall with a regular foundation waterproofing compound. It is important that your wall "breathe," a function that waterproofing will retard.

If you are able to locate a mason who has had previous experience with SCR construction, you will be fortunate indeed, because he will be able to quote you a complete price for the job. If a mason has not had previous experience he will probably be reluctant to submit a price quotation. Thus, the following statistics should help you when dealing with your mason.

Time and motion studies conducted by the Structural Clay Products Research Foundation have shown that a good mason can easily lay 450 bricks per day. In our home and quite a few others that call for extra corners and a more than average number of windows, we found a 350-brick per day average commendable. Any expert mason should easily be able to duplicate this figure. Setting up the corners, building in the flashing, accurately positioning the furring strips, making the weep holes, tooling the joints, erecting the scaffolds, and placing the roof anchor bolts in position are all part of the job, and each task must be expertly and accurately done. Don't rush your job; the saving, if any, is questionable.

If your mason prefers to work on a per-day basis, the figures above should serve as a guide. However, if SCR is being used in your area, a per-thousand price has undoubtedly been established.

Rates vary, depending upon the individual, and the complexity of the job, but you should expect to pay $140 per thousand as a minimum.

Jerry Candrilli sets a garage window frame in place before plate was bolted to top. Do not start any brick work unless all of your window units are on the job. Window sills can be brick or stone.

BRICK

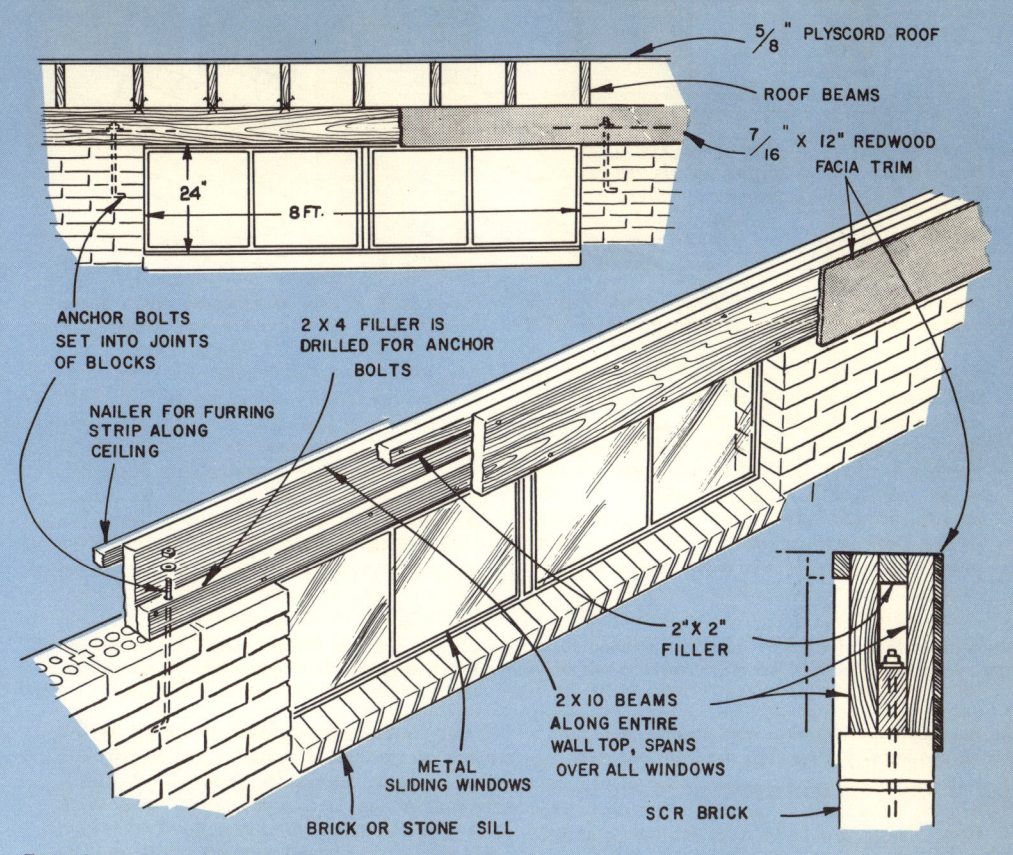

Typical window lintel and head plate construction. Single 2x4 is first bolted to top of wall, then 2x10s are added to both sides and a 2x2 filler to top. This method of construction eliminates costly steel work.

The metal flashing that extends ½ inch from the front and passes through the entire wall, is bent up over the furring strips. Take care not to puncture the flashing when adding wall covering and base.

Typical window sill detail. When window sill height is reached, position window and build frame directly into wall. Use of wood or metal windows of one-foot multiples will eliminate cutting brick.

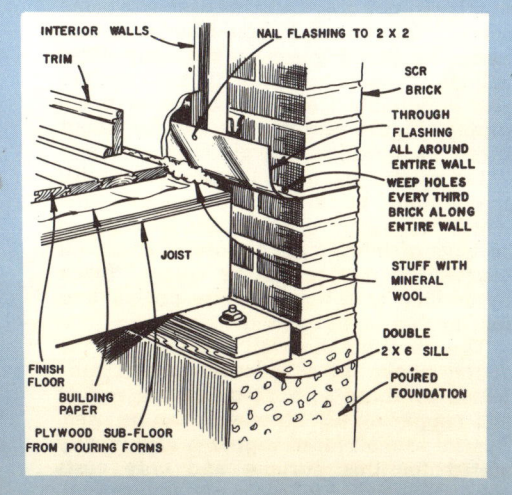

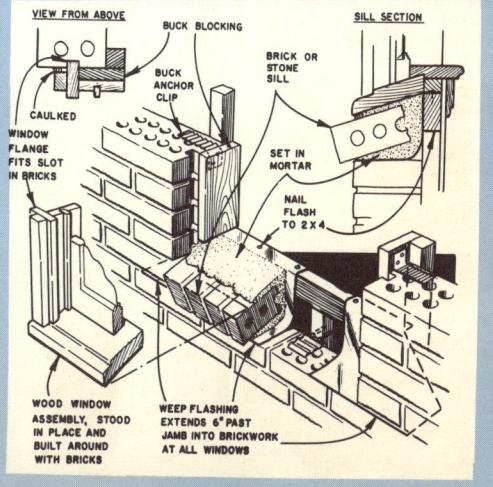

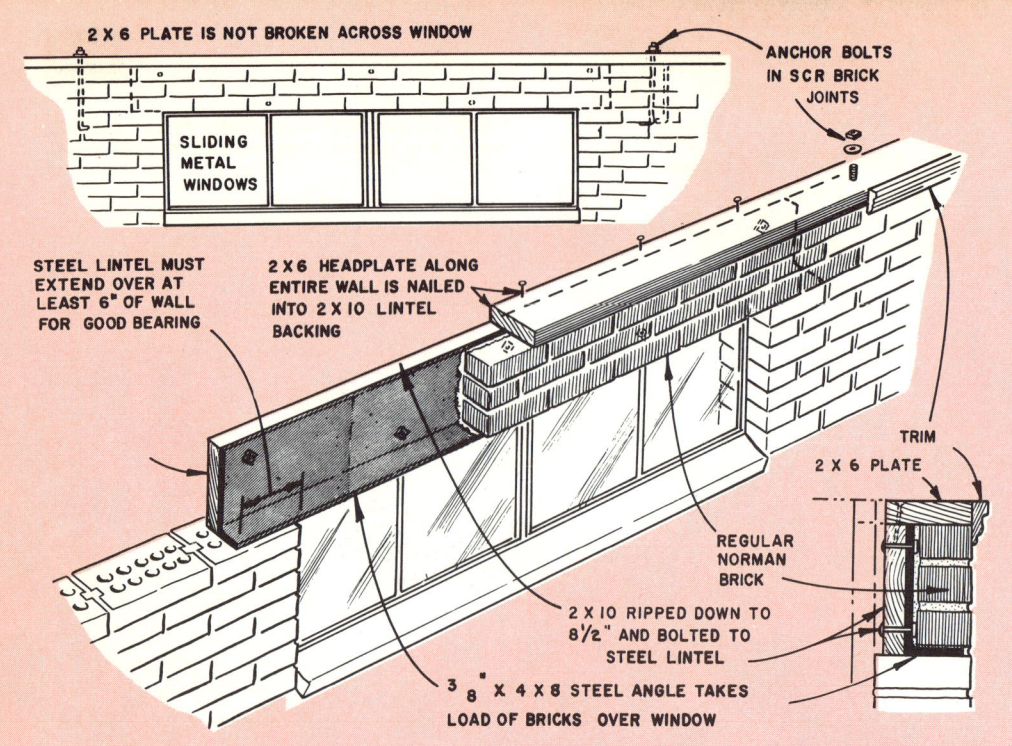

Labels on top diagram:
- 2 X 6 PLATE IS NOT BROKEN ACROSS WINDOW
- ANCHOR BOLTS IN SCR BRICK JOINTS
- SLIDING METAL WINDOWS
- STEEL LINTEL MUST EXTEND OVER AT LEAST 6" OF WALL FOR GOOD BEARING
- 2 X 6 HEADPLATE ALONG ENTIRE WALL IS NAILED INTO 2 X 10 LINTEL BACKING
- TRIM
- 2 X 6 PLATE
- REGULAR NORMAN BRICK
- 2 X 10 RIPPED DOWN TO 8½" AND BOLTED TO STEEL LINTEL
- ⅜" X 4 X 6 STEEL ANGLE TAKES LOAD OF BRICKS OVER WINDOW

Alternate method of window lintel construction that utilizes steel angle is recommended for spans beyond eight feet. The 2x10 bolted to angle is not necessary for short spans; furring can be nailed to plate.

Labels on lower diagrams:
On all corners and where a wall partition is to be placed additional furring clips are built into wall.
- 2 X 6 FULL HEIGHT BLOCKING
- 2 X 4 PARTITION STUD
- DOUBLE FURRING CLIPS BEHIND 2 X 6 BLOCK
- DRY WALL OR PLASTER
- SECURE 2 X 4 WITH NO. 10 NAILS
- 2 X 2 FURRING
- NO. 12 NAILS INTO 2 X 2
- 2 X 4 CORNER STUD SECURED TO ANCHOR CLIPS FIRST, THEN 2 X 4 IS ATTACHED
- DRY WALL OR PLASTER

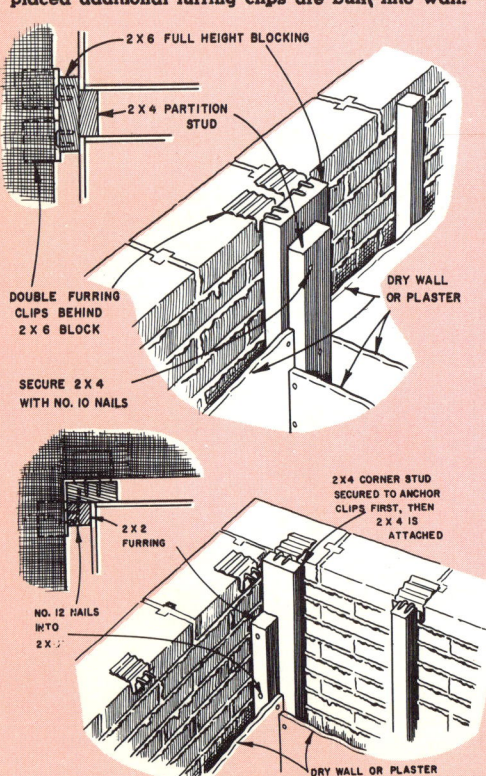

Your local masonry supply house is the source of your SCR brick. Cost varies the country over, depending upon brick color, transportation, and local conditions, with $125 per thousand being a good average. Unloading might cost you an additional $3 per thousand, which we recommend you pay, because unloading a trailer with 3,000 bricks adds up to unloading nearly 13 tons! When unloading brick have it placed in predetermined spots so as not to waste labor moving it to the wall area where it will be used. The 12-inch SCR brick (a smaller 8-inch size is also available in some parts of the country) should never be unloaded by dumping because too many edges will chip. Incidentally, the furring clips are also obtainable from the source of brick supply. Figure one furring clip for about every 3 square feet of wall area.

The mortar you use is the same used with conventional brick. Plan for ½-inch joints which will require anywhere from 14 to 16 bags of mortar per thousand brick. Of course, the mortar can be colored black by adding lamp black or else pre-colored mortar can be purchased.

The through-the-wall flashing on the course above the sub-flooring is not subjected to abuse so a 12-inch wide roll of .015 copper or .020 aluminum can be used. Special asphalt faced copper is also ideally suited for this purpose and only costs about 15 cents to 20 cents per square foot.

BRICK

Left: Sal Candrilli leveling sill of a garage window. Inside was cement plastered, did not need clips.

Completed masonry walls before windows and plate were added. Windows were not available at the time contractors scheduled job, but slot in each brick made it possible to slide windows in from top.

Even if you employ a professional mason to do the job, you should work very closely with him to make certain the weep holes are in the correct place, the furring clips are inserted at exactly 16-inch intervals and at the edges of room partitions, etc. You should also mark off the position of the windows and indicate at which brick course number the frames should be sent into the wall. While the slotted brick makes it possible to slip a window frame in from the top, it is best to have all the windows on hand so when the proper sill height is reached you can actually build the window into the wall.

The door bucks are set in place on the sub-floor height course and braced so they are absolutely perpendicular. Since the SCR brick is one foot long it is most economical to lay out the windows and door areas so you need not cut any bricks. This means you must use windows of even one-foot dimensions; the height does not make too much difference because the thickness of the sill can be adjusted. The important point is to make certain the top of the window frame is about 1/8 inch below the window lintel so the roof does not rest on the window. The 1/8-inch space is caulked.

An absolutely, level wall and accurately placed windows are achieved by use of a "story pole." Actually, this is merely a pole with each brick (2 3/16 inches plus the 1/2-inch thickness of the mortar joint) marked off.

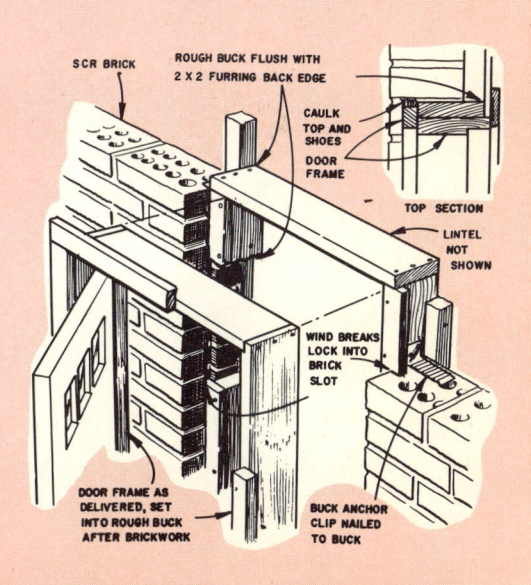

503

BUFFET

MATERIALS NEEDED

For the case:
3/4 in. plywood, 19 in. x 17 ft. 7 in.
1/4 in. plywood, 17 in. x 20 ft. 2 in.
For each drawer:
3/4 in. plywood, 6x18 in.
1/2 in. plywood, 5 5/8 x 48 in.
1 piece 1/4 in. plywood, 14 3/4 x 15-15/16 in.
2 pieces 1/4 in. plywood, 9/16 x 16 in.
For each tray:
3/4 in. plywood, 1 1/4 x 16-11/16 in.
1/2 in. plywood, 2 x 31 7/8 in.
1/4 in. plywood, 2 x 15-15/16 in.
For shelf (if desired):
1/2 in. plywood, 17-3/16 x 15-15/16 in.
For base:
2 pieces 3/4 in. plywood, 3 x 53 in.
2 pieces 3/4 in. plywood, 3 x 16 in.
1 piece 3/4 in. plywood, 3 x 14 1/2 in.
For doors:
2 panels 3/4 in. plywood, 18 5/8 x 25 1/8 in.
Hardware:
Sixteen 1 1/2 in. No. 8 flathead screws
2 in. finishing nails
1 in. finishing nails
3/4 in. brads
1/2 in. corrugated fasteners
36 in. of wood-tape, to match plywood
2 pair of offset hinges to fit 3/4 in. wood
4 medium drawer-pulls
2 large drawer-pulls

Modern Buffet

An unusually simple design, it is easily constructed and offers you a generous amount of storage space

BUFFET

ALTHOUGH designed as a buffet, this handsome, simply-built piece of furniture will meet your storage needs in any room.

We used plywood, which enabled us to get the modern, large-panel effect. But if you wish, you can glue ¾-inch hardwood stock to make the ends, doors and drawer-fronts. And, as a final touch, you can add a plastic laminate top to the case for a durable surface.

For a finish, use your own taste. We used a coat of lacquer sealer and two coats of water-white lacquer.

Making the Case

Cut an 18x55⁷⁄₁₆-inch panel of ¾-inch plywood for the top; 17¼x54¾-inch panel for bottom; two panels 17¼x25¼-inches for ends, and a panel of ¼-inch plywood 25¼x54¾ inches for the back.

Cut rabbets in one edge of the top, bottom and two end pieces, and across one end of each end piece. Dado two grooves ¼ inch deep and ¾ inch wide across bottom piece 17⅝ inches from each end of it. Dado the same grooves across the top, 18⁵⁄₁₆ inches from ends, stopping grooves ¾ inch from the unrabbeted edge.

Bore holes for No. 8 screws in ends of top, and in rabbeted ends of end panels, four holes to an end. Fasten partitions in bottom panel, put glue on ends of partitions and in grooves in top, and assemble them. Use clamps for tight joints. Put on ends with glue and screws; cap screws with pieces of dowel or plugs. Fasten in back panel with glue and ¾-inch brads.

Cut end shims and drawer spacers. Fasten a shim to each end panel.

Attach spacers for drawer glides. Start at inside of an end panel, fastening in a ⅜-inch strip. Using a ⅝-inch spacer, fasten in three of the 5½-inch pieces next. Add the 5⅛-inch piece tight against bottom. Do the same on other end and on both sides of the partitions.

Making the Drawers

Cut the required pieces as listed on opposite page. On the 6x18-inch plywood piece, rabbet each end ½ inch deep and 1⅛ inches wide. On same side, rabbet long edges ½ inch deep, ⅜ inch wide. Half inch from one end of two of the pieces of ½-inch plywood, dado grooves ½ inch wide and ⅛ inch deep. On third ½-inch piece, ¼ inch from edge, dado a groove ¼ inch wide and ¼ inch deep. Cut panel for bottom and strips for glides.

Fasten glides to upper edge of drawer-sides, on ungrooved surface. Assemble drawer with glue and 1-inch finishing nails.

Table-top-high, it offers four spacious drawers, and sliding trays that simplify the hunt for dishes.

BUFFET

Make the pieces shown at the left. They will form the case. Cut ¼x⅜-in. rabbet in one edge of top, bottom and both ends. Cut rabbet ¾x⅜ in. across one end of each end piece. Dado the grooves ¼x¾ in., spaced as shown, in bottom piece. Also dado similar grooves across the top.

BUFFET

Square the ends of the dadoes in the top piece, which stop ¾ in. from the unrabbeted edge of the piece. Do this with a chisel or mortise. Now assemble the case with glue, nails and screws. Partitions go in bottom grooves first, with glue and nails. Holes are bored for screws in ends of top, and rabbeted ends of end panels. Put on top; then ends and back.

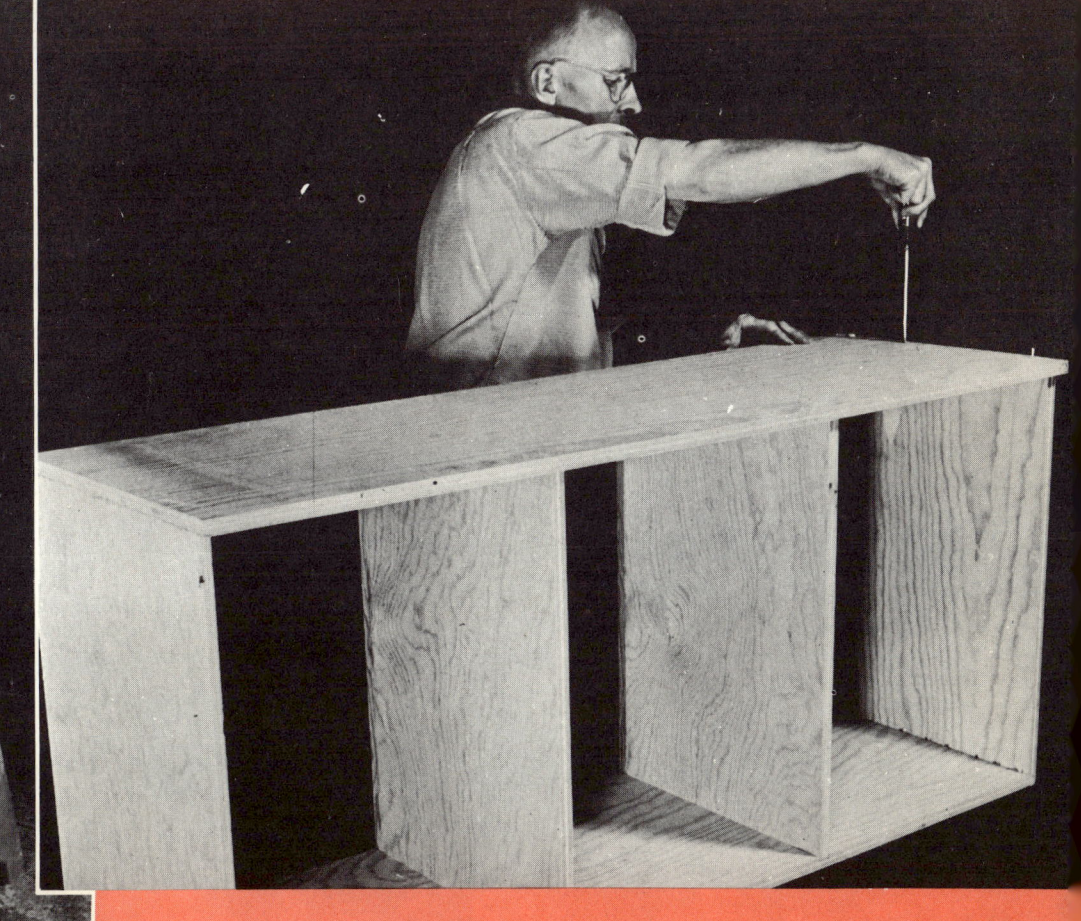

BUFFET

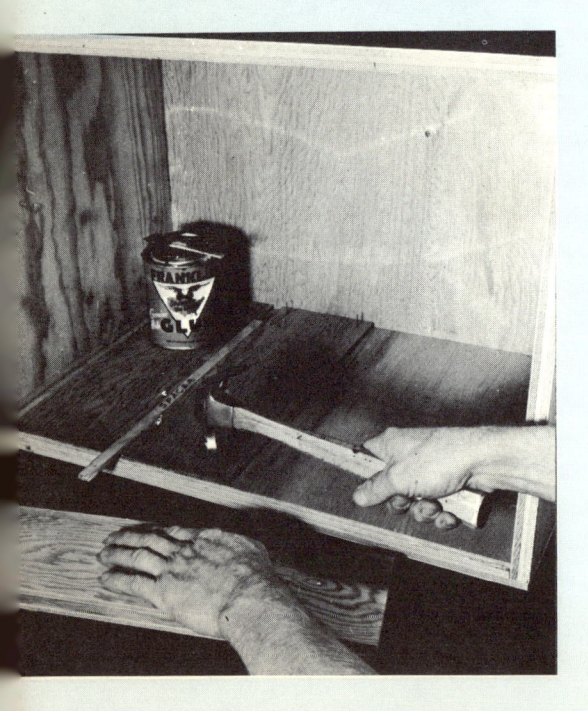

From ¼-in. plywood, make 2 end shims 17x24½ in.; 6 pieces 17x5⅛ in.; 18 pieces 17x5½ in., and 6 pieces 17x⅜ in. Next step is to fasten shims.

One shim is fastened to each end panel of the case with glue and ¾-in. brads. These shims fatten the ends for ease in sliding the trays.

With glue and brads, attach spacers for the drawer glides. Start at top with ⅜-in. strip, work down with 5½-in. pieces, and one 5⅛-in. piece.

Similar sets of spacers go inside each end panel and on both sides of partitions. Cover the edge grain of plywood with wood-tape, and sand case.

508

BUFFET

Buffet Tray, Base and Doors

Rabbet the piece of ¾-in. plywood on both ends and one edge, ½ inch wide and ½ inch deep.

From ½-inch plywood, cut a piece $17\frac{3}{16} \times 15\frac{1}{8}$ for bottom, and three pieces $2 \times 15\frac{1}{8}$ for sides and back. On two of the latter, ½ inch from one end of pieces, dado grooves ½ inch wide by ⅛ inch deep. Cut off a corner of opposite ends at 45° angle.

Assemble tray by first fastening sides to back with glue and 1-inch finishing nails. Glue and nail bottom to this assembly, so that it sticks out ¼ inch on each side. Then fasten on front.

Miter the ends of the four longest base-pieces so they can form a rectangle. Assemble the base, with 14½-inch divider piece across the center to strengthen it.

Take the two door panels (see materials list), and gain them for offset hinges. Cover their edges with wood-tape and attach them to ends of buffet case.

Now, sand and put finish on the buffet. •

Cut drawer pieces. Piece of ¾-in. plywood is front; three pieces of ½-in. wood are sides and back. Groove these pieces as explained in text.

Cut 15x16-3/16-in. piece of ¼-in. plywood for drawer bottom, and two glides 9/16x16 in. Lay pieces out on bench, to look like those below.

Fasten glides with glue and ¾-in. brads to upper edges of drawer sides, on ungrooved surfaces. Assemble drawer with glue, nails. (Turn page.)

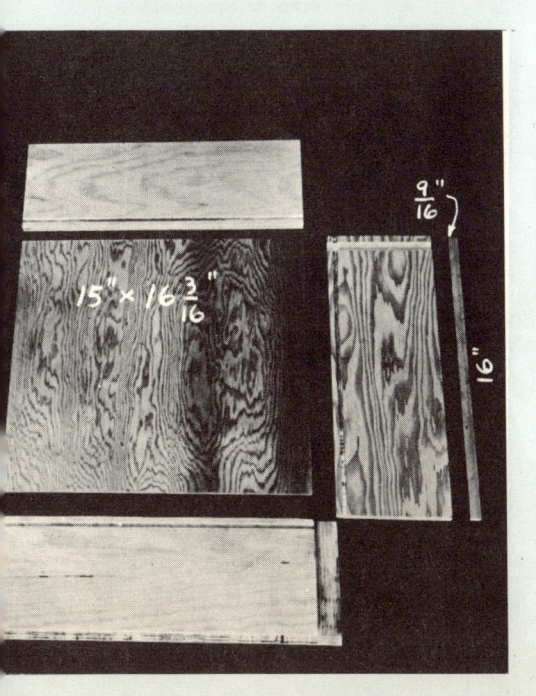

BUFFET

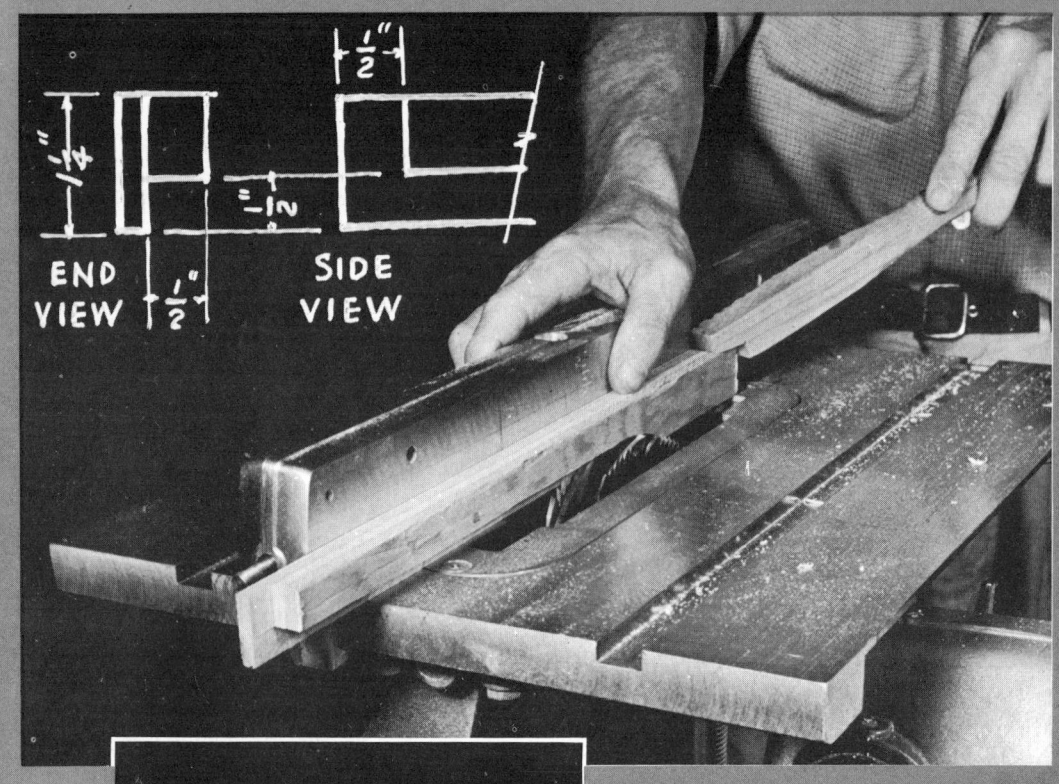

Cut a 1¼x16-11/16-in. piece of ¾-in. plywood for the front of the tray. Rabbet both ends and one edge of the piece ½ in. wide and ½ in. deep, as shown above.

Cut ½-in. plywood pieces for tray bottom, sides and back, as explained in text. Make the necessary dadoes, cut off ends at 45° angle, and lay out as at left.

Next, you assemble the tray by fastening sides to back; then glue and nail on bottom, leaving ¼-in. lip on each side. Then fasten on the front of the tray.

BUFFET

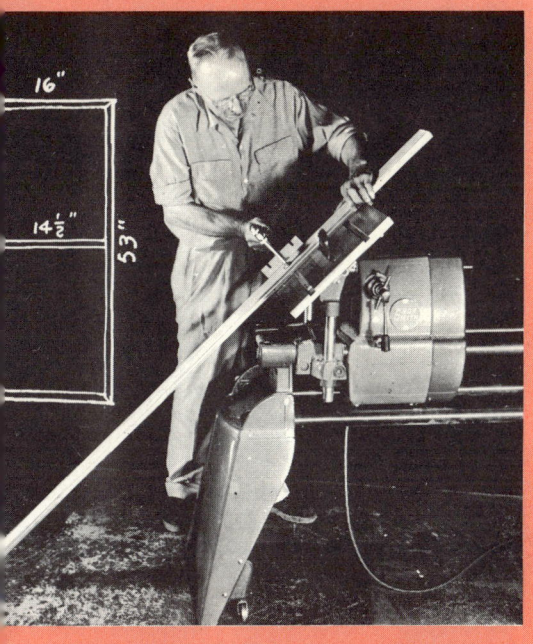

Cut 2 pieces of ¾-in. plywood 3x53 in. and 2 others 3x16 in. Miter the ends so they will make rectangle. Cut another piece 3x14½ in.

Assemble the frame with glue and fasteners. Put the 3x14½-in. piece across center of base. The base will give support and toe room to case.

Cut 2 door panels of ¾-in. plywood, 18⅝x25⅛ in. Next you gain them for offset ¾-in. hinges.

Cover the edges of the doors with wood tape, and attach to case. Put on drawer and door pulls.

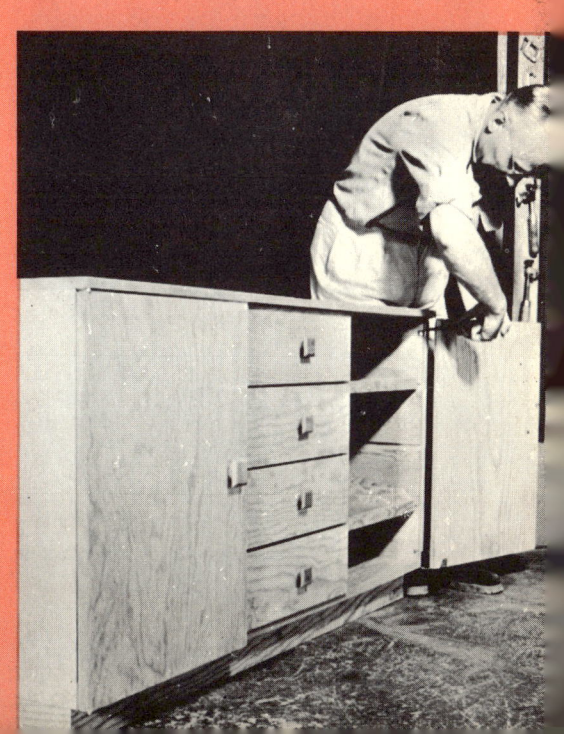

BUILT-INS

ideas for BUILT-INS

Built-ins will double your storage space and eliminate the necessity of buying new furniture every five or ten years.

THE contemporary home makes the most of every cubic inch of space and one of the major space-saving practices is to first plan the placement of a piece of furniture or cabinet and then "build it in."

With new home construction you literally have a once-in-a-lifetime opportunity to install space-saving and labor-saving equipment and furniture at a time when walls are bare and wiring, plumbing and heating lines can be detoured. If you must have built-ins, plan them—in fact, even BUILD them—before you start your home and then set them into their respective locations at the proper time.

The excellent designs appearing on these pages are a few of the more popular creations by designer-architect-artist Egil Hermanovski. Plans for all are available at nominal cost as directed below. •

PLANS For these Built-Ins are available for the nominal sum of $1.00 each. Specify order number and send remittance to Fawcett Publications, Dept. 337, Fawcett Building, Greenwich, Connecticut.

BUILT-INS

Left: A handy bed built-in. The top folding bed has a wood-paneled foundation that matches the other wood room trim when bed is folded. Note the bookshelves. An ideal built-in for den or guest room. No. 2A.

At right, a double wardrobe closet can serve as the basis for this huge and roomy built-in unit. Note the large number of drawers, the center mirror flanked by two door mirrors, and the pull-out tie rack. No. 5A.

One of designer Hermanovski's most novel built-ins is the revolving closet pictured above. It is built into a corner, pivots to make the most of available space. No. 14A.

This pass-thru is lined with upper and lower storage cabinets on both sides and is fitted with frosted glass sliding panels. It is set off floor, will not collect dust. Design can be adapted for any width. Order No. 21A.

BUILT-INS

Above: A complete closet built-in such as this one eliminates chests of drawers in room. No. 4A.

Closet built-in has folding sections for shoes, small clothing items, is topped by a large mirror. No. 3A.

Left: A novel revolving bar, which pivots and fits flush in wall. It can be made any size, depending on wall space available. One shelf, with ice bucket, is notched for glasses. No. 12A.

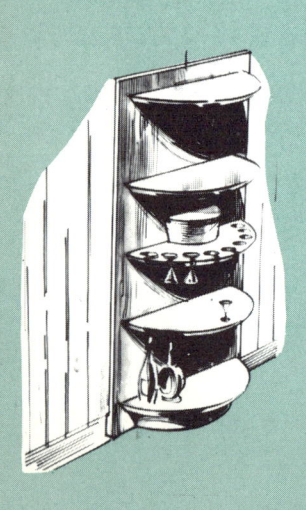

TV sets can become space-hogging eyesores in the living room. This is one way of beautifying home and adding space; fine for hi-fi units. No. 7A.

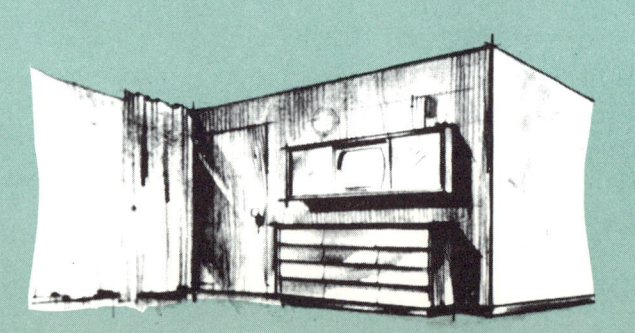

BUILT-INS

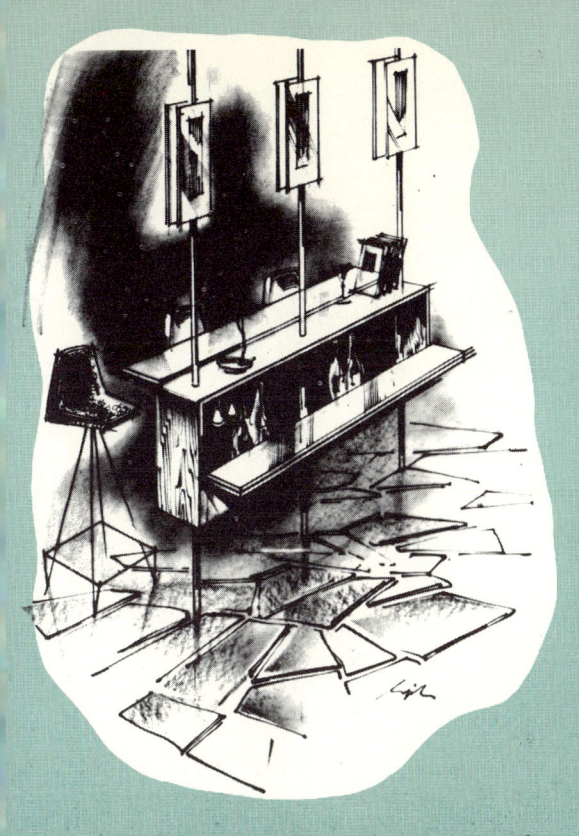

Combination bar and storage unit is set on rods on which pictures can be mounted. No. 10A.

Built-in bar has recessed indirect illumination, ample shelving for glasses, etc. Order No. 11A.

Storage of canned goods is no problem with the storage unit illustrated at right corner. There's enough room for a season's canning. No. 20A.

Below: A desk which swings into dividing counter. This desk is a good one for kitchen-dinette area; its top is of plastic or any other kitchen counter material. Note the adequate drawer space. Order building plan No. 15A.

515

BUILT-INS

Dining Room Wall Unit

by Bill Baker

It's extremely functional, features new style plastic-molded drawers.

FOR a striking new approach in dining room furnishing, this wall unit will certainly fit the bill. Its clean, modern lines and striking color contrasts between the cabinet shell and its front parts will create immediate acclaim.

Space-wise, this unit is well balanced with sufficient drawer space for linens as well as silverware. The new type molded plastic drawers add to the functional characteristics of this cabinet.

Behind the sliding doors an adjustable shelf divides ample space for your dinnerware. Most important of all this unit does away with unnecessary stress in reaching and stooping. It is a pleasure to keep clean.

The unit is 8 feet long, but can be made shorter by eliminating either one of the drawer units.

The unit can also be made longer by adding on more units in sections.

A few weekends will see the workshop hobbyist through this worthwhile addition to the home. •

COMPLETED CABINET looks like a million, provides much-needed storage in dining room.

BUILT-INS

CUT OUT all parts following diagram, mark guide lines, drill the necessary holes.

RABBET top and bottom edges of outside panels, as indicated in the diagram here.

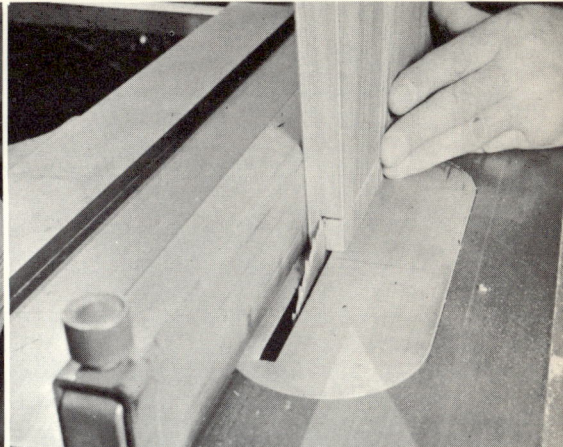

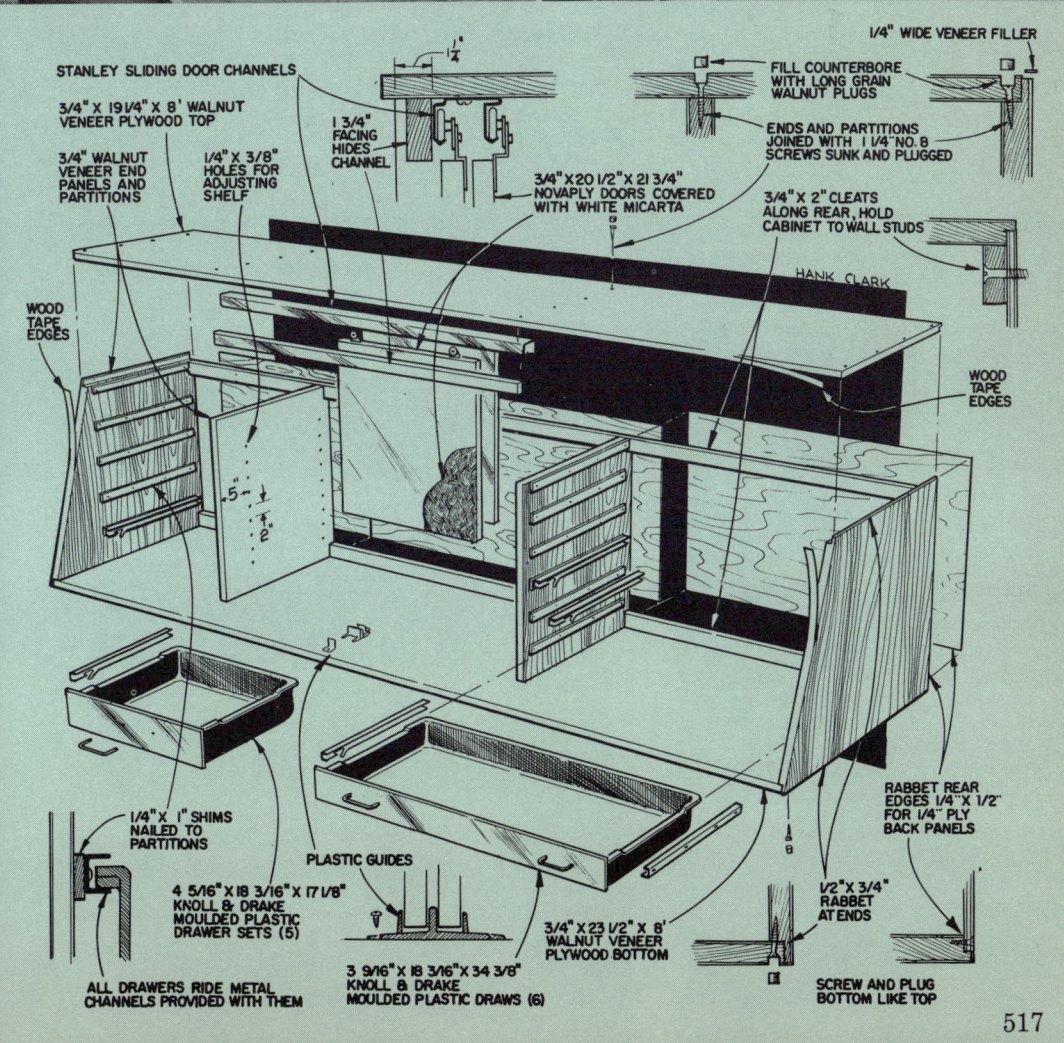

Labels on diagram:
- STANLEY SLIDING DOOR CHANNELS
- 3/4" X 19 1/4" X 8' WALNUT VENEER PLYWOOD TOP
- 3/4" WALNUT VENEER END PANELS AND PARTITIONS
- 1/4" X 3/8" HOLES FOR ADJUSTING SHELF
- 1 3/4" FACING HIDES CHANNEL
- 3/4" X 20 1/2" X 21 3/4" NOVAPLY DOORS COVERED WITH WHITE MICARTA
- 1/4" WIDE VENEER FILLER
- FILL COUNTERBORE WITH LONG GRAIN WALNUT PLUGS
- ENDS AND PARTITIONS JOINED WITH 1 1/4" NO. 8 SCREWS SUNK AND PLUGGED
- 3/4" X 2" CLEATS ALONG REAR, HOLD CABINET TO WALL STUDS
- HANK CLARK
- WOOD TAPE EDGES
- WOOD TAPE EDGES
- 1/4" X 1" SHIMS NAILED TO PARTITIONS
- 4 5/16" X 18 3/16" X 17 1/8" KNOLL & DRAKE MOULDED PLASTIC DRAWER SETS (5)
- ALL DRAWERS RIDE METAL CHANNELS PROVIDED WITH THEM
- PLASTIC GUIDES
- 3 9/16" X 18 3/16" X 34 3/8" KNOLL & DRAKE MOULDED PLASTIC DRAWS (6)
- 3/4" X 23 1/2" X 8' WALNUT VENEER PLYWOOD BOTTOM
- 1/2" X 3/4" RABBET AT ENDS
- SCREW AND PLUG BOTTOM LIKE TOP
- RABBET REAR EDGES 1/4" X 1/2" FOR 1/4" PLY BACK PANELS

517

BUILT-INS

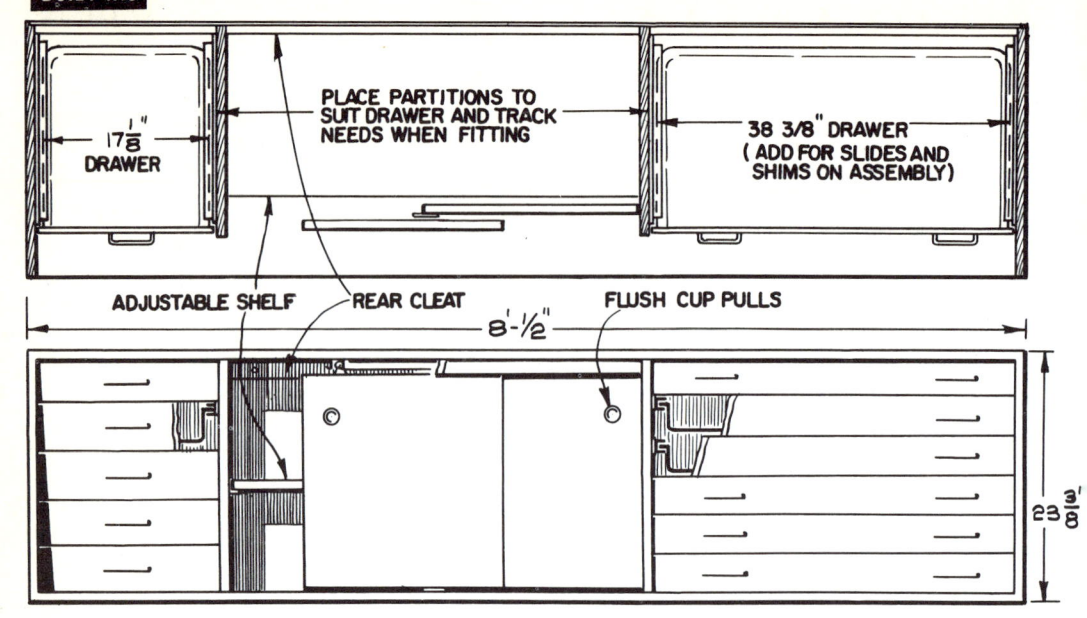

[Diagram showing cabinet construction with labels:]
- 17 1/8" DRAWER
- PLACE PARTITIONS TO SUIT DRAWER AND TRACK NEEDS WHEN FITTING
- 38 3/8" DRAWER (ADD FOR SLIDES AND SHIMS ON ASSEMBLY)
- ADJUSTABLE SHELF
- REAR CLEAT
- FLUSH CUP PULLS
- 8'-1/2"
- 23 3/8"

CLOSEUP of end assembly shows 1¼-inch, No. 8 flathead screws mounted through ½-inch holes in top and bottom pieces. If necessary, fine finishing nails may be used to hold ¼-inch lip in place.

BACK of cabinet is made of three parts which join in the center of each upright partition. The center panel is made of matching plywood; for outside panels, inexpensive ¼-inch plywood can be used. Fit center portion first to keep cabinet in square position.

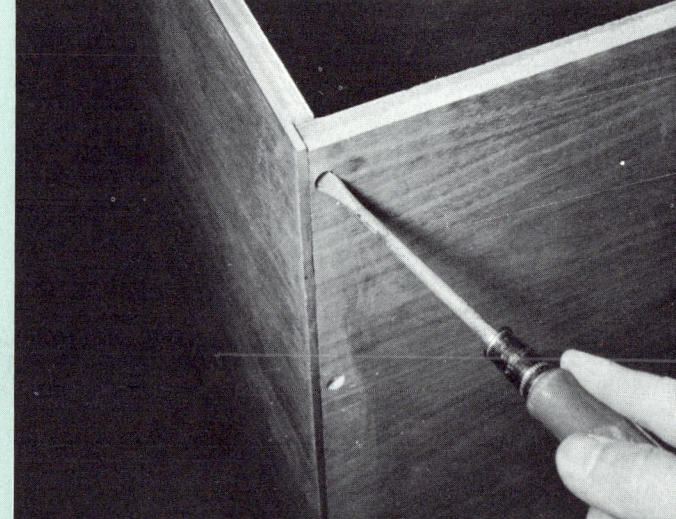

BUILT-INS

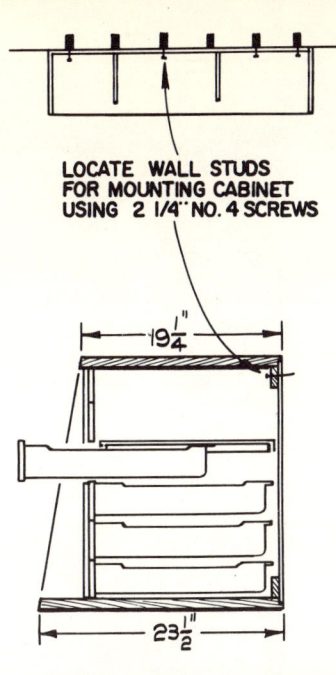

LOCATE WALL STUDS FOR MOUNTING CABINET USING 2 1/4" NO. 4 SCREWS

19 1/4"

23 1/2"

PLANE front edges flush, straight. Cover them with matching Weldwood Wood Trim, using Contact Cement. Miter the corners.

MOUNT steel slides, using spacer and making sure they are mounted level. It's best to mount slides for one drawer at a time.

DRAWER must be tilted upward when inserting. It's advisable to rub paraffin on steel slides to assure smooth operation of drawers.

MOUNT remaining rear panels to cabinet once all the drawers operate properly. Use ¾-inch head nails, but use no glue.

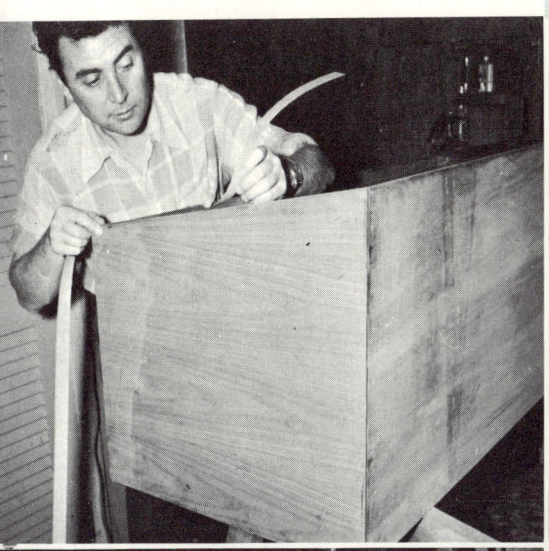

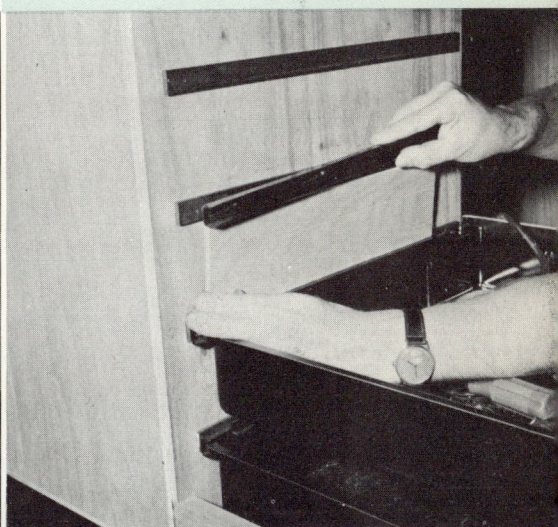

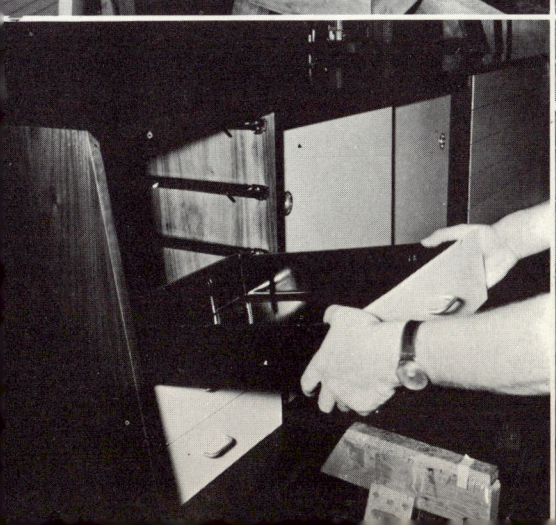

BUILT-INS

SLIDING door panels are tried for fit. Then left and right door edges and front surfaces are covered with white Micarta, as shown.

TO KEEP doors from warping, cover inside surfaces with Micarta backing. Excess Micarta is taken off with Porter-Cable router.

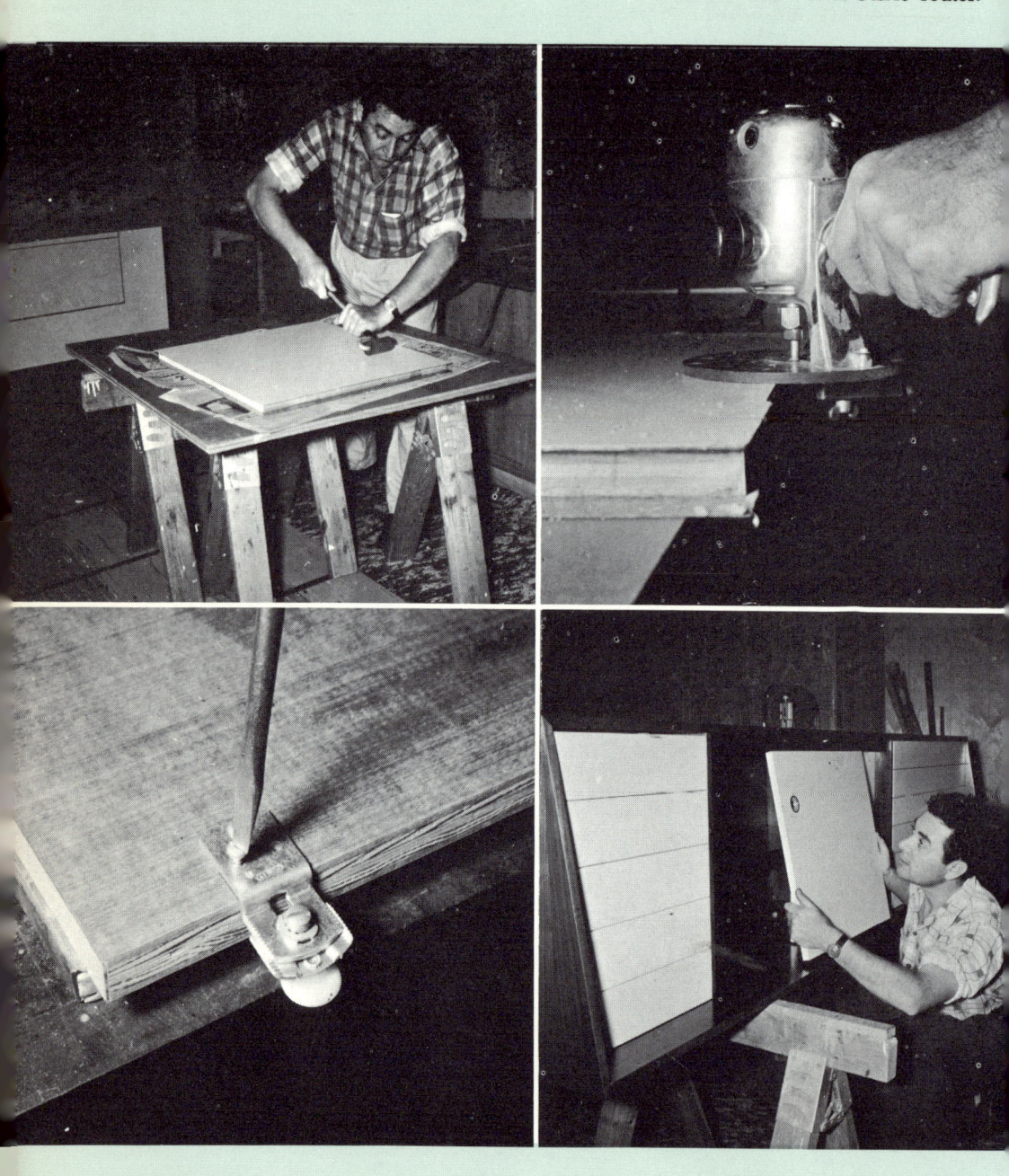

SLIDING door rollers and brackets are mounted 2 inches from side edges of doors as in diagram and mfg's instructions.

MOUNT doors, then adjust wheel brackets so edges of doors line up with upright partitions, have ¼-inch clearance on bottom.

BUILT-INS

MOUNT plastic floor guides. To assure proper clearances use piece of thin cardboard between door surface and the guides.

MAKE a jig for boring ¼-inch holes to mount brass handles. Hold jig snugly in place in order to assure perfect alignment.

PARTITIONS for drawers is 3/16-inch Dekaulux, notched halfway in each piece, lined up with the grooves inside of the drawers.

PARTITIONS are assembled before mounting in drawers. Front cross partition is not necessary, can be excluded if so desired.

521

BUILT-INS

Built-In TV Hi-Fi

MOUNTED on roll-out slides, the various units are readily accessible for inspection.

"HI-FI FEVER" is sweeping the country—and it's an enjoyable epidemic. One of the fringe ideas stirred by the upswing in hi-fi interest is the establishment of the built-in television and hi-fi center in the home.

An outstanding example of this entertainment center idea, shown above, is located in the home of a Portland, Oregon, couple. The development of this installation was a cumulative process, starting about one and one-half years ago. At that time, the couple decided to modernize the living room. This included a complete paneling of the room with natural-finish redwood. Coincidently, they had a chance to pick up, at a great saving, a color television set which had suffered cabinet damage.

The obvious conclusion was, "Why not build it into a permanent cabinet?" A few sketches later, the plan was complete. Not only was the TV set to be built in, but also a hi-fi radio-phonograph, a complete set of speakers, record storage space and room for later expansion (recently used for a stereophonic sound installation with tape player.)

Actual construction of the cabinet was routine, something most do-it-yourself handy men can handle. (But have the power equipment or it's mighty slow work). Half of the battle is won once the dimensions have been decided. This means reconciling the amount and size of your equipment with the available

BUILT-INS

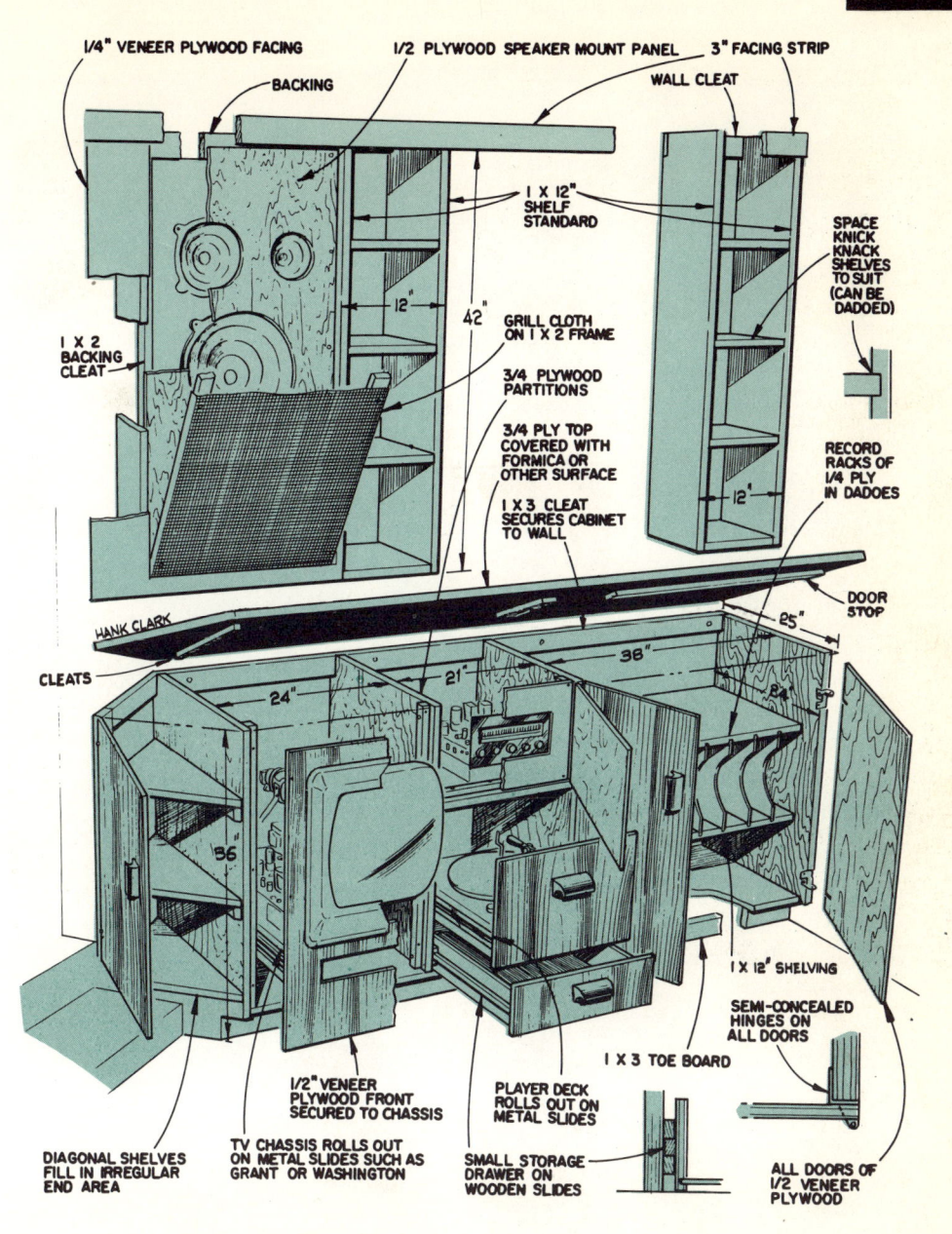

space. After completion, the cabinet (and the walls) were finished with two coats of hand-rubbed wax.

To save a lot of trouble later, the TV and hi-fi components were placed on slide-out bases for easy access.

The accompanying drawing shows the dimensions of this installation. While a certain amount of flexibility is necessary to account for different equipment sizes, the dimensions shown will serve most purposes and provide a good working diagram.

One of the advantages of using redwood, aside from its attractive color and grain, is the ease with which it is worked. According to Georgia-Pacific Corporation, one of the world's largest producers of redwood lumber, this wood has few equals when it comes to working qualities. Another factor is its high dimensional stability. •

523

CABANA

shoreside cabana

It proves that a storage house need not look makeshift

THIS handsome Cabana demonstrates that a storage house need not look makeshift. This design features a unique roof constructed of fir plywood panels bent into a series of arches. Only the roofed area contains storage but adjoining fences on each end add attractively to the Cabana's scale and effectiveness as a wind screen.

Follow the step-by-step procedures as enumerated below for fastest and simplest construction:

Determine size of concrete pad required. Roughly level off the ground surface so the concrete will have about 3½-inch thickness throughout. Excavate a trench approximately 4 inches below this leveled

CABANA

PHOTOS ABOVE show storage units which are housed neatly behind folding doors of shoreside cabana. Storage units have plenty of space, will accommodate all kinds of garden and terrace equipment. Unique roof is constructed of plywood bent into a series of arches. Unit is very easy to build. Study detailed drawings on the following pages before you undertake project.

area to provide for perimeter footing. Set 2x8 forms in trench at the proper depth to provide for a slope of $\frac{1}{8}$ inch per foot away from Cabana to all edges of the concrete pad. Install 2x4 screeds along post lines front and rear. Pour concrete mixed to the following proportions into form: 1 part cement, 2 parts sand, 4 parts gravel, with enough water to form a thick, fairly dry mix. Strike off surface along screeds with a wood float giving it a rough, non-skid surface texture. After concrete has set up sufficiently, set $\frac{1}{2}$x5-inch steel dowels 2½ inches into concrete at position of posts. Forms may be removed in 24 hours.

Cut and notch 2x6 rafters as shown in elevation. Drill $\frac{9}{16}$-inch holes into the bottom end of all posts to receive ½-inch dowels. Lay each post and rafter assembly flat and nail rafters to front and rear of posts with 16d galvanized nails. Be sure to insert blocking where required. Notice the center post in front is notched and nailed to the rear rafter only, to provide clearance for accordion door track. Treat bottom ends of posts against moisture with creosote. Added protection is gained by slipping a ⅛-inch thick painted steel plate with a hole drilled for a ½-inch dowel, under vertical posts before assemblies are raised into position.

After checking with carpenter's level for vertical alignment of posts, brace structure temporarily with diagonals at end walls. Gutters can be made by notching

525

CABANA

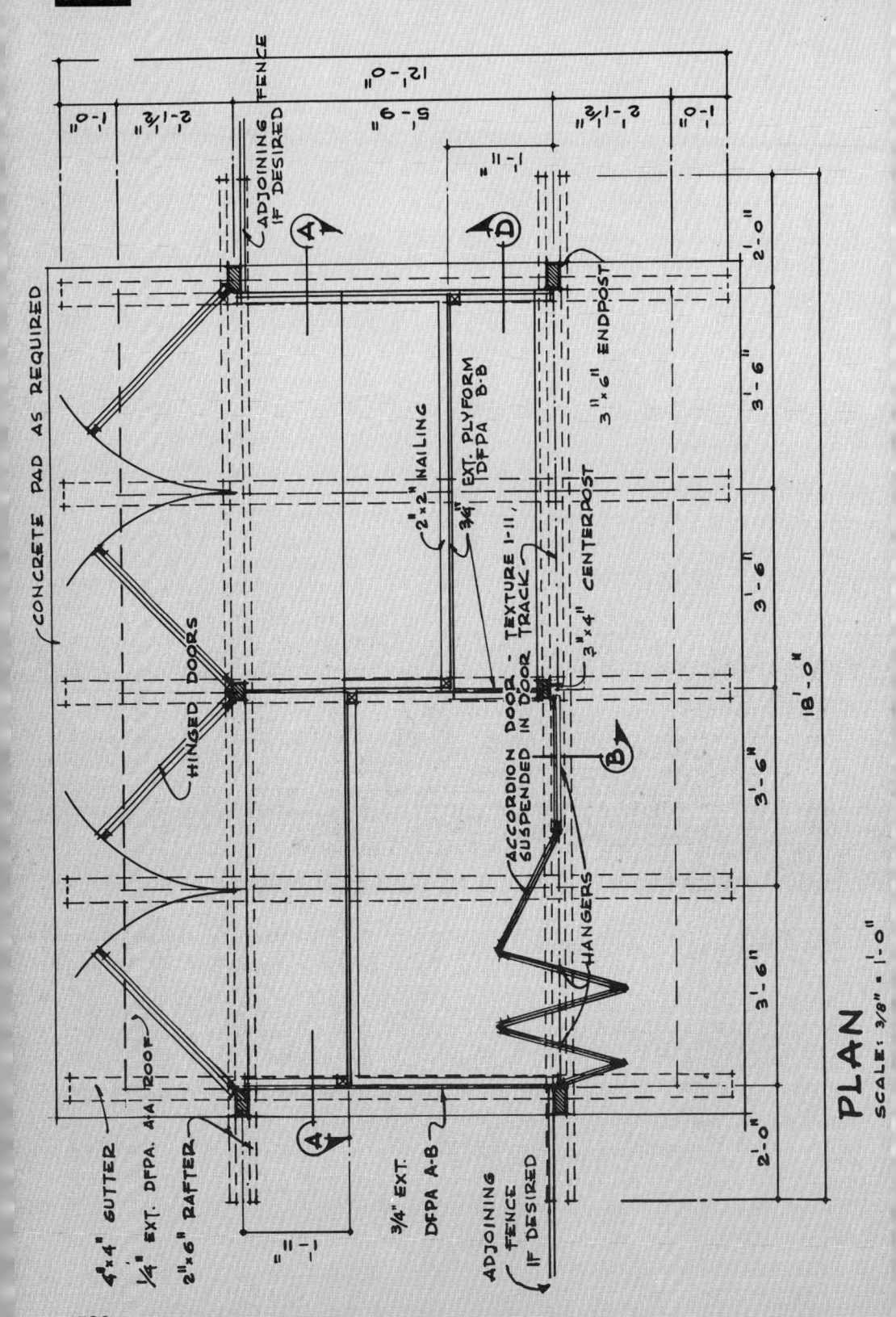

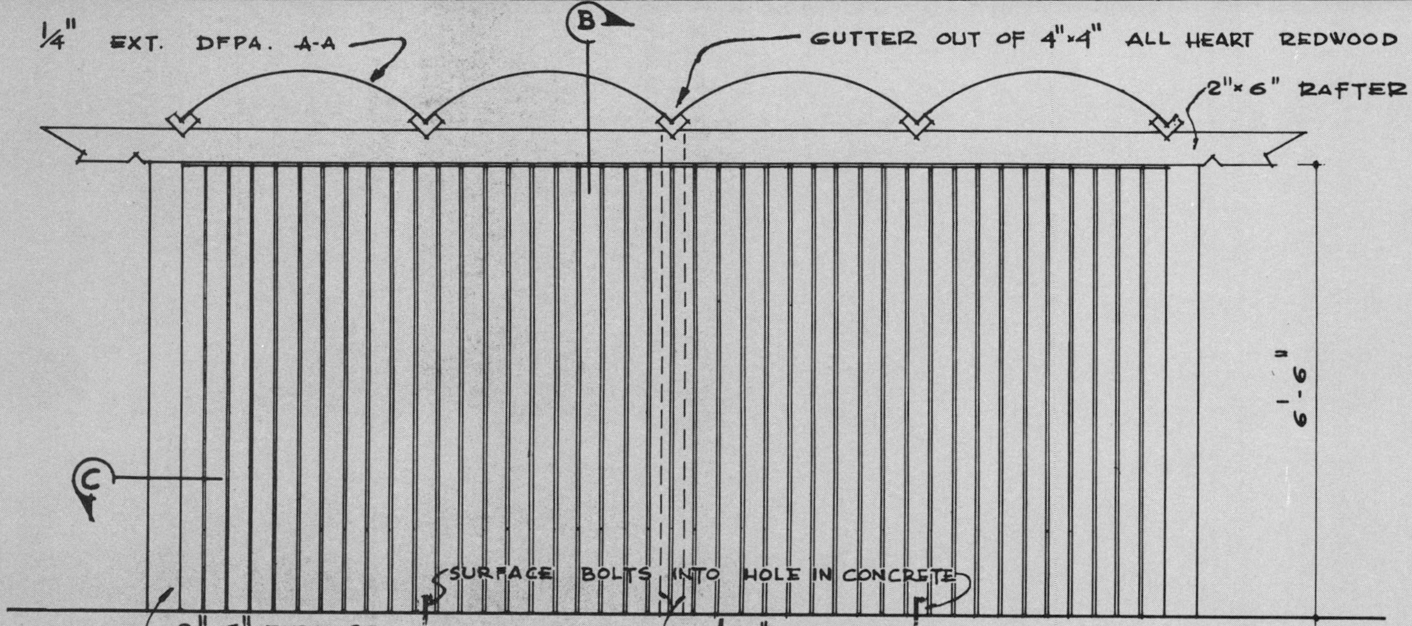

ELEVATION

SCALE: 3/8" = 1'-0"

ACCORDION OR HINGED DOORS

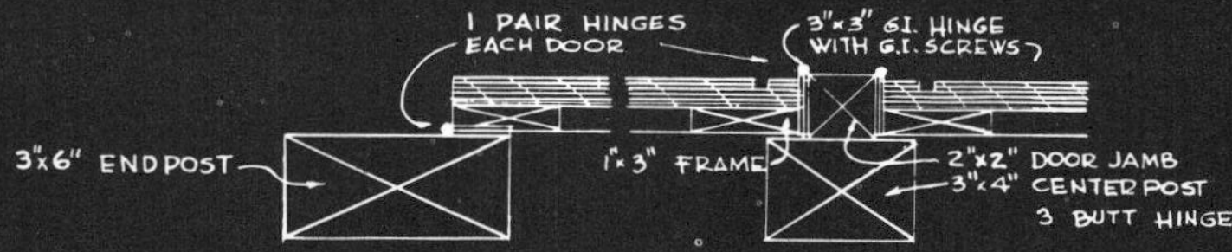

DETAIL HINGED DOORS

SCALE: 1 1/2"=1'-0"

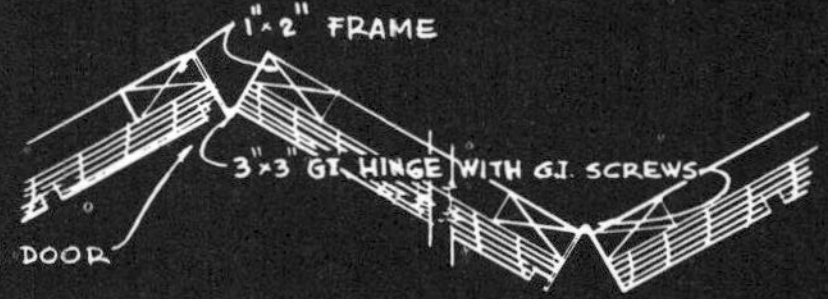

DETAIL ACCORDION DOOR

SCALE: 1 1/2"=1'-0"

DOOR DETAIL

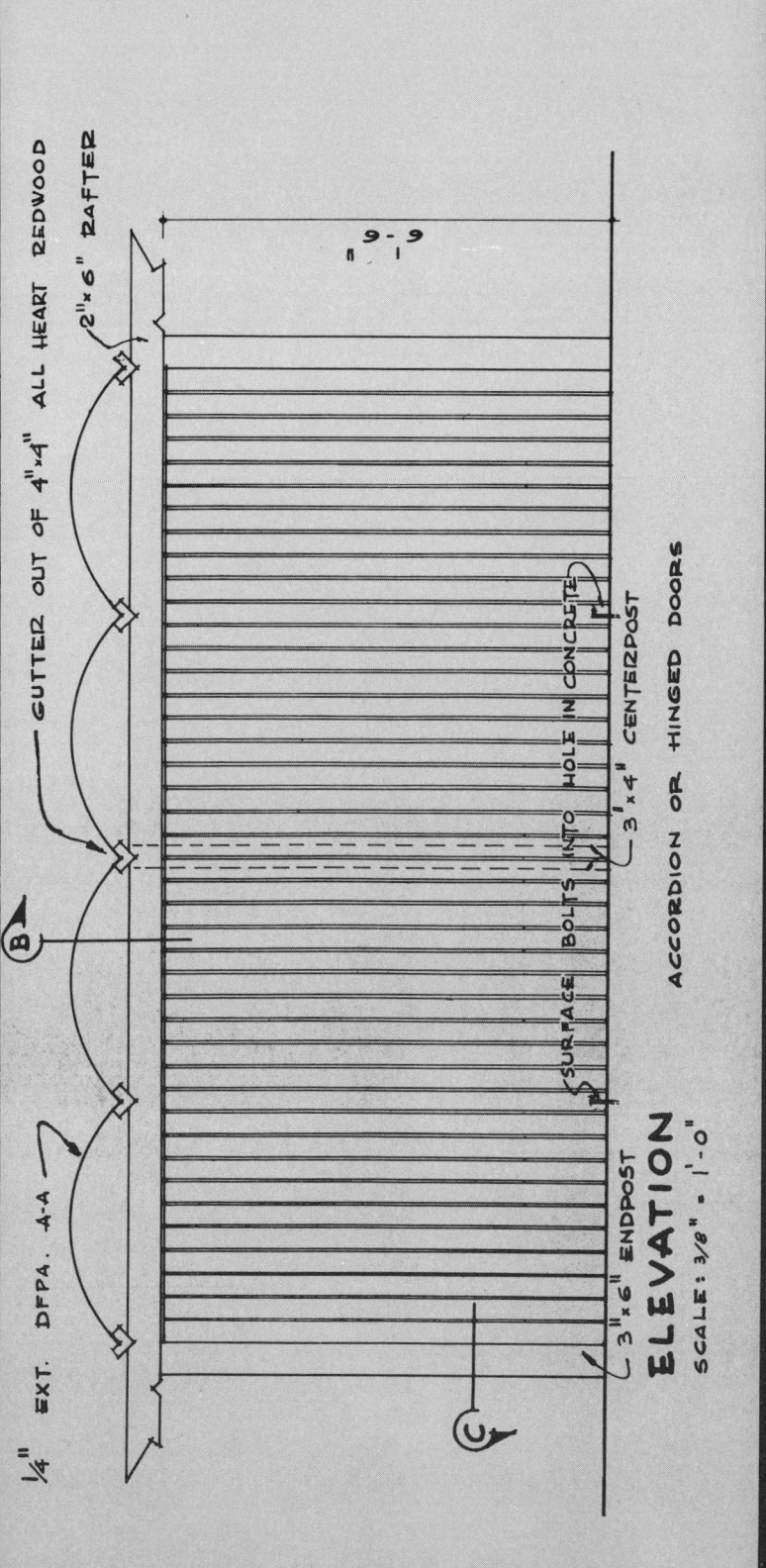

CABANA

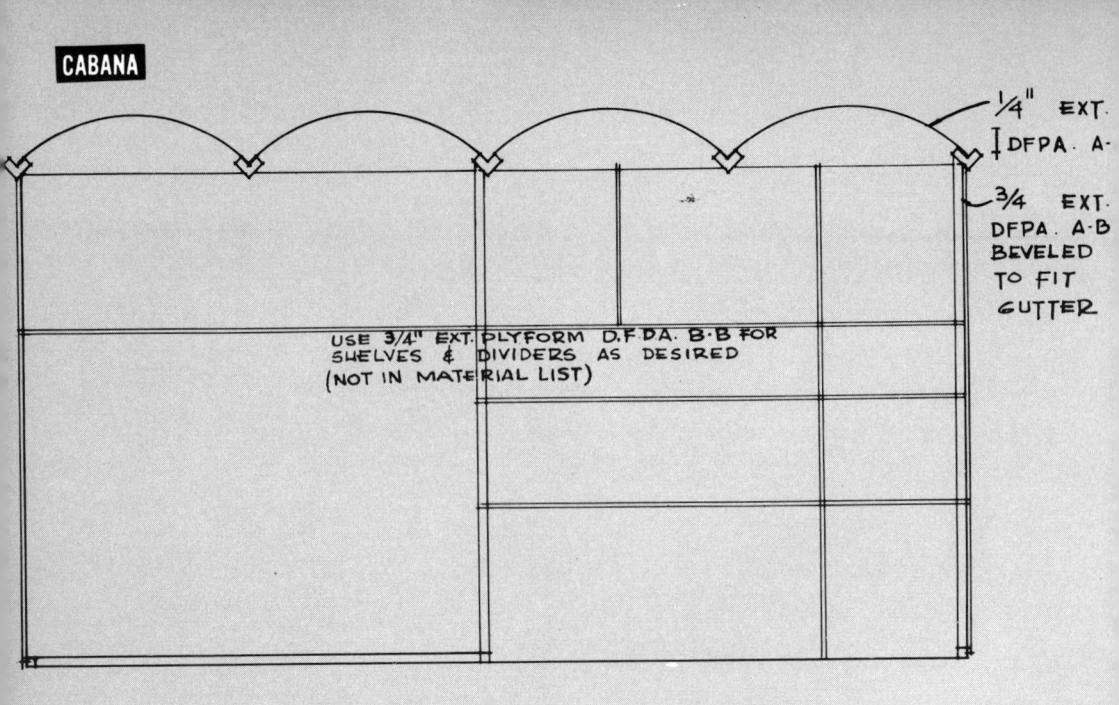

SECTION A-A
SCALE: 3/8" = 1'-0"

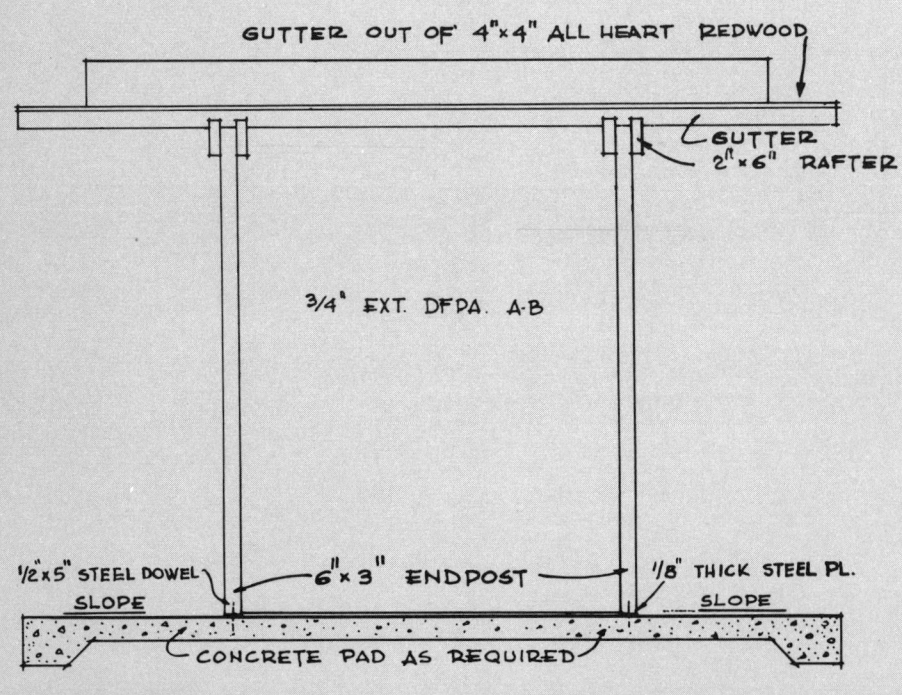

- 1/4" EXT. DFPA. A-
- 3/4" EXT. DFPA. A-B BEVELED TO FIT GUTTER
- USE 3/4" EXT. PLYFORM D.F.P.A. B-B FOR SHELVES & DIVIDERS AS DESIRED (NOT IN MATERIAL LIST)

GUTTER OUT OF 4"x 4" ALL HEART REDWOOD
GUTTER
2"x 6" RAFTER
3/4" EXT. DFPA. A-B
1/2 x 5" STEEL DOWEL
SLOPE
6"x 3" ENDPOST
1/8" THICK STEEL PL.
SLOPE
CONCRETE PAD AS REQUIRED

ELEVATION SIDE
SCALE: 3/8" = 1'-0"

CABANA

FIRST STEP in building shoreside cabana is to put up the framework, as photo here shows.

PLYWOOD sides and roof then go in place. Roof arches are bent into place, then nailed down.

ROOF pieces need not be wet when they are bent into place. Plywood bends easily by hand.

CABANA

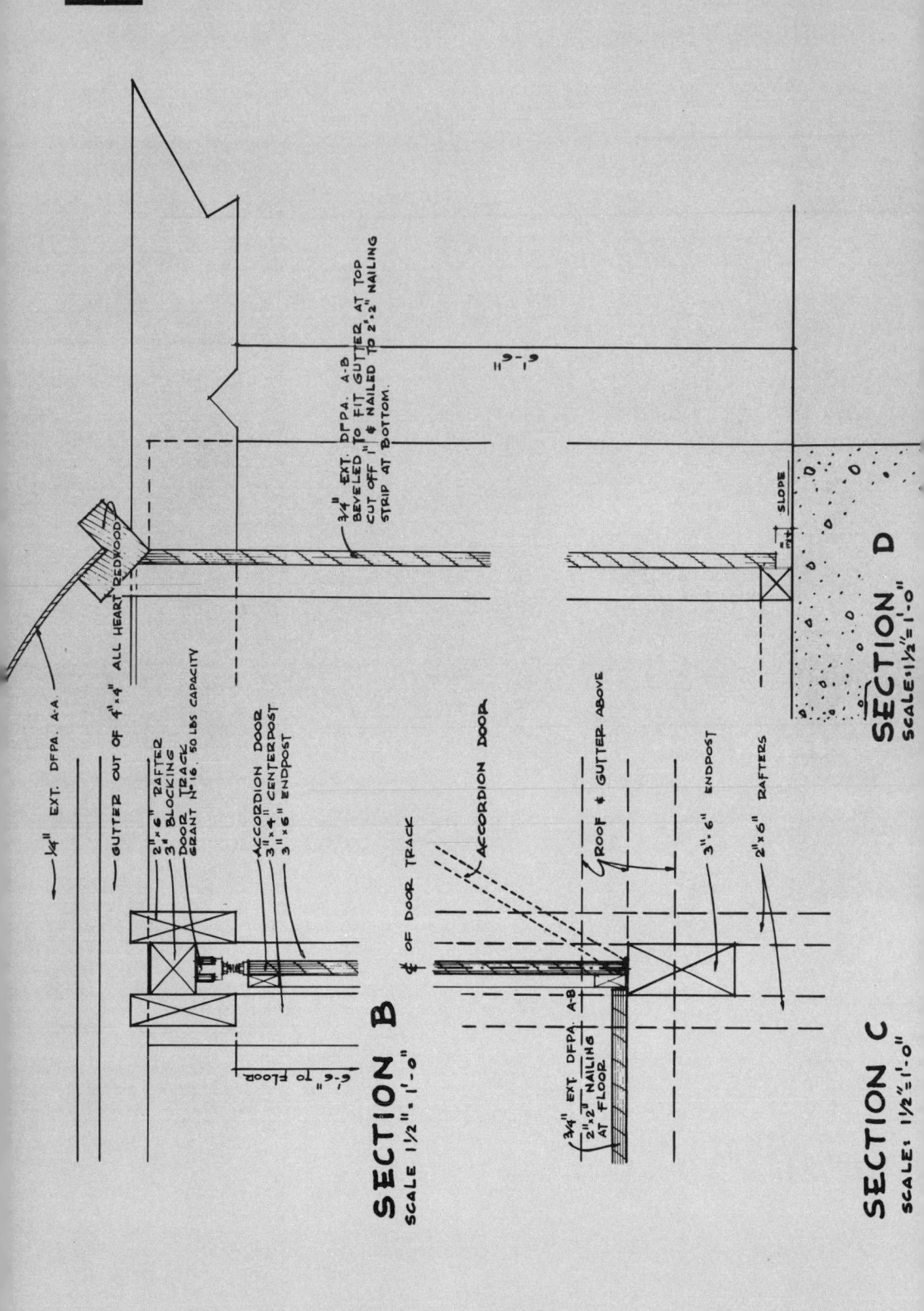

CABANA

MATERIAL LIST:

4 Pieces	2"x6"	Rafters	18'-0"	Fir
4 Pieces	3"x6"	Endpost	7'-0"	Fir
2 Pieces	3"x4"	Centerpost	7'-0"	Fir
5 Pieces	4"x4"	Gutter	12'-0"	Redwood
	2"x2"	Nailing	84'-0"	Fir
	3"x3"	Blocking	28'-0"	Fir
4 Panels	¼" Plywood		4'-0"x10'-0"	
3 Panels	¾" Plywood		4'-0"x 8'-0"	
6 Panels	¾" Plywood		4'-0"x 8'-0"	
12 Panels	⅝" Plywood		2'-8"x 8'-0" Texture 1-11 - Pattern 32/4	
	1"x2"	Door Frames	72'-0"	Fir
	1"x3"	Door Frames	56'-0"	Fir

Concrete, Hardware and Finishing Materials as Required

CABANA provides a beautiful backdrop for a swimming pool, also serves as a windscreen for the pool. And it has storage features.

a four by four with a "skill" or table saw. Place gutters into notched rafters and fasten with 16d galvanized nails. Give gutters a gentle slope to shed water by notching rafters slightly deeper at back.

Cut plywood for end walls and nail to posts making certain that vertical joints will occur at nailing strips. Set nailing strips on concrete pad with 16d concrete nails.

Beginning at the center, nail ¼-inch exterior plywood roof arches into gutter along each edge with 4d galvanized screw nails. Bend into position and nail opposite edges into gutters on each side of center one. Repeat for remaining roof arches. The plywood need not be wet when bent. Next install interior plywood partitions using nailing strips as shown.

Hinged doors are constructed using Texture One-Eleven plywood to which a 1x3-inch frame is applied. Detail shows how doors are hung.

The accordion door hinged to the post at left is made from a half-width panel of Texture One-Eleven plywood. All others are made from full-width panels except the first at right, which must have approximately 8 inches cut from its width to adjust total length of doors for fit. Apply the 1x2-inch frames and hinge doors as shown in detail. Install the door track and hang doors, carefully following manufacturer's instructions.

Finish in paint and stain closely following recommendations of manufacturer. Be sure to seal all door edges well and finish both faces alike. If adjoining fence on both ends is desired, order extra material and finish to match doors of the Cabana. •

CABINETS

SMALL PARTS CABINET

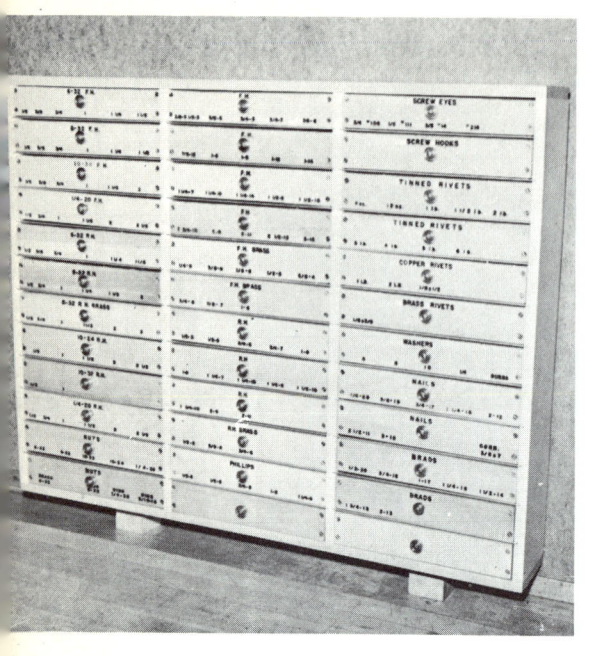

THE practice of keeping screws, nuts, nails, washers, etc., in jars or cans might be a fine temporary measure, but for permanent, neat storage, nothing compares to a properly indexed parts cabinet of the type shown here.

The plans and dimensions given are for guidance only; they can easily be modified to suit individual needs and space requirements. Construction is relatively simple—any type of available lumber may be used for the wood frame with its ¼-in. plywood back. One novel feature is the use of aluminum sheet for drawer supports, making the whole cabinet much lighter and giving the drawers a trouble-free and easy sliding action.

All wood surfaces get at least two final coats of top quality flat varnish. The finished unit can either be hung up on a wall or stood up on wooden supports. •

—C.M.

CABINETS

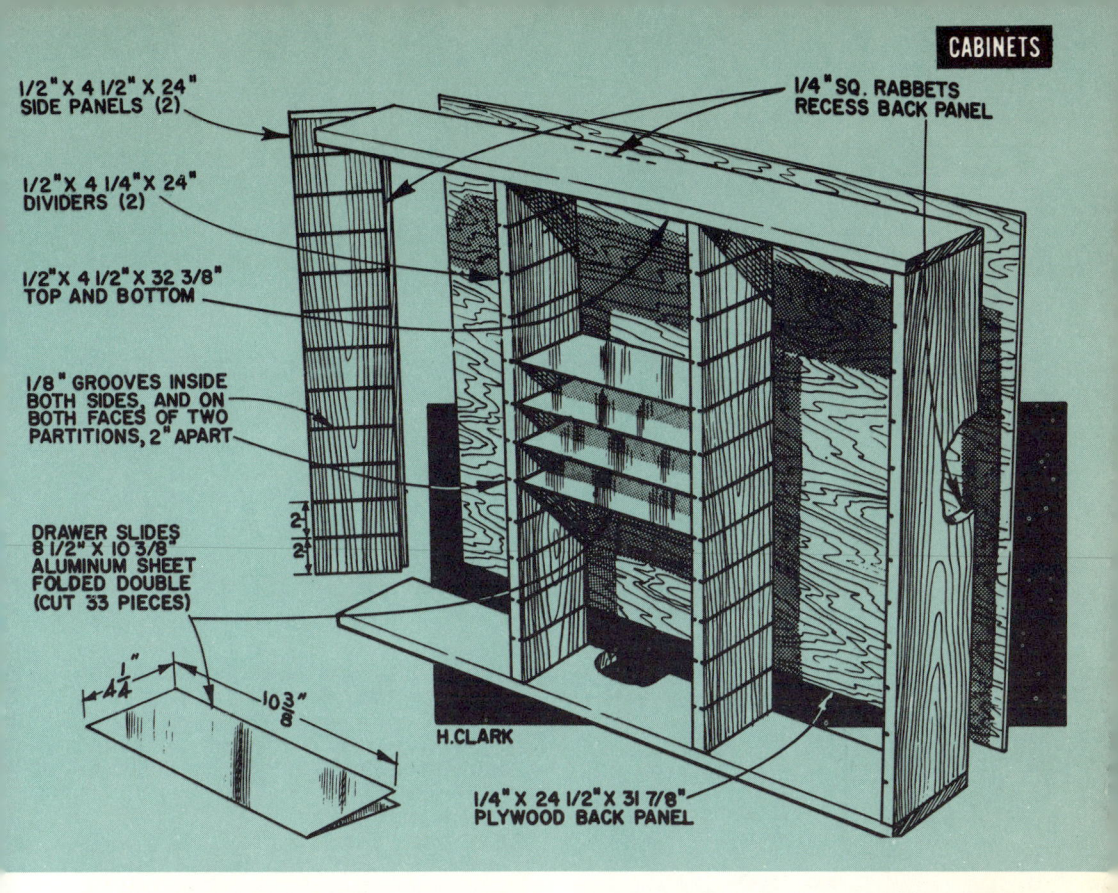

- 1/2" X 4 1/2" X 24" SIDE PANELS (2)
- 1/2" X 4 1/4" X 24" DIVIDERS (2)
- 1/2" X 4 1/2" X 32 3/8" TOP AND BOTTOM
- 1/8" GROOVES INSIDE BOTH SIDES, AND ON BOTH FACES OF TWO PARTITIONS, 2" APART
- DRAWER SLIDES 8 1/2" X 10 3/8" ALUMINUM SHEET FOLDED DOUBLE (CUT 33 PIECES)
- 1/4" SQ. RABBETS RECESS BACK PANEL
- 1/4" X 24 1/2" X 31 7/8" PLYWOOD BACK PANEL

H. CLARK

A simple drilling jig is handy for any job where a large number of holes are drilled.

Neat lettering can be accomplished with the help of a Leroy lettering device, as shown.

CABINETS

Vegetable Cabinet

This versatile piece does triple duty.

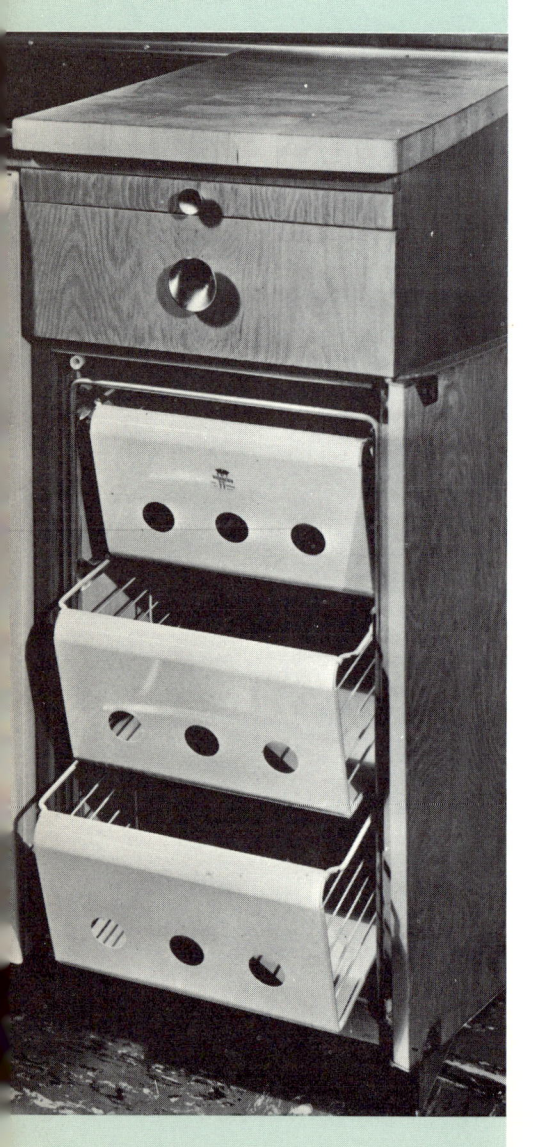

Storage cabinet takes up only 2 square feet of floor space, and can blend in with other units.

ALTHOUGH this cabinet is only two feet deep and 15 inches wide, it has three roomy vegetable bins plus a drawer and an attached cutting board. It can be used in combination with others or as a single unit you can place anywhere. The metal vegetable bins and any other hardware called for is available in most any hardware store and at some lumber dealers. It's a good idea to have the metal bins on hand before you start construction—then you can check cuts against mating parts to assure a good fit.

Start off by cutting the cabinet parts to the sizes called for in the materials list. If you make a layout of all parts on the plywood panel, be sure to allow for saw kerfs between pieces. If you plan to finish the cabinet in natural tones, plan cutout of the face strips, the drawer front and the door so the grain pattern will match over the entire front.

After cutting, sand edges carefully and check parts against each other. Now is the time to make any necessary adjustment—it will be too late after assembly. The cabinet bottom should be nailed to the base and to the ledger strips first, using glue and 6d or 8d finishing nails.

Add the side panels to the bottom, base and ledger strips, then install the ¼" back panel in the rabbeted edges of the sides. Check carefully for fit by putting the parts in position, and when you are sure they're okay, attach the frames and guides for the drawer and the sliding cutting board.

Before going further, place the cabinet in position and check for levelness. If floor is uneven, compensate by adjustment on base of cabinet.

Cut the parts for the drawer to size, dadoing as required and assemble with glue and 4d finishing nails. Hang the door and install the face strips as indicated in the drawing details.

After the cabinet is finished, install the metal vegetable bins, the laminated cutting block and the handles. Be sure that all plywood edges are carefully sealed and that the inside and outside faces of the door have equal coats of finish.

The laminated cutting block should be made from a hardwood such as maple or birch. Matching pieces should be cut and then rejoined with plenty of glue in the joints, and held tightly together under clamps until the glue is really dry. Make the board a little oversize so you can trim down just right to fit the cabinet.

A good finish for the cutting board, is to first sand very smooth, then apply several coats of good olive oil rubbed in by hand. •

By R. J. DeCristoforo

CABINETS

Exploded view labels:

- (F) FACING STRIP
- (G) CUTTING BOARD
- (H) FACING
- (D) THREE FRAMES FOR TOP, CUTTING BOARD, AND DRAWER SUPPORT FROM 3/4" X 1 1/2" COMMON STOCK
- (A) SIDE
- 1/4" X 1" GUIDE
- SEMI-CONCEALED WASHINGTON HINGES NO. 1031
- (I) DOOR
- WASHINGTON LINE VEGETABLE BIN UNIT SECURES TO BOTTOM
- (C) KICK BOARD
- (O)
- (B) 3/4" PLYWOOD BOTTOM
- 1/2" GUIDE WITH 1/4" X 1" GROOVE
- (L) 3/4" FRONT PANEL DADOED FOR BOTTOM AND SIDES
- (K) 1/2" SIDES
- (N) BOTTOM IN 1/4" DADOES
- 1/4" STOCK DIVIDERS
- (M) DRAWER BACK
- 1/4" X 1/2" RABBET DOWN EDGES
- (A) SIDE PANEL (2)
- (E) 1/4" PLYWOOD BACK PANELS
- 3/8" DOWELS JOIN TOP TO FRAMES
- (J) 1 1/8" CUTTING TOP OF ONE PIECE OR BUTTED UP STOCK

Dimensions shown: 24", 14 1/2", 13", 22 1/4", 2 5/16", 4 7/8", 13", 12 3/4", 4 3/4"

HANK CLARK

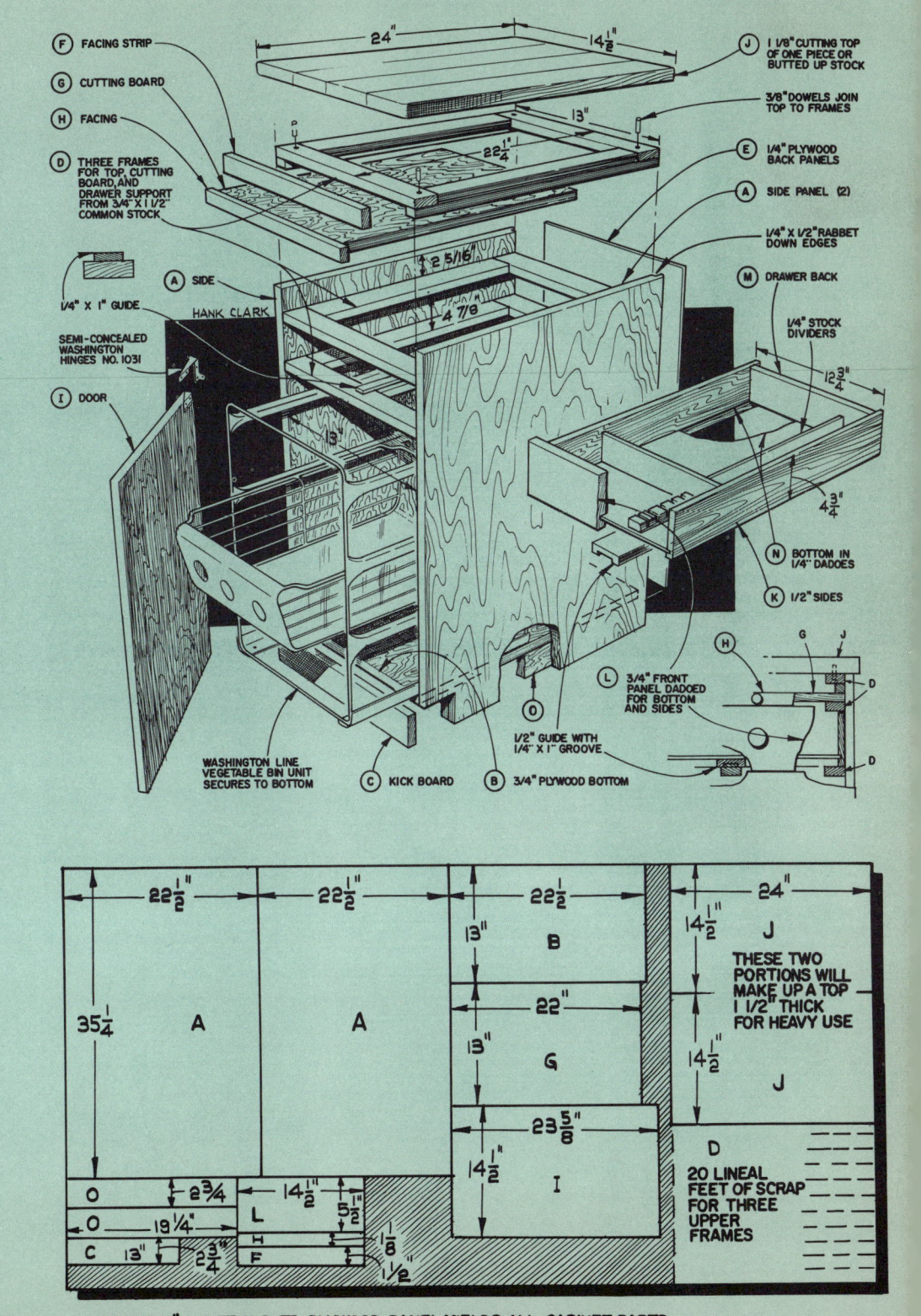

Cutting layout (lower diagram):

ONE 3/4" X 4 FT. X 8 FT. PLYWOOD PANEL YIELDS ALL CABINET PARTS

- A: 22 1/2" x 35 1/4" (two panels)
- B: 22 1/2" x 13"
- G: 22" x 13"
- I: 23 5/8" x 14 1/2"
- J: 24" x 14 1/2" (two) — THESE TWO PORTIONS WILL MAKE UP A TOP 1 1/2" THICK FOR HEAVY USE
- O: 2 3/4"
- O: 19 1/4"
- C: 13"
- L: 14 1/2" x 5 1/4"
- H: 2 3/4"
- F: 1 1/8", 1/2"
- D: 20 LINEAL FEET OF SCRAP FOR THREE UPPER FRAMES

535

CABINETS

Spice Cabinet

by John Prechtl

It's ideal for handling those often-misplaced spice cans and containers

THE cost of materials for this project will not exceed $3. The cabinet is of ¼-inch plywood and ½x3-inch pine. The antique screws and the brass knobs and hinges can be purchased from any well-stocked hardware store.

Start with the plywood back and shelves. Drill ⅜-inch mounting holes in the back, then bevel and sand the edges with medium and fine sandpaper.

The top, bottom, sides, and two doors are now cut to length; the top and bottom facings are cut from the remaining material. Slot both doors to a depth of ⅛ inch and bevel their edges to about 60°.

The dadoes are cut to a depth of ⅛ inch. The sides bordering the mirror are relieved ⅛ inch to accommodate the ⅛-inch mirror. A felt pad will later be inserted behind the mirror to prevent condensation. Now sand all parts with fine sandpaper.

Glue and interlock the outer and inner sides with the top, top facing, bottom, bottom facing, and shelves, but don't use glue when attaching the back wood screws.

The brass hinges are now mounted to the doors and the doors placed in position on the cabinet. Outline the hinges on the cabinet and then notch out this area, as shown in diagram.

Finally, replace the mirror, attach the doors, install the brass knobs, and apply one more coat of wax for a really lustrous and long-lasting finish. •

CABINETS

Highly-polished spice cabinet makes a bright and worthwhile addition to any wall.

Components of cabinet are laid out, ready for assembly in photo below, across page.

Cutaway drawing below shows how cabinet is assembled, gives dimensions for pieces.

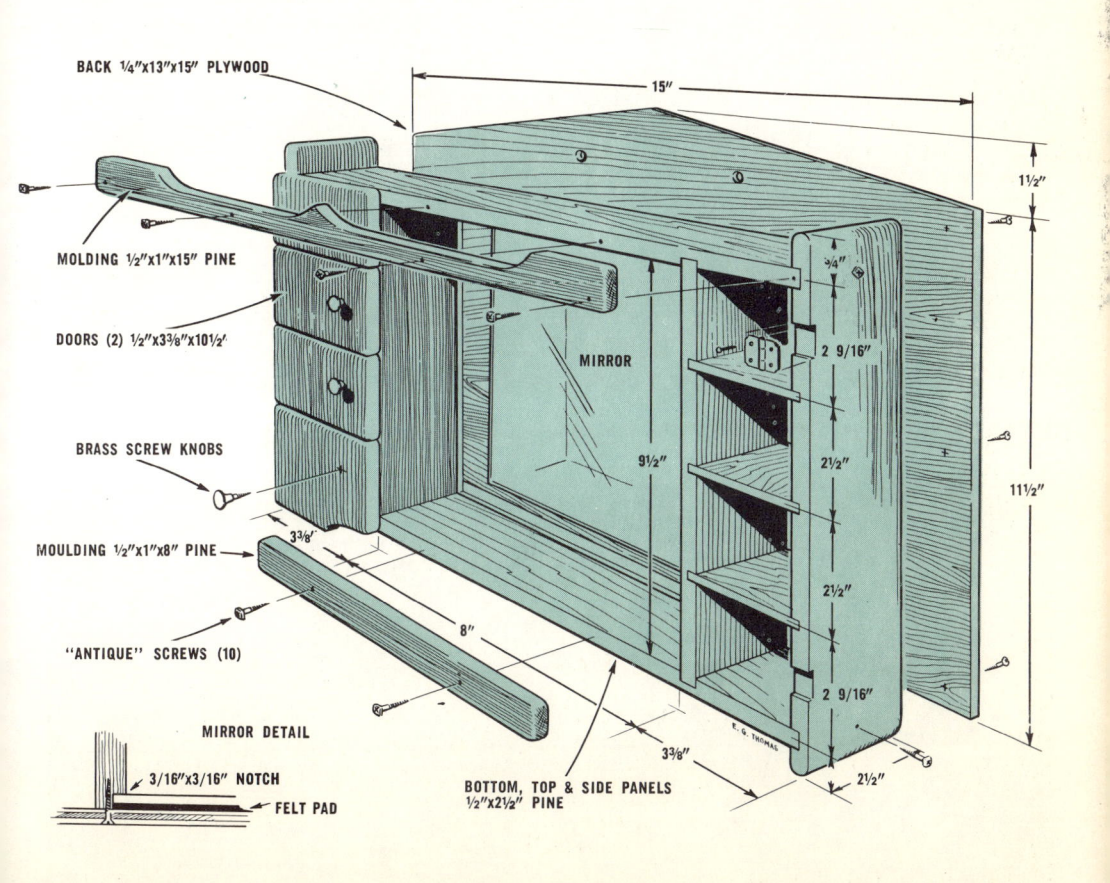

BACK ¼"x13"x15" PLYWOOD
MOLDING ½"x1"x15" PINE
DOORS (2) ½"x3⅜"x10½"
BRASS SCREW KNOBS
MOULDING ½"x1"x8" PINE
"ANTIQUE" SCREWS (10)

MIRROR DETAIL
3/16"x3/16" NOTCH
FELT PAD

BOTTOM, TOP & SIDE PANELS ½"x2½" PINE

15"
1½"
¾"
2 9/16"
2½"
9½"
2½"
2 9/16"
11½"
3⅜"
8"
3⅜"
2½"

537

CABINETS

All dishes and glassware are stored on shelves.

Table folds up into a cabinet with shelves.

Kitchen Cabinet

... stores dishes, and unfolds into a table for dining.

CABINETS

HERE'S A CABINET which will solve a number of problems in a crowded kitchen. It provides a storage space for dishes and glassware. It affords table space for four. The table folds away to within eight inches of the wall and gives the room an uncluttered, modern look. The small shelves on both sides may be used, of course, for small green plants or flowers.

Birch plywood was used to make the entire cabinet. Two sheets were necessary; one of three-quarter inch thickness and one of one-quarter inch thickness. The table leaf, sides and shelves were made of the thicker stock while the back of the cabinet and a small top piece were made of thinner stock. A long piano hinge was used to connect the table leaf to the cabinet. The two rods which hold the dishes upright are aluminum. The table leaf was covered with pink formica on one side and three edges.

Glue and screws were used to join the various pieces of the cabinet and wooden plugs were used to cover the heads of the screws wherever the heads might have been visible. The entire cabinet was screwed to the wall studs with four three-inch long chrome plated screws. The outer edge of the table leaf is supported by a one-inch maple dowel which has a machine screw (the head removed) embedded at one end. This machine screw is screwed into a fixture just under the handle on the front of the cabinet before the leaf is lowered to form a table.

The cabinet was finished with one coat each of linseed oil, varnish, and wax. This transparent finish left the cabinet very light in color with the strong natural grain of the birch a dominating factor.

Begin to make this cabinet by carefully marking the location of each piece on the big sheets of plywood. When you are sure that the grain is running in the right direction on each piece and every piece is included, then saw them out. After all pieces are sawed to the correct measurements assemble them loosely and check your plan for the location of the pieces.

The first step in the final assembly of the cabinet is to mark the location of the shelves on the two side pieces. Then drill the screw holes in the side pieces. Two holes are needed for each screw. One hole is for the shank of the screw and the other for the head of the screw and the wooden plug which covers it. Since one-half inch plugs were used the plug holes were drilled one half inch in diameter and at least three sixteenths of an inch in depth. Next, glue was applied to the ends of the shelves and to the cabinet sides and the screws were driven into place. Plugs were cut from a

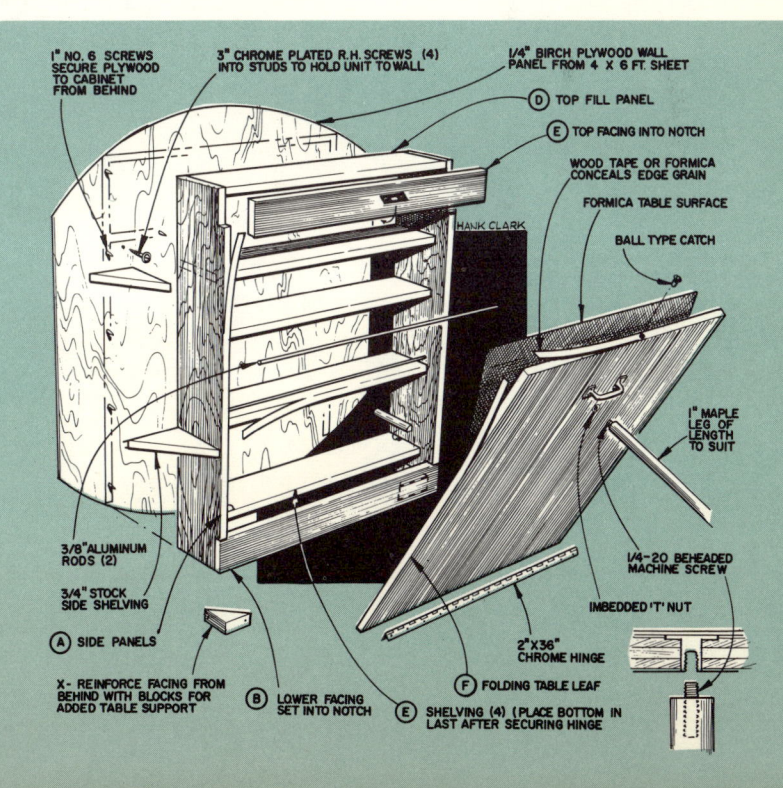

CABINETS

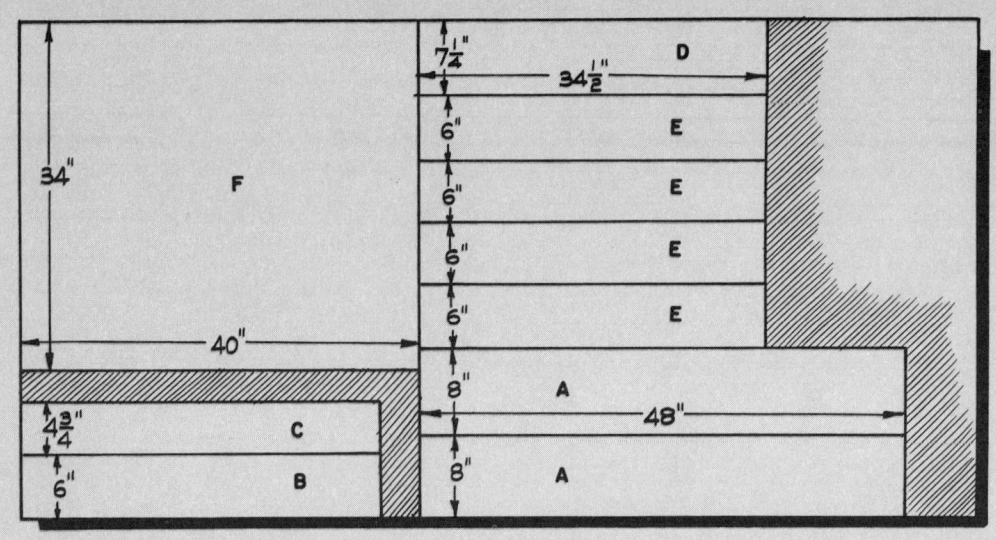

3/4" X 4 FT. X 8 FT. BIRCH VENEER PLYWOOD YIELDS ALL EXCEPT BACK PANEL

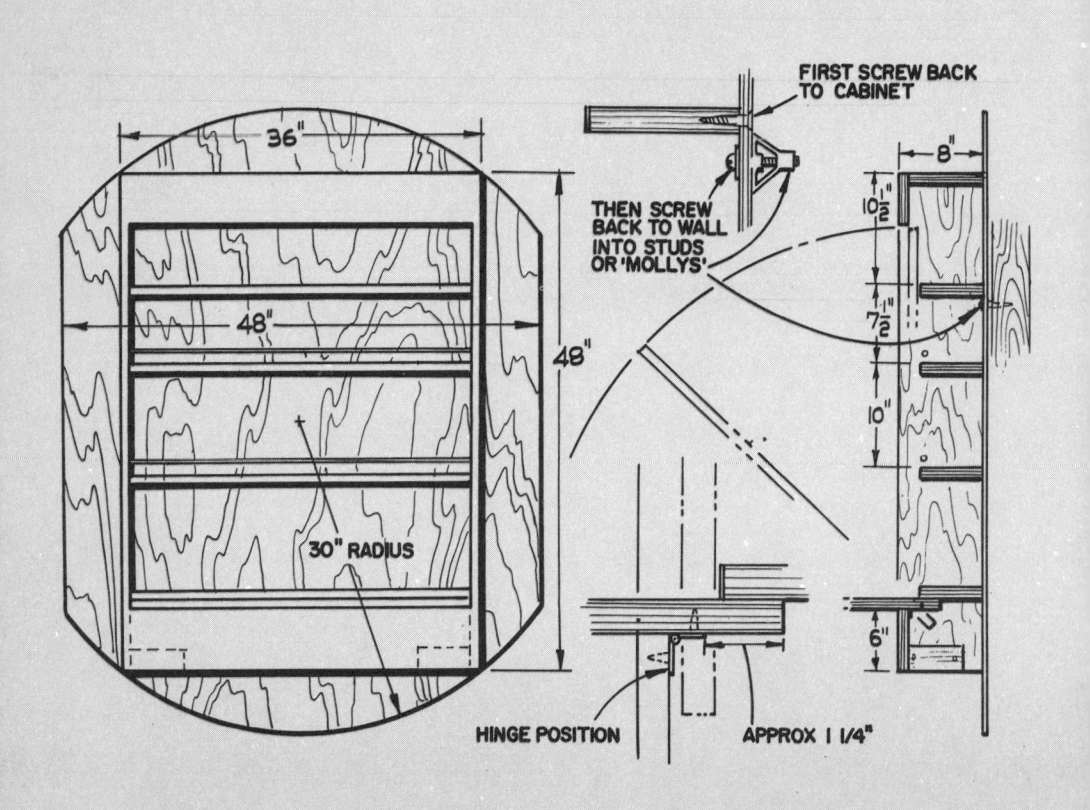

FIRST SCREW BACK TO CABINET

THEN SCREW BACK TO WALL INTO STUDS OR 'MOLLYS'

30" RADIUS

HINGE POSITION

APPROX 1 1/4"

540

solid scrap of birch with an inexpensive plug cutter which fastens in a carpenter's brace. Plug cutters are available, of course, for electric drills and will do an even faster job. A spot of glue was added to each plug hole before the plug was tapped into position. Each plug was also made long enough to protrude a fraction of an inch above the surface of the wood so that it could later be sanded down flush with the surface. If no solid birch wood is available from which to make plugs, a scrap of maple of the right color will serve the same purpose. Drive the plug into position so that the grain matches the wood into which it is being driven.

After the shelves are anchored in place the two front pieces are added. Notches must be cut for these in the side pieces. Remember, when cutting the notches that wood tape will be added to the front edges of the sides and must be included in the measurement of the notches.

At this point, place the table leaf in its proper position and mark the location of the piano hinge.

Now cover the one surface and three edges of the table with Formica. Mark your Formica so that it will be about $\frac{1}{32}$ inch larger in each direction after being sawed. This Formica was cut by hand with a keyhole saw having twenty-four teeth to the inch. These saws are sold in the hardware stores for the purpose of cutting bonded laminates of all kinds. The Formica used here was glued to the wood with contact cement which eliminates the use of clamps or weights. After the Formica was glued to the wood, the edges of it were filed down with a double cut bastard file. A single cut smooth file was used to finish off the edges.

The piano hinge was then screwed to the table leaf and the leaf placed in its extended position. The holes for the other half of the piano hinge were marked, drilled, and the screws driven tight to the lower front piece of the cabinet. Next the corner blocks and metal corner braces were added to the bottom of the cabinet so that the piece on which the table leaf rests is strongly tied to the rest of the cabinet. The handle and the ball bearing cabinet catch were then added to the front of the table leaf and the top of the cabinet.

Installing the cabinet back is an easy job. The location of the shelves and sides were marked on the back piece with the cabinet in position. Holes were then drilled for the screws. Then glue was added carefully and the back placed in position for the screws to be driven.

Birch wood tape, one inch in width, was next applied to all of the exposed edges. Contact cement again was brushed to both the exposed edges and tape itself and allowed to dry for thirty minutes. Then the tape was pressed onto the edges and tapped with a mallet on a block of wood to secure it in position. A file was used to remove the excess of wood tape which extended beyond the edges.

The small triangular pieces which form the shelves on the sides of the cabinet were glued and screwed into place with an ordinary white polyvinal glue before the edges were covered with wood tape.

The wooden dowel which serves as a table leg is one-inch diameter maple. A rubber tip was added to the floor end to prevent slippage. A ¼-20 machine screw,

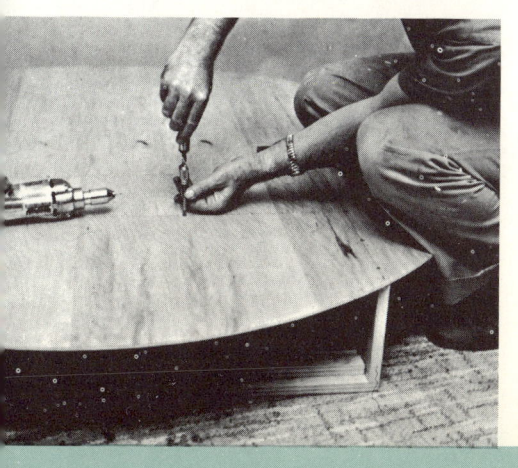

Shelf frame is fastened through the back. 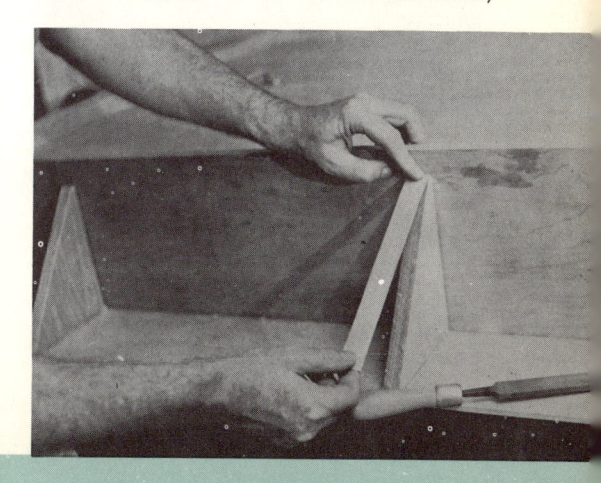   **All exposed plywood edges are tape covered.**

541

CABINETS

Plugs for covering the countersunk screws are cut from a solid block of matching wood.

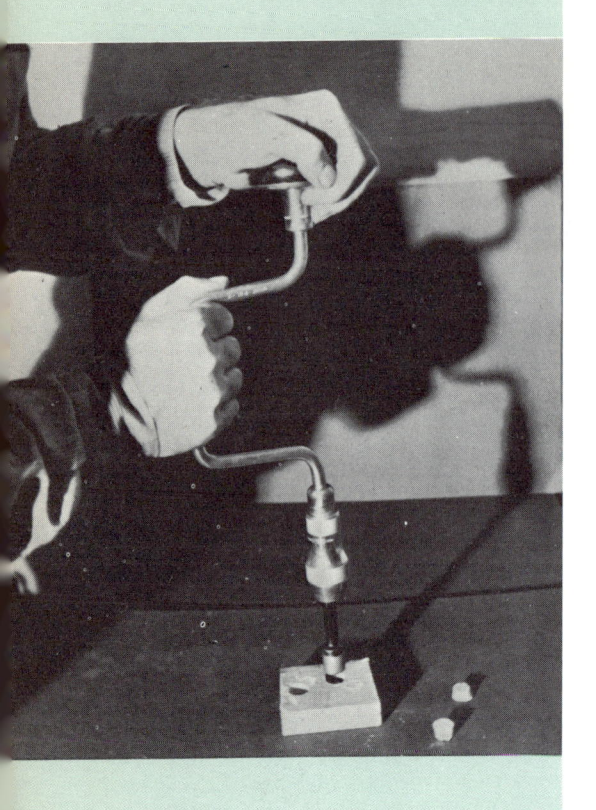

Dry-fit parts together and check for fit and squareness before finally fastening down.

one inch long, with its head removed, was tightly screwed into a drilled hole in the top end of the dowel. Three threads of the screw were left extending out of the rod. A 1/4-20 tee-nut was driven in a hole in the front of the table leaf just below the handle. This tee-nut has inside threads which receive the machine screw at the end of the dowel rod.

Because of the natural beauty of the wood a simple transparent finish was selected. Linseed oil was liberally applied and rubbed into the wood only after the entire cabinet had been sanded and steel wooled and all glue marks removed. After the oil had been allowed to soak into the wood for more than 24 hours and all surface oil had disappeared, a thick coat of varnish was brushed over the entire cabinet.

Then the varnish was steel wooled to remove all bubbles and bumps and a paste wax was applied to the entire cabinet. This was rubbed hard when dry until a good gloss appeared. Of course, other coats of wax may be easily added from time to time as they are needed.

With this natural wood finish, and perhaps made of walnut or mahogany instead of birch, this cabinet might also be used as a book cabinet and study table. The back pieces might also be redesigned to fit the decor of any room. Instead of Formica or any plastic laminate the table surface might be given a natural finish to match the rest of the cabinet. Of course, if the unit is to match existing cabinets that are painted, a cheaper grade of plywood can be used. • *By Bill Moore*

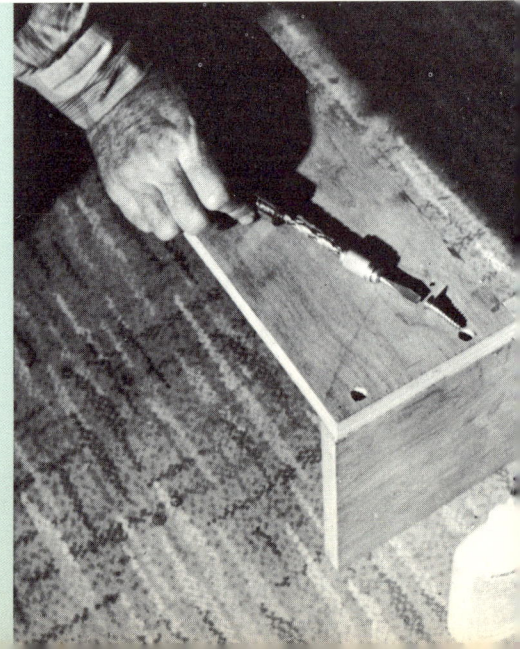

CABINETS

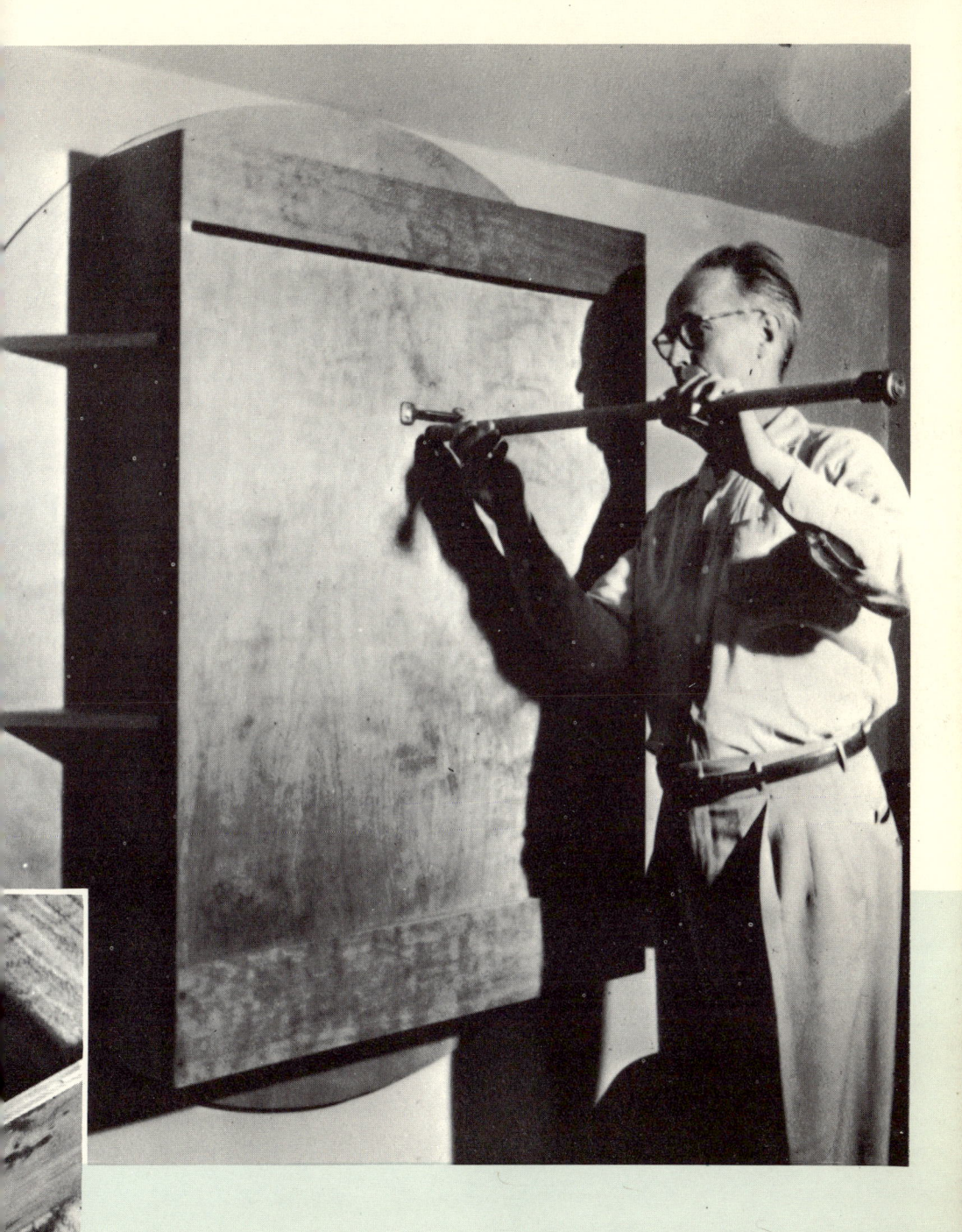

Screws for the two facing pieces are countersunk and counterbored for matching plugs.

The supporting leg screws in below the handle and is stored inside when not in use.

CABINETS

Record Cabinet

Keep records neatly stored away

Despite the popularity of hi-fi and stereo, there are thousands of families who still prefer the conventional consolette or table model record player. But whether they own a complete hi-fi system or a small player, all music fans have one problem: record storage.

Here's a compact record cabinet which holds records and provides a handsome resting place for your table model record player. It is designed small, since most homes do not have a lot of wall space for

CABINETS

music equipment. The cabinet, itself, without sliding doors and record spacers, can be cut from one panel of ¾-inch fir plywood.

The cabinet can also be used to hold small hi-fi or stereo components, with the speaker nearby. Installation of the components doesn't cut down the record storage space—there is room behind the records for the amplifier and pre-amp system.

Construction calls for simple butt joints glued and nailed. Sliding doors can be hardboard or hardwood plywood. Any type of commercial legs, sold at hardware stores and lumber yards, can be used. An extra scrap piece of ¼-inch plywood or hardboard can be used for dividers and drawer bottom.

Inside the cabinet, half the space is devoted to long-play record storage, and the remainder has space for the 45-speed records and a small drawer. The 45s fit into small racks which are available in any music, hi-fi or record store.

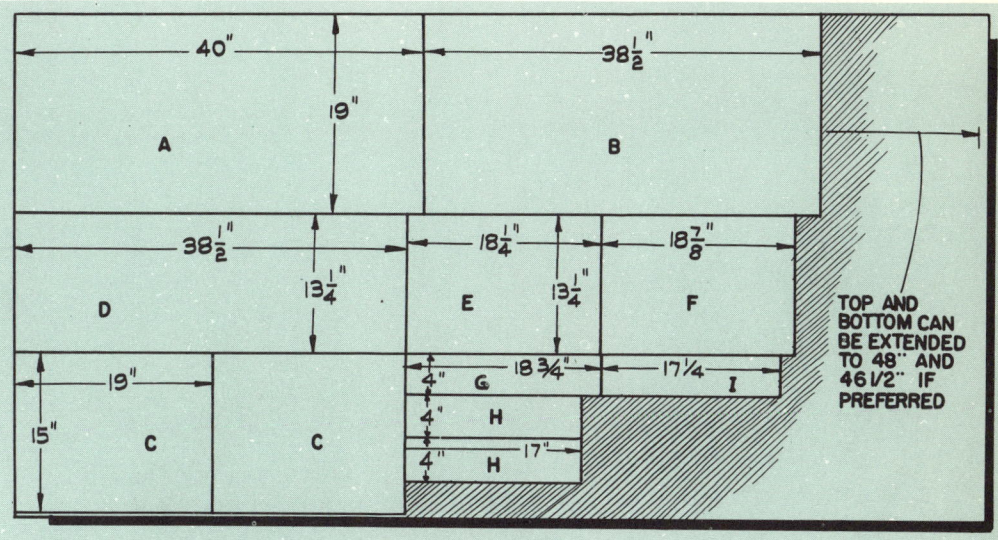

As simple to make as a box, this record cabinet provides an ideal place for a table-model record player and storage space for the 33-speed and 45-speed discs.

Compartments for large long-play records hold them vertical, in the approved storage position. Each divider is spaced to hold 18 records, a cabinet total of 108.

CABINETS

END CROSS SECTION

- 13"
- STOP TO HOLD RECORDS FORWARD IN RACK
- 9/32" DADO 1/4" DEEP FOR RECORD DIVIDERS

RECORD COMPARTMENT DIVIDER

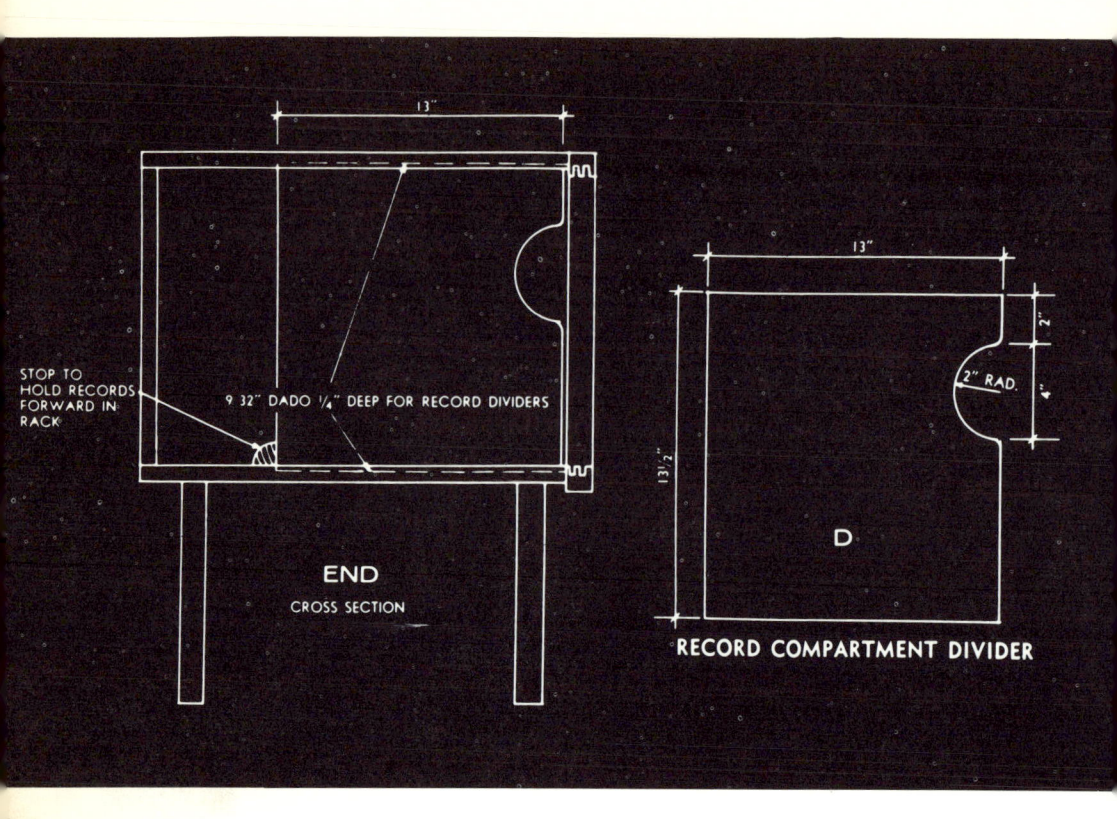

- 13"
- 2"
- 2" RAD.
- 4"
- 13½"
- D

One half of the record cabinet contains a shelf for standard racks which hold the 45 rpm records —the most efficient way to store them. Below the shelf is a drawer to hold record-playing accessories.

CABINETS

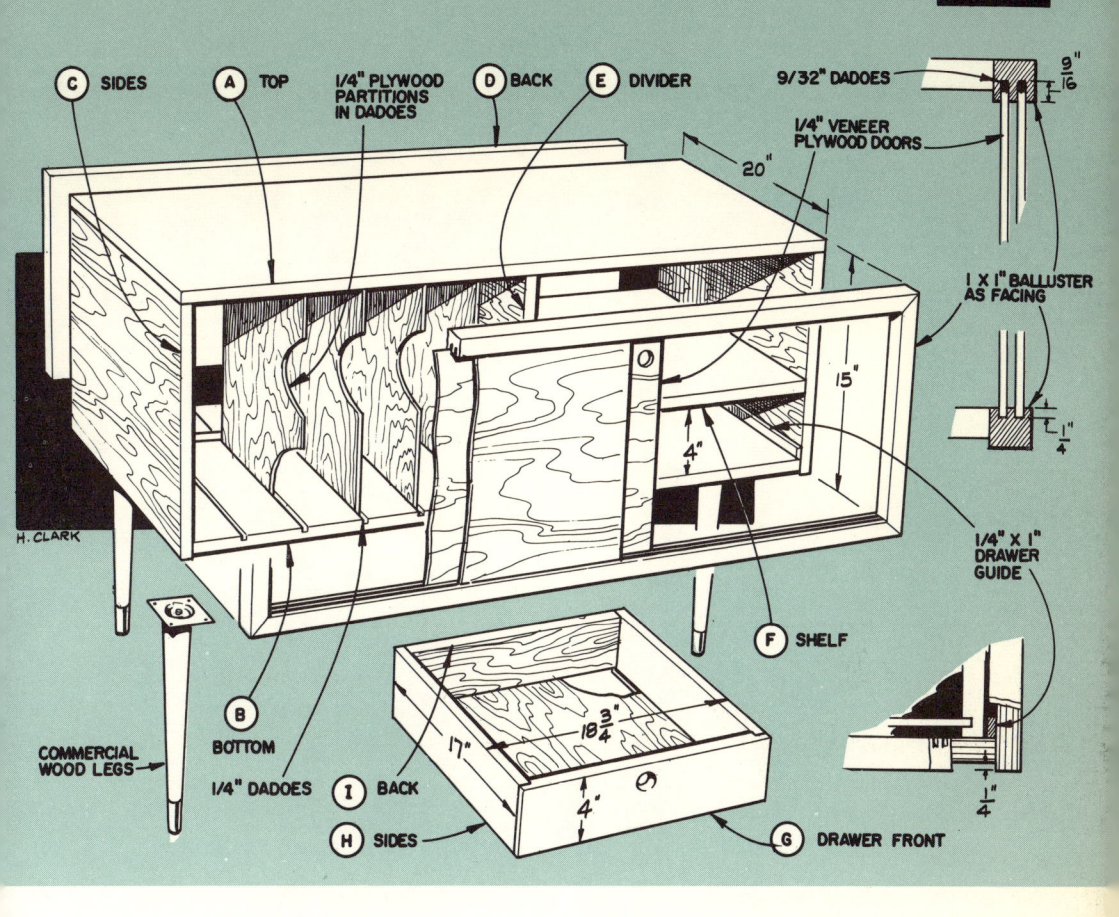

If the job is done with hand tools, it will be safer to combine the glue with 2-inch No. 10 screws. Be sure to predrill for the screws to avoid splitting and to obtain maximum strength. Sink the screw heads just far enough to allow smooth patches to be made with plastic wood.

Cut out the parts, following the cut-out diagram. Make dado cuts for the record compartments, or fabricate grooves.

Assemble by nailing the top to the sides, then the sides to the bottom. Then nail the back into the top, sides and bottom. Sink nails and fill holes with water-mix putty.

Install the central divider and the shelf that covers the drawer space. Paint the inside of the cabinet and the space above the shelf. Next, cut out the dividers for the record compartments and paint them.

Cut the grooves in the 1 by 1 balluster used for facing pieces in which the sliding doors move.

When the paint has dried, put the compartment dividers in their grooves. Now, nail on the balluster facers, with glue, fitting the corners with careful miters. Pull the record compartment dividers forward till they strike the facers, then reach through and tack a length of quarter-round behind them as a stop to hold the records forward in their spaces.

Cut out the sliding doors and bore holes in the upper corners for "handles."

Finish the outside of the cabinet with two or more coats of semigloss enamel, and with two or more coats of varnish on the sliding doors if they are of a cabinet wood. As shown in the photographs, the cabinet is white with walnut doors. It would be equally attractive in white with enameled doors—one gray, the other blue—or any color combination that strikes your fancy.

Install the legs. Be sure to use the largest screws possible without having them come through the bottom, so as to achieve the maximum strength. Stain or enamel the legs to match the finish of the sliding doors.

Last, assemble the drawer, paint it inside and out with a good semigloss enamel, and the cabinet is completed. •

CABINETS

sewing cabinet

"Finger-tip" storage is the big feature of this easy-to-build household unit

USE a straightedge to lay out the fir plywood panels as shown in the cutting diagrams and parts schedule. Be sure to allow for saw kerfs.

Cut plywood parts to exact size with a table saw. In determining size of the cutout in sub-top, allow at least ¼-inch clearance for the base of the sewing machine on three sides with adequate clearance at the power end for electrical connection. Locate cutout 6 inches from front edge and approximately 12 inches from right end. To provide rabbet for flush removable cover, make cutout ½ inch larger in counter top. Cut a hole in bottom "D" to allow for entry of electrical cord and in back "O" for wall plug. All cutouts can be made by drilling holes at corners and removing material with a saber saw or band saw.

Cut 5/4x2-inch blocking to length and apply to bottom "D" with 6d nails and glue. Similarly, fasten sub-top over, flush with edge of blocking. Position counter top on sub-assembly and drill holes near each corner for countersunk bolts. Insert bolts and then apply plastic laminate to counter top and removable cover. A saber saw with a special blade is required to remove plastic laminate for cutout. Make a rough cut first and then use a router with a carboloy bit to trim cutout. Similarly, trim outside edges of counter top and removable cover. Most plastic laminate applicators will do this job if these special tools are not available.

Bolt well assembly to counter top as shown. Then apply 1x2-inch door stops to left end and counter top. Nail and glue brackets and cleats in position and install shelves on inside of each end standard. Use 6d finish nails and glue to fasten back and ends in place. Nail bottom edges to floor with 1x2-inch cleats, being careful to keep cabinet assembly square.

Cope bottom shelf for caster leg, and fasten to end standard. Assemble standards and shelves of storage door. Apply ¼-inch plywood back and face frame cutout. Drill holes for dowels and then nail and glue spool rack in place, as shown.

Hang door using loose pin hinges. Remove pins, and lay door flat to fasten shelf assembly with screws through ¼-inch back. Install caster on 2x2-inch leg. Then apply hardwood counter edging. •

ITEMS which often become lost are stored in full view in this cabinet. Wood dowels on sloped surface hold spools; lipped shelving holds scissors, patterns, etc. Machine is stored when not used.

PARTS SCHEDULE

CODE	REQ'D NO.	SIZE	PART IDENTIFICATION
A	1	24" x 41½"	Top
B	1	23½" x 40"	Sub-Top
C	1	28" x 40"	Door
D	1	As Required	Bottom of Well
E	1	As Required	Cover
F	2	8" x 16"	Shelf
G	2	4½" x 8"	Bracket
H	2	24" x 29¼"	Side
J	1	23½" x 36"	Shelf Back
K	5	5" x 17¼"	Shelf
L	1	5" x 35"	Shelf
M	2	5" x 23½"	Divider
N	1	5" x 22¾"	Divider
O	1	29¼" x 40"	Back
P	1	15" x 36"	Face Frame
Q	1	10" x 17¼"	Rack
	5 Lin. Ft.	3/16" Dia.	Dowel
	12 Lin. Ft.	½" x 1¼"	Hardwood Edge
	14 Lin. Ft.	1" x 2"	Door Stop & Cleats
	1½ Lin. Ft	2" x 2"	Leg
	6 Lin. Ft.	5/4" x 2"	Blocking
	4	¼" x 4"	Bolt & Nut
	1 Ea.	1¼"	Swivel Caster
	1½ Pr.	1½"	Semi-Concealed Hinges
	1 Ea.		Friction Catch
	1 Ea.		Door Pull

MISCELLANEOUS—4d and 6d finish nails, screws and glue finishing materials.

CABINETS

DIAGRAMS shown here give complete dimensions for construction of unit.

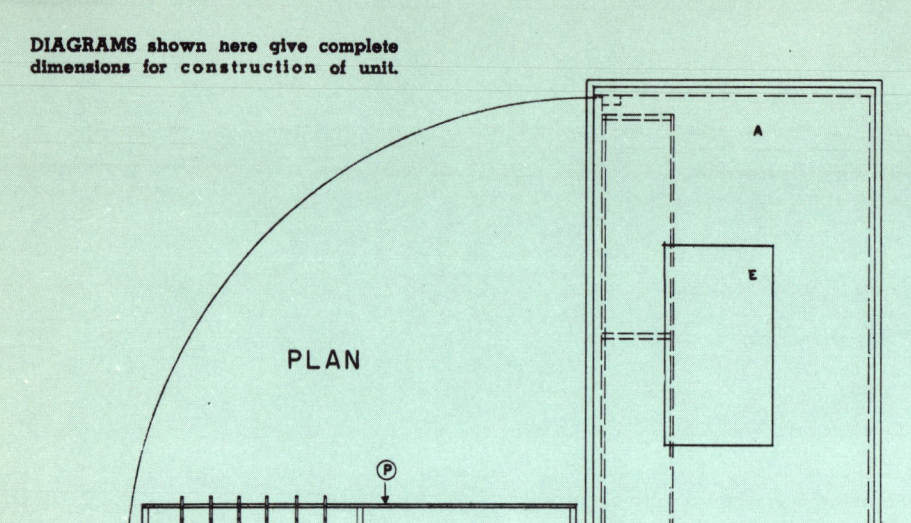

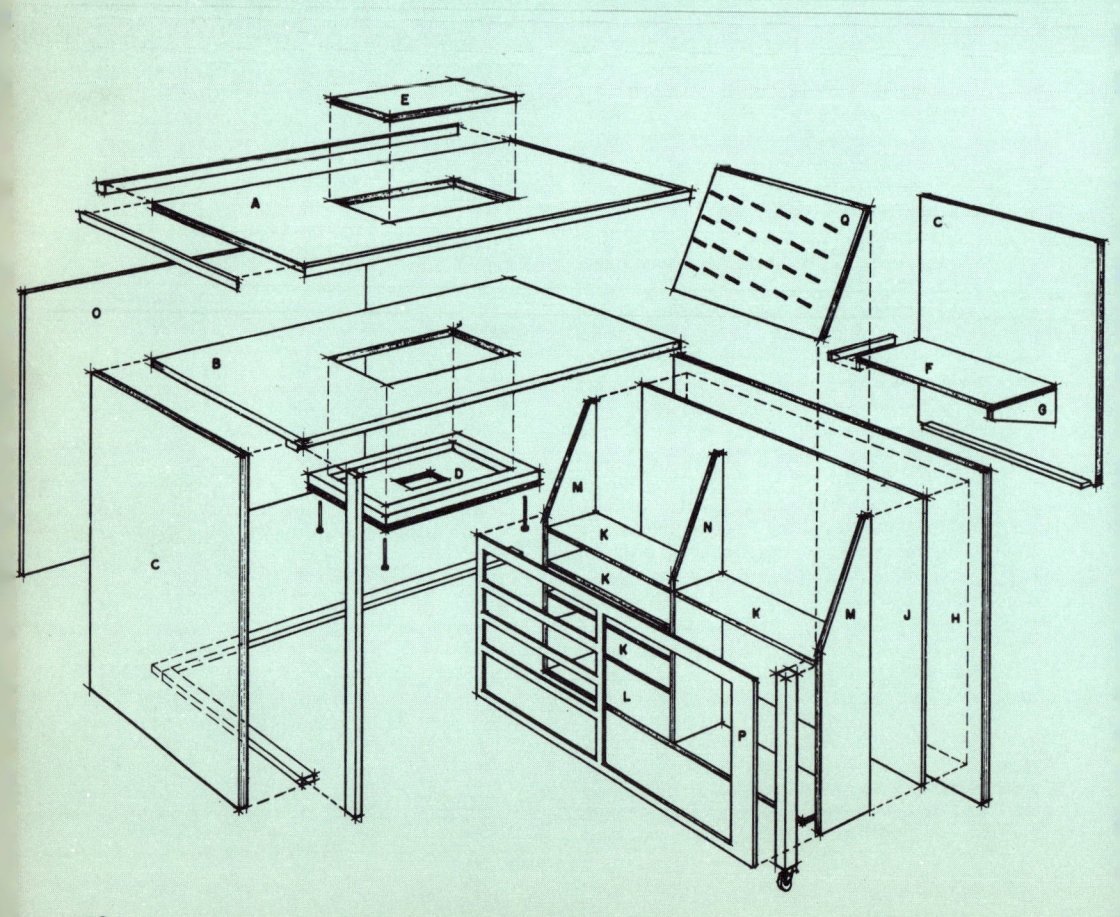

PLAN

CABINETS

CUTTING DIAGRAMS

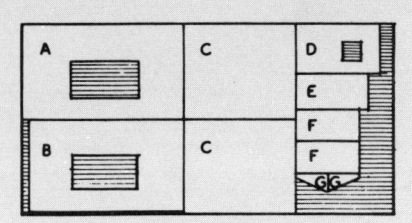

¾" x 4'-0" x 8'-0" PLYPANEL A-D • DFPA

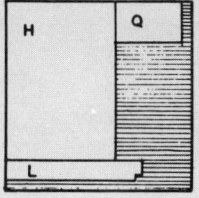

¾" x 4'-0" x 4'x0" PLYPANEL A-D • DFPA

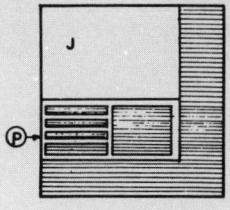

¼" x 4'-0" x 4'-0" PLYPANEL A-D • DFPA

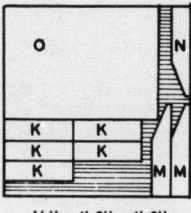

½" x 4'-0" x 4'-0" PLYPANEL A D • DFPA

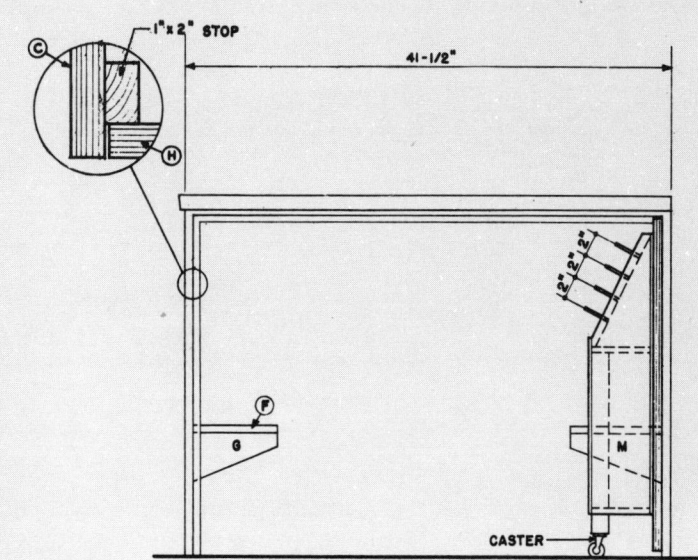

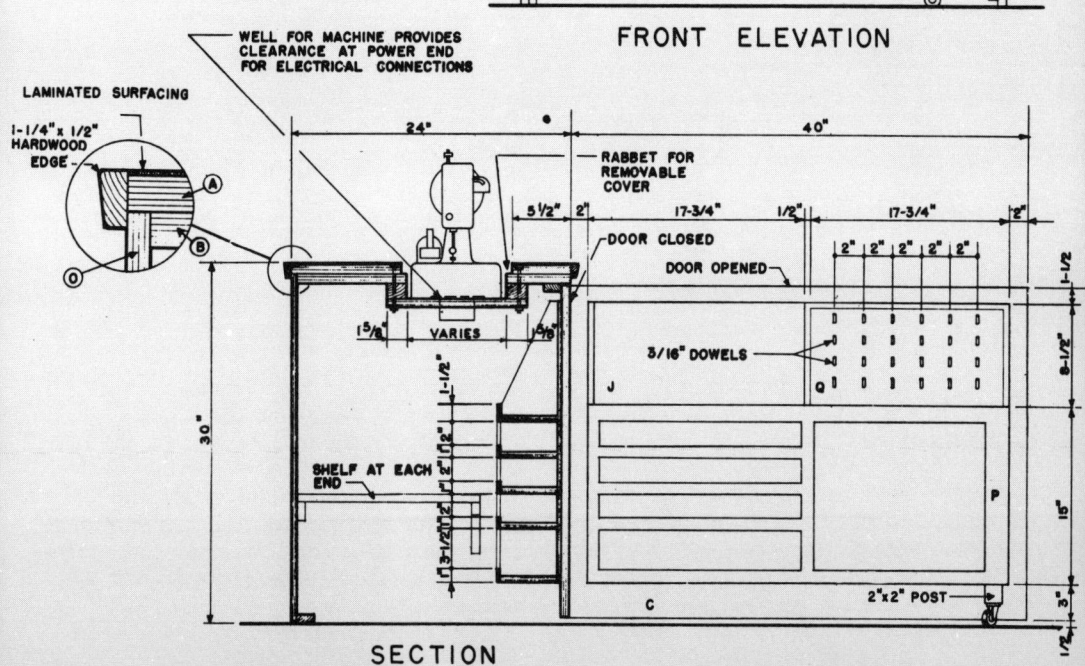

FRONT ELEVATION

SECTION

551

CABINS

ONE-ROOM CABIN can house guests, a darkroom, workshop, radio shack—you name it.

Guest Cabin

Build an "extra room" in the form of a cabin separate from the house.

by Bart Goldrath

THE DESIGN of your home, local building codes and other factors may rule against your adding another room to your house. However, if your lot dimensions are somewhat more than minimal you will be able to solve your space problem by building your "extra room" as a separate cabin apart from the house. An ideal little guest house offering maximum privacy, it can serve alternatively as a den, workshop, radio shack or playhouse for the kids.

Although costs will vary from one locality to another, this particular cabin cost the author only $680, or about $5.00 per square foot including labor and underground electrical wiring. The job was completed in three days with the help of a carpenter.

Keep costs down by selecting a stand-

CABINS

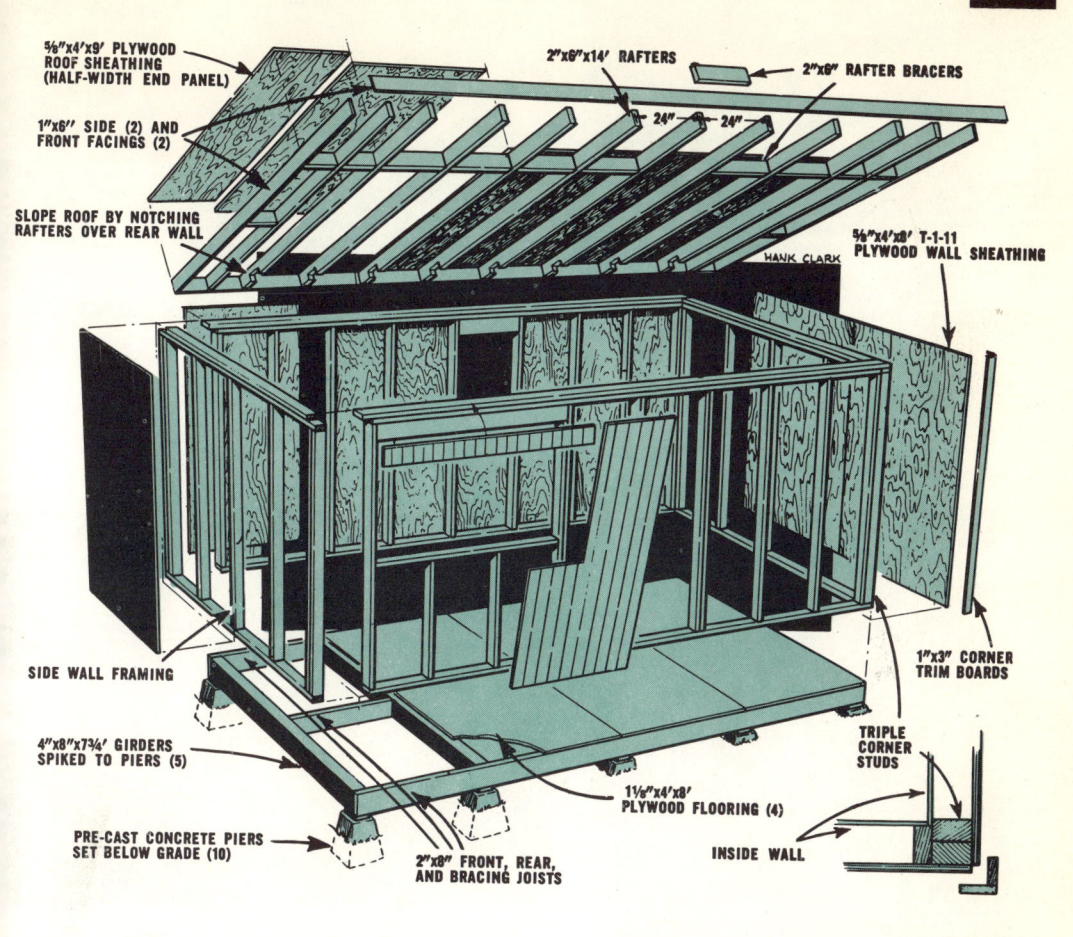

Exploded view labels:
- 5/8"x4'x9' PLYWOOD ROOF SHEATHING (HALF-WIDTH END PANEL)
- 2"x6"x14' RAFTERS
- 2"x6" RAFTER BRACERS
- 1"x6" SIDE (2) AND FRONT FACINGS (2)
- 24"
- SLOPE ROOF BY NOTCHING RAFTERS OVER REAR WALL
- 5/8"x4'x8' T-1-11 PLYWOOD WALL SHEATHING
- 1"x3" CORNER TRIM BOARDS
- SIDE WALL FRAMING
- TRIPLE CORNER STUDS
- 4"x8"x7¾' GIRDERS SPIKED TO PIERS (5)
- 1½"x4'x8' PLYWOOD FLOORING (4)
- PRE-CAST CONCRETE PIERS SET BELOW GRADE (10)
- 2"x8" FRONT, REAR, AND BRACING JOISTS
- INSIDE WALL

ard, durable building material that can be bought cheaply in quantity. In this case fir plywood was used, not only for exterior and interior walls, but for the roof and floor as well. Note too that the structure—measuring 8x16 feet—is designed to take advantage of standard 4x8-foot plywood panels.

The high cost quoted for a concrete slab foundation dictated the need to build on precast concrete piers. These were set into shallow holes containing four inches of fresh concrete. With the four corner piers squared and leveled, remaining piers were then set in place.

Five 4x8-inch girders were spiked to the piers in parallel rows the width of the building and four feet on center. Then the 2x8-inch blocking was nailed between girder ends on both the 16-foot sides and down the center to provide a grid of four-foot squares over which the

FOUNDATION is of precast concrete piers set in holes containing some fresh concrete.

CABINS

FOUR-BY-EIGHT girders, in four-foot rows, are spiked to blocks precast in the piers.

FLOOR GRID of 2 x 4's (or 2 x 8's) between girders provides a base for the flooring.

GIRDERS must be carefully leveled. If necessary, shim them with shingle wedges.

FOUR 4x8-foot panels are of 1⅛-inch plywood nailed to grid to complete the floor.

plywood floor is laid. Before nailing down the floor, the understructure was painted with a coat of wood preservative to deter termites and mildew.

Wall framing is conventional with 2x4's placed 24 inches on center instead of the usual 16 inches as in residential construction. Each wall frame may be built as a unit on the deck and then raised into place. Otherwise the corners may be set up first and braced and the walls then framed in place; in this case a 2x4-inch sill is nailed to the floor all around the perimeter. A double top plate of flat 2x4's is required by most local codes. Be sure to use three studs at each corner to give you an inside nailing surface for the wall paneling.

Use two studs at the window and door for the necessary rigidity and structural support. A 2x6-inch header was nailed over the six-foot-wide window to take the weight of the roof off the window frame; and 2x4-inch studs placed beneath the windows help to distribute the load.

Place 2x6-inch rafters two feet on centers across the width of the building. The overhang provided for in this instance is one foot on either end and at the rear, and five feet at the front; the 2x6 rafters are thus 14 feet long. To slope the roof, notch the rafters to a depth of two or three inches where they rest on the top plate along the rear side. To frame for the overhang on the ends, spike 2x6's at right angles to the rafters from inside the walls. Now 2x6 blocking

CABINS

ERECT triple studs at each corner following the installation of the 2x4-inch sill.

FOUR WALLS go up in a few hours, then are topped with a double plate of 2 x 4's.

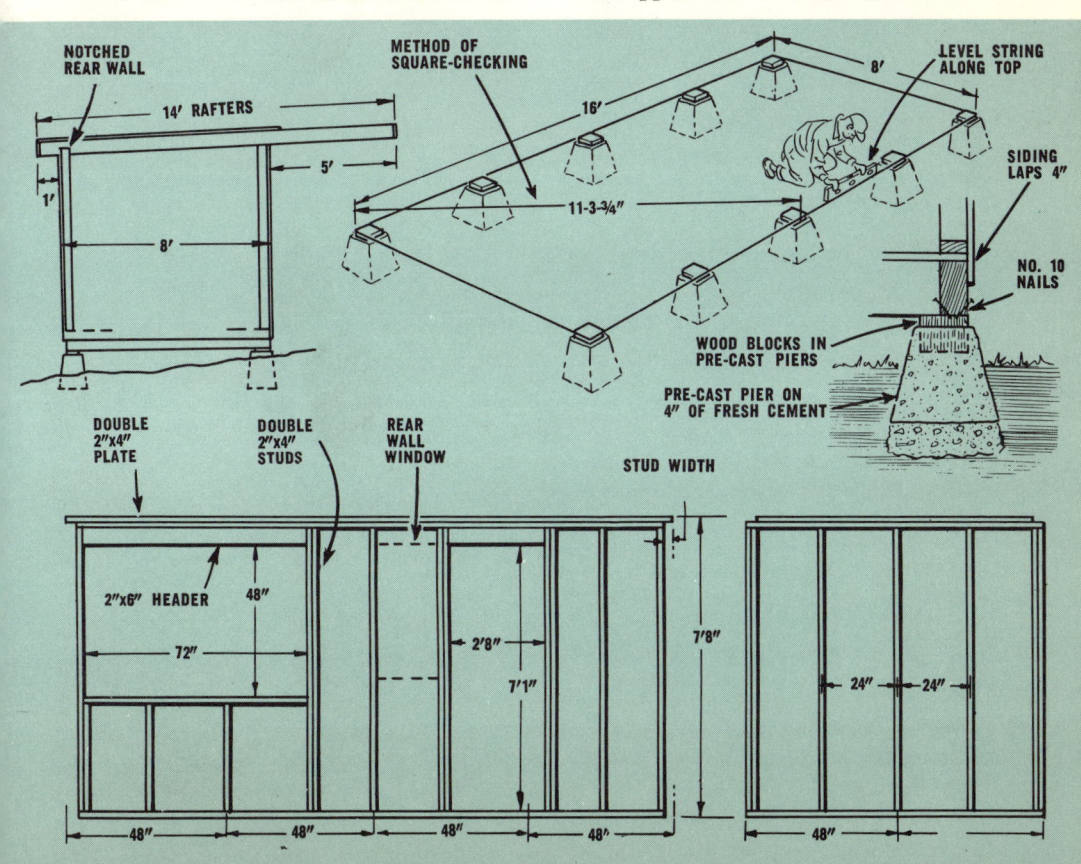

555

CABINS

PORTABLE electric saw makes quick work of cutting out the two window openings.

IT'S PLANNED on a four-foot module, so cabin's plywood panels need no trimming.

SHORT 2 x 6's are framed in for the overhang extending over each end of the cabin.

TOP VIEW of cabin shows overhang of the 2 x 6-inch rafters on their 24-inch centers.

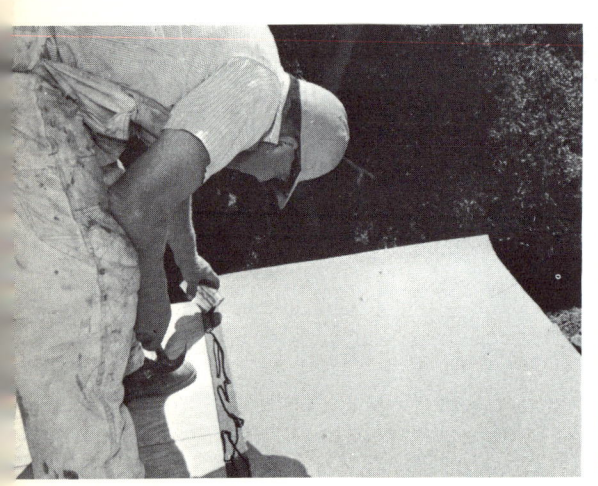

SEALING COMPOUND waterproofs the lap joints between strips of roofing material.

ROOFING PANELS are of ⅝-inch plywood and fit exactly in place over the rafters.

For a luxurious touch, include air conditioning, heater, and telephone.

must be carefully cut and nailed between the rafters all around.

The 4x8-foot exterior wall paneling is then applied. Texture One-Eleven fir plywood is vertically scored and displays pleasing shadow effects. No end trimming is necessary since the wall height is exactly 92 inches, the extra four inches extending down below the floor to form a skirt. Two-by-fours all around the bottom of structure give it a finished appearance.

The exterior plywood walls are fastened with six-penny galvanized nails, six inches apart to take full advantage of the 5/8-inch thickness of Texture One-Eleven so that diagonal bracing is unnecessary. This building does not even require felt paper under the siding because the edges of the plywood panels are lapped and make a tight seam. Corner bead of 1x2-inch corner trim is nailed at the corner of each outside wall from top to bottom.

Once the walls are completed it's a simple matter to cut out the window openings. Jalousies were used because they permit about twice as much ventilation as conventional windows and the aluminum frames require no maintenance. Fins on the window frames were nailed directly to the siding, then covered with 1x2-inch trim.

Putting on the roof is simply a matter of nailing down the 5/8-inch plywood panels. By shopping around you should be able to buy these in nine-foot lengths, thus eliminating piecing. Roll roofing with a mineral surface goes down over the roof deck.

Start at the higher side of the roof (in this case, the front) and let the leading edge of the first strip hang down a couple of inches so you can nail a batten over it. Then apply sealing compound to each edge before lapping the next strip. Nail every four inches for a tight seal.

Calk with a cartridge-type gun all around each section of 2x6 blocking and around the windows, especially in the grooves of the plywood. For additional rain protection, install flat or corrugated plastic sheets on the large front overhang.

The building will acquire a smart finished appearance by applying a 1x6-inch fascia all around. This ties together the rafters protruding along the front side of the building. To lend some style to your cabin you may want to taper the overhang—as was done here—from the extreme depth of five feet to two feet at the other end.

The interior is finished off with quarter-inch interior-grade fir plywood on the walls. It nails right into place with a minimum of cutting due to the four-foot module design. Practically no trim is necessary, except around windows, where quarter round makes a finished edge. The ceiling is half-inch prefinished white insulation board, also in 4x8-foot panels. Redwood battens cover the seams. The floor may be painted or covered with tile or rush squares.

Three electric outlets were installed for wall fixtures and for a small fan-type heater. The current can be switched off and on either from within the cabin or from a switch in the kitchen of your house. A telephone and buzzer system provides communication with the house, and all wires are run through conduit to preserve the natural setting.

The area was landscaped with low-spreading shrubs that conceal the base of the building but do not cut off ventilation. A few fast-growing pines and cypresses, planted six or eight feet apart will provide a fragrant woodsy setting.

You may call your little auxiliary room a teahouse or a poolside cabana. But even if you don't have a pool and are strictly a coffee drinker you'll get plenty of enjoyment and privacy from this cabin for many years to come. •

CABINS

COZY CABIN is a hideaway anyone can build at the mere loosening of a purse string.

BUILD A
VACATION HOME FOR $275

By Ralph S. Wilkes

THIS little hunting cabin and weekend retreat was built by the author for $275. It can later be expanded as time and finances permit. The cabin can be erected on 2x12-inch skids should you anticipate moving it at some future time to make the site available for a larger house. With this in mind, the porch was added in such a way that it is readily detachable from the cabin.

Siding for the cabin consists of four sheets of half-inch Homasote—two 8x12 feet, and two 8x14 feet. Four inches are gained each way by leaving two inches of exposed studs—to which the trim is nailed—at each corner. Therefore, the 2x12-inch "runners" (lengthwise sill pieces) will be 14 feet, 4 inches long and the cross-sills and floor joists 12 feet long.

The cabin's basic frame forms the sill. It rests on six large flat rocks and must be carefully leveled. A more stable foundation would require the construction of concrete piers below the frostline. Anchor bolts set in the piers would then hold the sill.

Rough lumber can be used for the sill and joists. Including the outside sill pieces, there are ten joists spaced every 19 inches. Nail cross bracing between the joists to "firm" the floor. For this cabin, one-inch matched flooring was laid and the ends trimmed along the outer edge of the sill with a portable power saw. The flooring was obtained from a house-wrecking concern for ten dollars (new material would have cost about three times as much).

Once the floor is down, a level surface is provided on which to construct the front and back walls. Planed 2x4's are used for the framing. The walls are built flat on the floor, then erected, spiked in place, and held upright by scrap boards nailed diagonally from the corners to the side of the sill.

With front and back walls vertical and parallel, the rafters then go into place after first being tapered to 2½ inches at the ends. The slight pitch of the rafters may make notching unnecessary, although in this case the plate was notched about a half inch at the point of contact to give each rafter greater bearing surface. Space the eight rafters evenly over the 14-foot, 4-inch plates so that they're a bit over 24 inches on center. The overhang is about eight inches at the back and ten inches at the front. The tapered rafters will allow four-inch roof trim boards to be used on all four sides.

Along the side walls 2x4's are spiked to the floor from front to back and marked for the studs which are placed 16 inches on center. Use a level or plumb bob to be sure each stud is vertical, then mark each stud at the rafter and notch it (or the rafter) to fit before nailing in place.

The location, size and type of windows are matters each builder will decide for himself. Secondhand windows were installed in this cabin at a cost of $1.50 per sash and are the separate sashes of upright double-sash windows, trimmed to fit and turned sidewise for mounting.

2"x12" SILL measures 12'x14'x4". Arrange large, flat rocks under corners to support and level sill.

FLOORING is nailed crosswise to joists. Used flooring cost only $10.

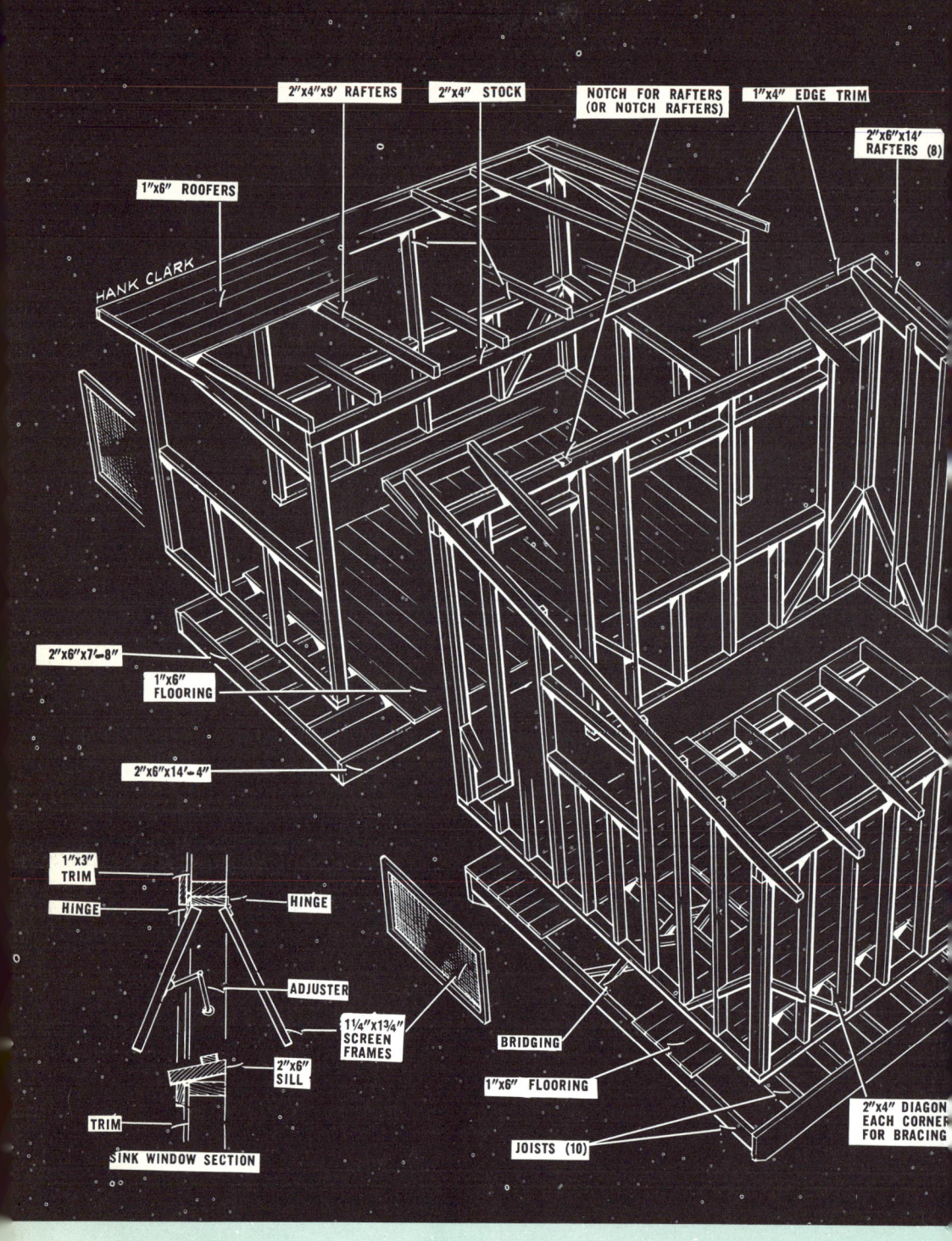

The lower edge of the sash over the sink is beveled to fit the sill, then hinged at the top and equipped with a storm-window adjuster to hold it at the desired position for ventilation.

The front windows are two-pane sashes installed horizontally with a single-pane sash hinged below each so it will tilt outward. Window installation is left until the late stages of con-

CABINS

Diagram labels:
- FRONT WINDOW SECTION
- FIXED SASH
- SASH HINGE
- SCREEN INSIDE
- 1"x6" ROOFERS
- NAIL SOLE TO FLOORING
- 2"x12"x14'-4" SILL
- JOISTS REST ON 2"x2" CLEAT

FRAMING for rear wall is nailed together on cabin floor. Note doubled 2x4's at sides and top.

RAFTERS (eight 2x6's) are cut to size, tapered at their ends, notched, then nailed into place.

"PRE-SHRUNK" (see text) 8'x12' Homasote sheet is positioned and nailed into place on framing.

struction but framing must be planned in advance to provide proper openings for the door and sash frames.

The first step in applying the

561

CABINS

DROP PORCH FLOOR about six inches below cabin floor so that cabin roof will overhang porch roof.

ASPHALT roll roofing is lapped, then nailed down over roof boards.

Homasote—or any other exterior insulation board—demands careful reading of the manufacturer's directions. Homasote must be expanded before use, so lightly sprinkle each sheet on both sides with water. They are then laid flat on top of each other overnight, but not more than 48 hours before use.

A section of Homasote is now set into position while the upper edge is scored and cut to fit snugly under the rafters. The piece is then raised and nailed into place by framing it in with lengths of trim at the corners as shown in the drawing. Then use the rustproof nails to fasten this material to the frame.

When all four sides are up, saw out the openings for door and windows. After this, the roof boards go on. Trim their edges, then apply the 1x4-inch trim before laying the asphalt roll roofing.

Close the openings between the rafters by fitting pieces of Homasote in them. Screening can be installed over three rafter openings at the middle, front and rear to provide ventilation.

Roll on a coat of white undercoat paint before applying the trim. After that apply a second coat of outside paint and two coats to the trim.

Smooth the floor with a rented floor sander before laying down the linoleum or other floor covering.

Advice should be obtained from the local power company as regards wiring specifications, since inspection will be required before power is supplied. Wiring this cabin is a simple job. It consists of installing four outlets around the room, a ceiling light over the sink, and an outside floodlight. Switches are located inside the door. If a hot plate will be used instead of a range, two-wire service of 120 volts will be sufficient.

No provision has been made for heat-

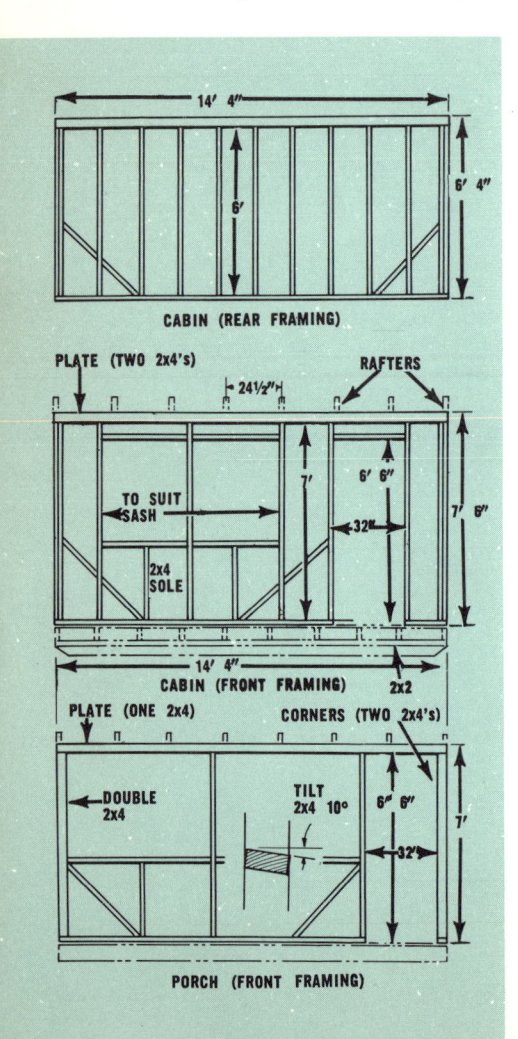

CABINS

NAIL fitted cuts of Homasote under ends of porch roof and around porch railings.

COMPLETED CABIN, including the porch, has total floor space of over 280 sq. ft.

ing the cabin. Due to the tight construction and good insulating properties of the siding, a portable electric heater with circulating fan will keep the cabin comfortable in cool weather.

A porch can be added whenever desired. It is attached with bolts and lag screws which can be removed in a few

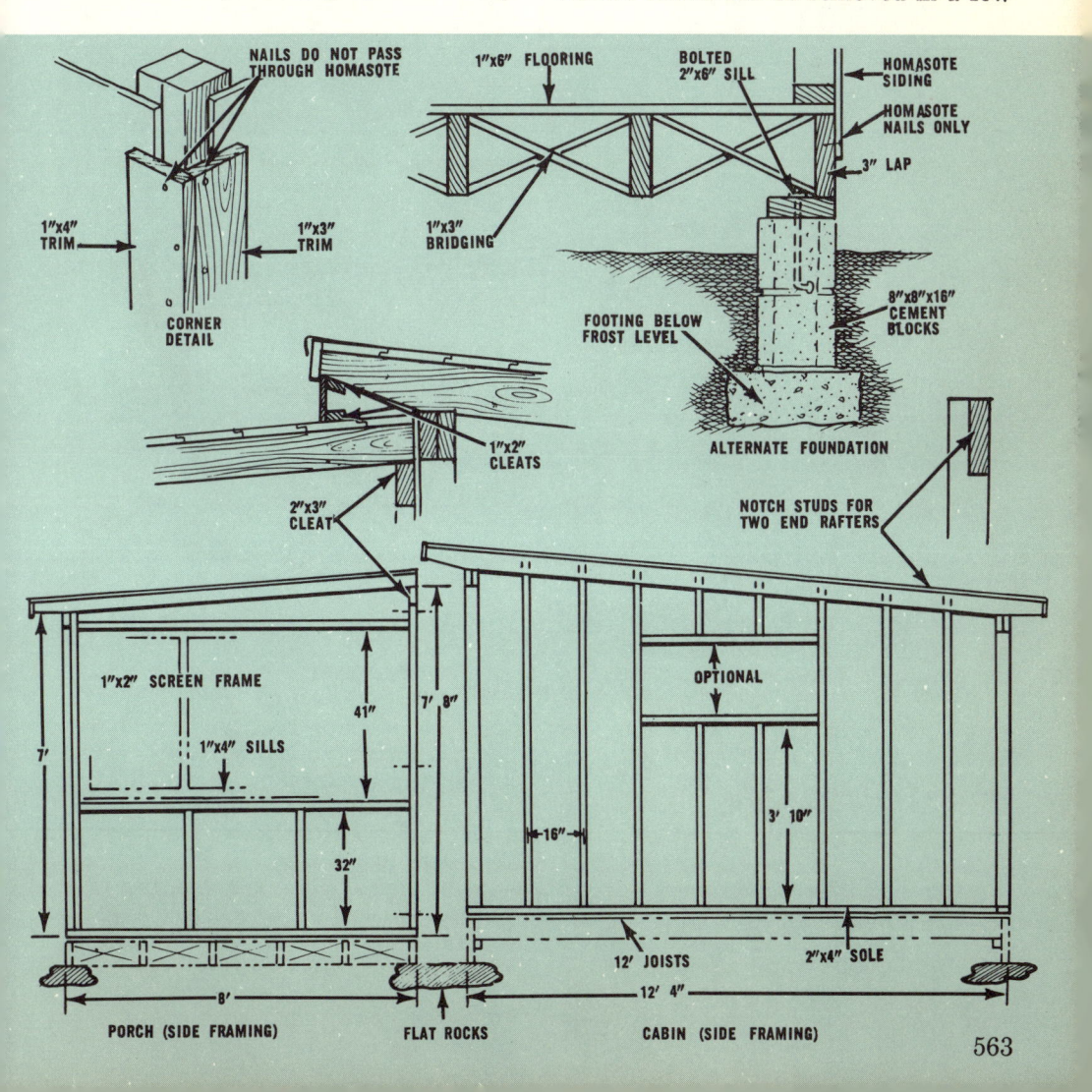

563

CABINS

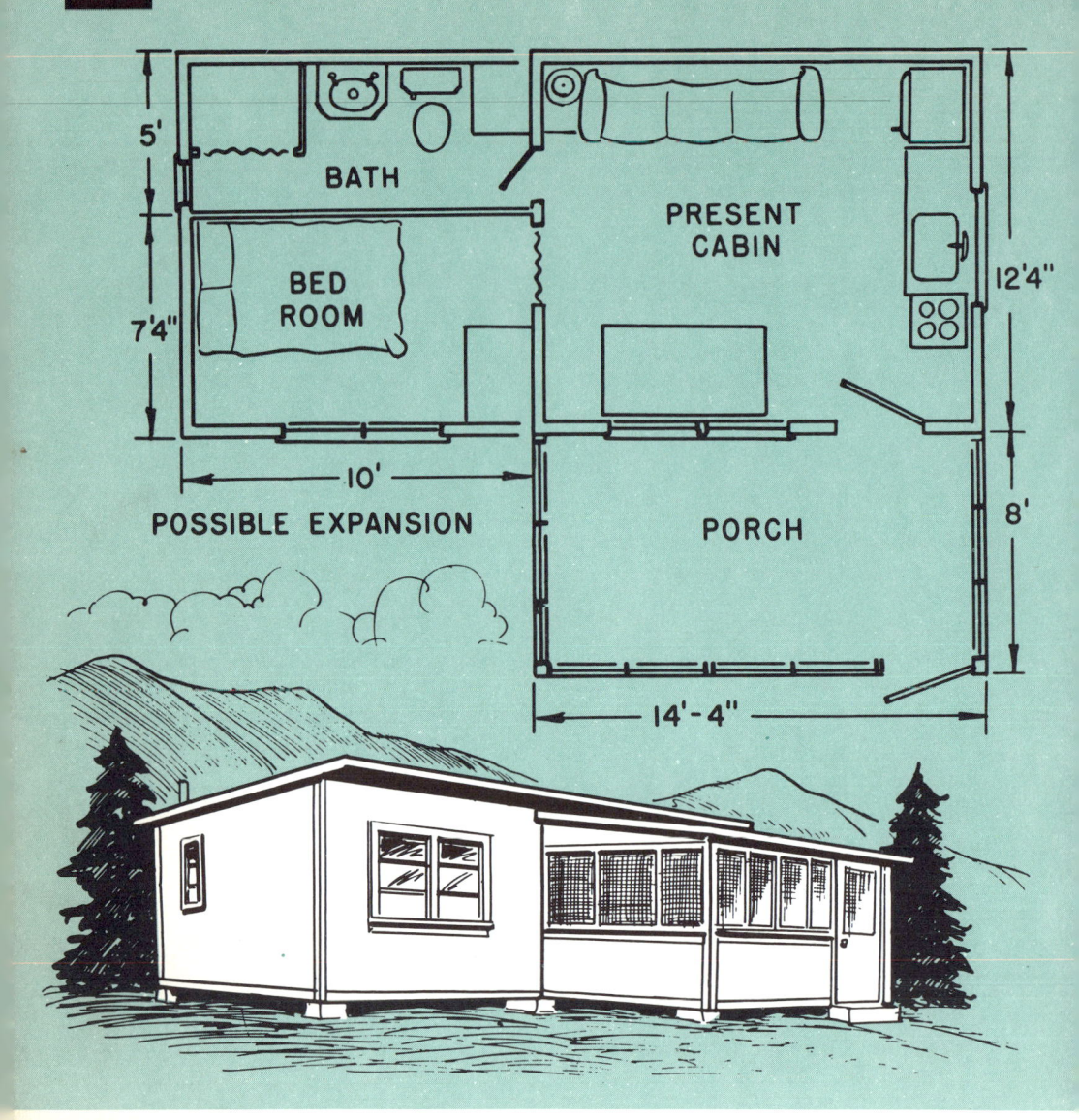

minutes to permit the two units (cabin and porch) to be moved separately.

The porch is the same length as the cabin and eight feet wide. The floor drops six inches below the cabin-floor level so that the porch roof is overlapped by the roof of the cabin. The sill and joists are 2x6's with cross-bracing bridging the joists to make the floor more rigid.

After the sill has been spiked together and blocked in place, four holes are bored to allow for bolting it to the cabin sill with ½x6-inch carriage bolts.

A 2x3-inch piece is now attached to the front of the cabin above the door and windows with lag screws. It is placed just far enough below the overhang of the cabin roof to allow attaching the rafters and roof boards. Then erection of the framing and application of roofboards and roofing are attended to in that order. Finally, the siding is nailed in place.

At a later date a bedroom and bath can be added to this cabin, also a water system and sewage disposal in most instances. •

CABINS

BILL OF MATERIAL — CABIN

Quantity	Size - Material	Use
2	2"x12"x16' rough	Sill (Rough lumber)
2	2"x2"x16' "	" " "
10	2"x6"x12' "	Sill, floor joists (Rough lumber)
2	2"x4"x16' planed	Framing (floor plate)
2	2"x4"x12' "	" " "
13	2"x4"x6' "	Studs
26	2"x4"x8' "	Studs
4	2"x4"x16' "	Plate
5	2"x4"x12' "	Misc. framing
8	2"x6"x14' "	Rafters
1	2"x6"x12' "	Window sills
225 board feet	1"x4" matched	Flooring
230 board feet	1"x8" unmatched	Roof boards (Add ¼ if matched)
200 linear feet	1"x4"	Trim
60 linear feet	1"x3"	"
2 sheets	½"x8'x12' Homasote	Siding
2 sheets	½"x8'x14' "	"
1 sheet	4'x8'	Boxing under rafter overhang or piecing between rafters.
3 windows	Approx. openings 18"x42" (1) 38"x48" (2)	
1 door & screen dr.	2'6" or 2'8"x6'8"	
3 rolls	Slate surface asphalt roll roofing	

Miscellaneous: Nails, paint, plumbing, wiring, material for kitchen cabinets, steps, etc.

BILL OF MATERIALS — PORCH

Quantity	Size - Material	Use
2	2"x6"x16'	Sill
2	2"x6"x8'	"
4	2"x6"x14'	Joists
1	2"x3"x16'	Plate for cabin end of rafters
1	2"x4"x16'	Plate
8	2"x4"x8'	Studs
6	2"x4"x8'	Framing
4	2"x4"x12'	"
8	2"x4"x10'	Rafters
150 bd. ft.	1"x4" matched flooring	Flooring
150 bd. ft. unmatched Or 190 bd. ft. matched		Roof boards
135 linear feet	1"x4"	Trim
50 " "	1"x3"	Trim
100 " "	1½"x2"	Screen frame
100 " "	¼"x1"	"
3	½"x4'x8'	Homasote
1	½"x4'x12'	"
1 (plus leftover from cabin)	Slate surface asphalt roll roofing	

Miscellaneous: Bolts, lag screws, nails, screen, paint, awnings, etc.
Use screen door from cabin.

Porch has two cots and a folding table. Rolled awnings on each side provide privacy and protection from the weather. Below is front and side exterior view of completed cottage.

CABINS

LOW COST COTTAGE

By Ralph S. Wilkes

CABINS

You can build this dream cottage at a cost of less than $1500 for materials.

FOR durable, fireproof building materials that are easy to maintain, it is hard to beat concrete and cinder block. Yet, in our latest building venture, we felt that a house built entirely of these materials would lack the warmth and beauty of pine, cypress or redwood. We therefore decided to combine the three materials, using concrete for the floor, block construction for three walls and wood for the front and gables. We chose pine.

It was our aim to provide for at least six people in a building a little over 20x30 ft., yet give the feeling of spacious living. This was accomplished by building three small bedrooms and a bath, leaving the rest of the building open as a living room, dining area and kitchen with the latter separated by a serving bar.

After drawing the plans and constructing a scale model from plywood and fiberboard (a safe way to correct mistakes), we were ready to start the actual construction job. Of course we already had the site picked out, but it is important to check local sanitation codes concerning sewage disposal. In our area, a sewage disposal bed must be at least 75 ft. from the high water mark of the lake which the cottage overlooks.

The first step consisted of laying out the foundation, squaring the corners and checking by measuring the diagonals to be sure they were equal. Then we dug a trench about 15 in. wide and 3 ft. deep. In warmer climates this depth might not be necessary but here

EXPOSED rafters over kitchen, living and dining area lend a feeling of extra spaciousness.

KITCHEN is set off from dining area by a serving bar built from leftover lumber.

READY for first pouring. Blocks laid sideways are temporary cover to keep out rain.

in the Finger Lakes region of New York the frost sometimes penetrates to this depth. We were fortunate in having a gravelly, well-drained soil. In heavy soil it is wise to go even deeper.

We planned to have a fireplace at the end of the living room so we also excavated for a 2 ft., 6 in. x 4 ft., 6 in. footing for this. After leveling the bottom of the trench, concrete was poured to a depth of about 14 in., using some small clean stones in it to cut cost. The exact location for the soil pipe and entrance water pipe must be determined at this time. We placed a six-inch diameter tin can in the wall, poured concrete over it and later removed it. Three courses of concrete blocks were laid all the way around to bring the wall up to a little above ground level. Because they are less porous than cinder blocks, it is always recommended that concrete blocks be used below ground level.

The fireplace footing is of solid concrete with some large clean stones imbedded in it. A frame was constructed

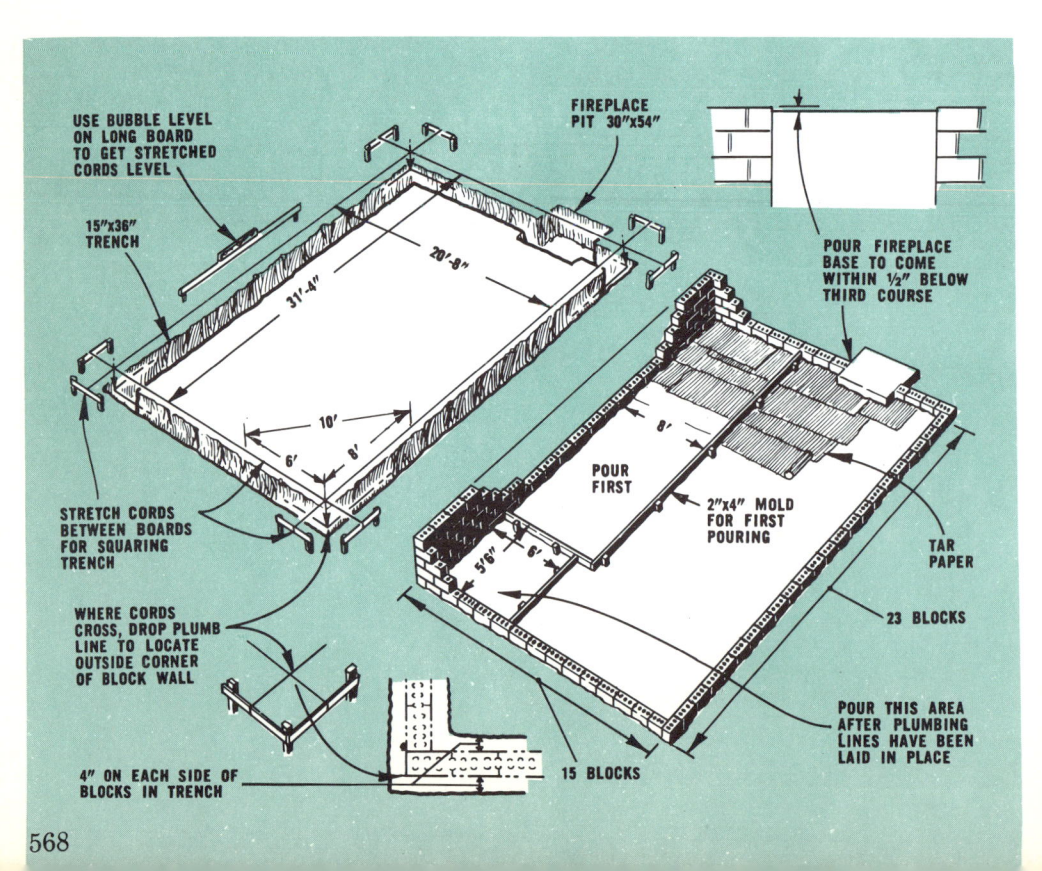

CABINS

around the upper portion so the edges would be straight. Ours was 2 ft., 6 in. x 4 ft., 6 in. but the exact size will depend upon the size of the circulating unit you decide to use. The surface was leveled off ½ in. lower than the height of the floor which was to be poured later.

The surface of the ground inside the footing was next leveled and covered with moisture-proof paper in preparation for the concrete floor. If the soil is poorly drained, lay the floor on a 4- or 5-in. bed of coarse gravel. The paper was pressed tight to the ground by walking over it before the concrete was poured. Pieces of thin beveled siding, four inches wide, were coated with oil and placed around the inside of the wall, thick edge up, then removed when the concrete had begun to set. After the concrete had cured, the slot was filled with hot asphalt to serve as an expansion joint. Some type of expansion joint is important to prevent cracking of the wall as the floor expands and contracts with changing temperatures.

While the cost of transit-mix concrete is greater than the do-it-yourself kind, the convenience and saving in time out-

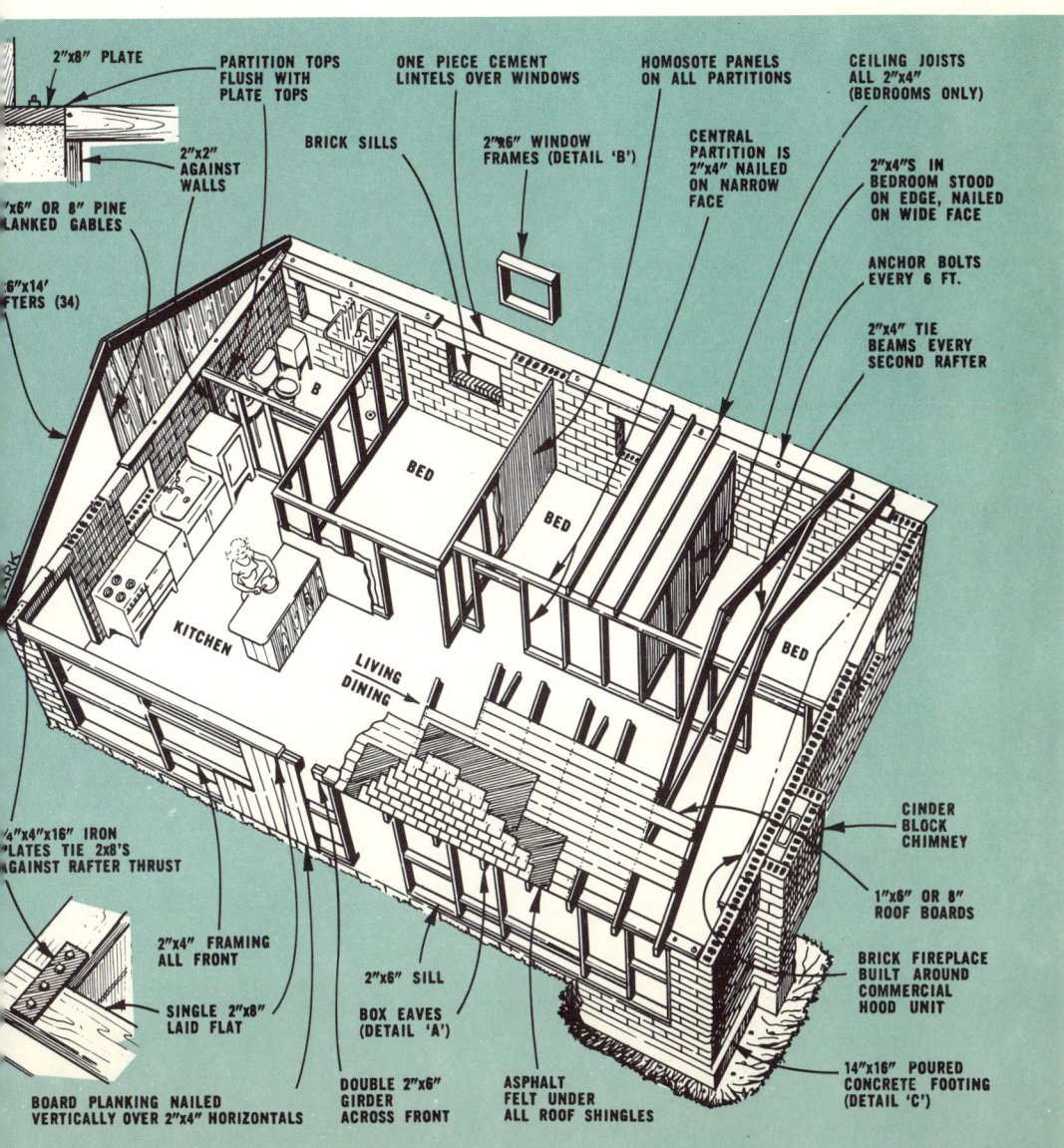

CABINS

weighed the financial disadvantage. By pouring a large amount at one time, one also avoids the unsightly appearance of a floor that is laid in small sections. To pour this large area, a 2x4 was set on edge and firmly secured by stakes along the line where the bedroom-living room partition was to be placed, eight feet from the back wall. This 2x4 at one side and the cement block wall at the other provide surfaces for the ends of the straight board used to strike off the surface before troweling. The bedroom area was poured one day and the living room-kitchen area the next. The bathroom was left until the cottage was completed and the plumbing was installed. The 2x4 was removed before the second pouring and ⅜x6-in. anchor bolts for the partitions were set in the fresh concrete of the second pouring. Use care in locating these so they will not inter-

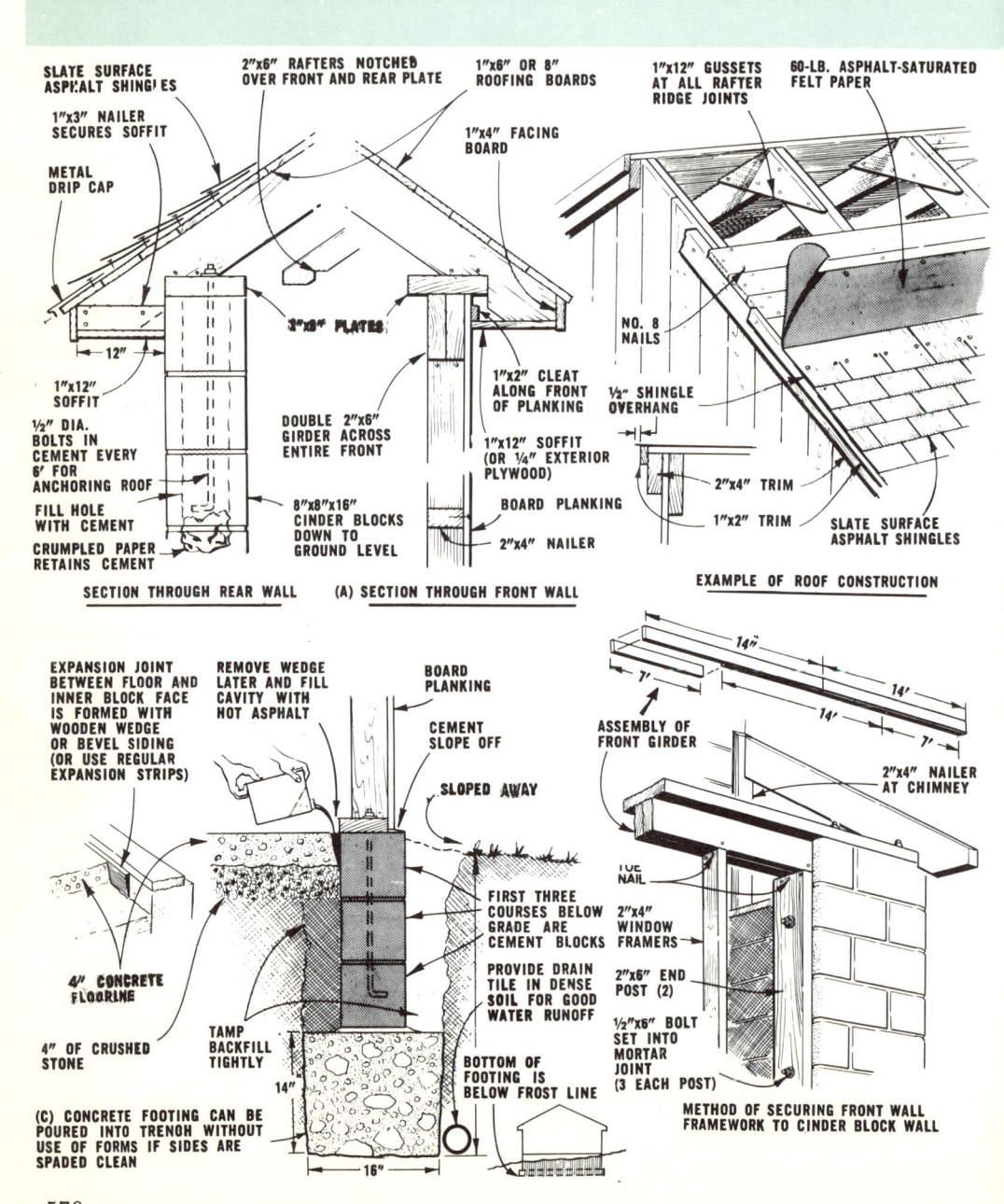

WINDOW FRAMES are fitted in as the blocks are laid. All openings are spanned with 48-in. lintels.

fere with a stud. For the other anchor bolts we later set expansion shields in holes made with a star drill and used 3/8-in. lag screws. A carbide-tipped concrete drill would have helped.

It was while pouring the footing and laying the first three courses of blocks that we decided we were more efficient carpenters than masons. Since we worked weekends and time was a factor, we decided to turn over the jobs of constructing the floor and laying the cinder blocks to someone more skilled, planning to take up the job

TEMPORARY pieces are nailed diagonally across rafters to make them rigid and hold the spacing.

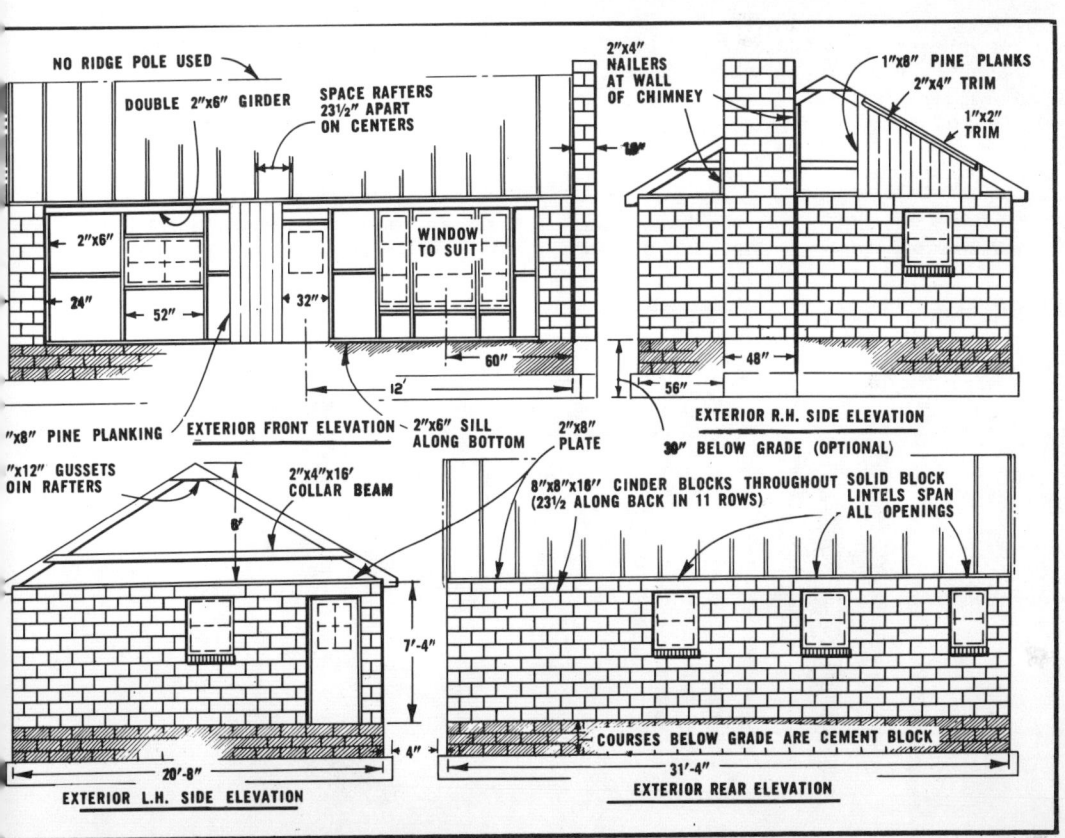

571

CABINS

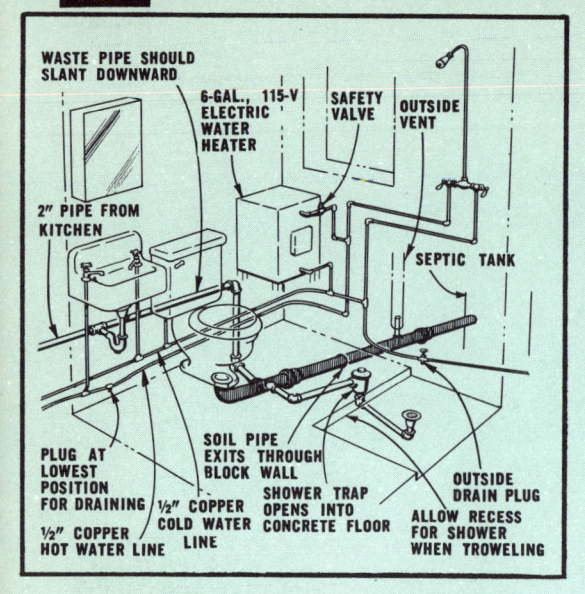

Diagram labels:
- WASTE PIPE SHOULD SLANT DOWNWARD
- 6-GAL., 115-V ELECTRIC WATER HEATER
- SAFETY VALVE
- OUTSIDE VENT
- 2" PIPE FROM KITCHEN
- SEPTIC TANK
- PLUG AT LOWEST POSITION FOR DRAINING
- SOIL PIPE EXITS THROUGH BLOCK WALL
- ½" COPPER COLD WATER LINE
- SHOWER TRAP OPENS INTO CONCRETE FLOOR
- OUTSIDE DRAIN PLUG
- ALLOW RECESS FOR SHOWER WHEN TROWELING
- ½" COPPER HOT WATER LINE

again at the carpentry stage. It was here that we realized the importance of shopping around for the skilled labor of a mason. The first one we contacted wanted $50 for the labor of leveling the floor. Since this seemed high, I made further inquiries and finally got the job done at an hourly rate of $15. The same man offered to lay the blocks at 12 cents each. He did the job, with a helper, in about two days at a total cost of about $75, including the fireplace chimney.

The end door and all windows except the bathroom window, which had to be made, had been previously obtained from a house wrecking concern. The windows are the separate sashes of double-hung windows, turned sidewise, hinged at the top in a 2x6-in. frame and provided with storm sash adjusters to hold them in any desired position for ventilation. A bit of trimming was necessary on the wide side and a narrow strip had to be added to the other but, after painting, they presented a neat appearance. At $1.50 apiece, this is an inexpensive way to solve the window problem. Window frames and door frames were set in place as the block laying progressed. Bedroom and kitchen window frames were 36 in. wide, so some block cutting was necessary.

For the sake of appearance, bullnose rounded-corner blocks were used at all corners and at the windows and door opening. Since the corners are rounded to a two-inch radius, six-inch width window and door framing fits well against them.

The fireplace chimney was built up around a commercially made unit (Price or Heatilator or others; ours was a Price) with a ½-in. blanket of insulating material laid on the unit before the blocks were installed. An

THE PARTITION framing in place. Note that interior studs and plates are turned sideways as opposed to conventional practice.

THE SILL for the large living room window is notched around the studs. It may be installed before or after putting in windows.

CABINS

8x12-in. tile flue was used as a liner, the spaces at the sides being filled with broken blocks.

As soon as the masons completed their work, we started the carpentry job that was to occupy most of our weekends over the next few months. We first laid 2x8s on the top edge of the cinder block walls, anchoring them about every five or six feet with long, ½-in. bolts set in concrete and extending about three blocks deep. In windswept areas it is recommended that one go somewhat deeper than this. It is advisable to first mark the location of the rafters along the wall before putting in the anchor bolts in order to avoid having any of them come at points where the rafters should rest.

The sill was next laid across the front, using a length of 2x6 each side of the doorway, flush with the inner edge of the block footing. This is anchored the same way as the plate only ½x6-in. bolts are used. The 2x6 uprights at the ends are next bolted in place on three ½x6-in. bolts that were set in the mortar between the blocks when they were laid. These also are even with the inner edge of the wall. At about this time, the holes in the blocks in the doorway were filled and a concrete threshold was

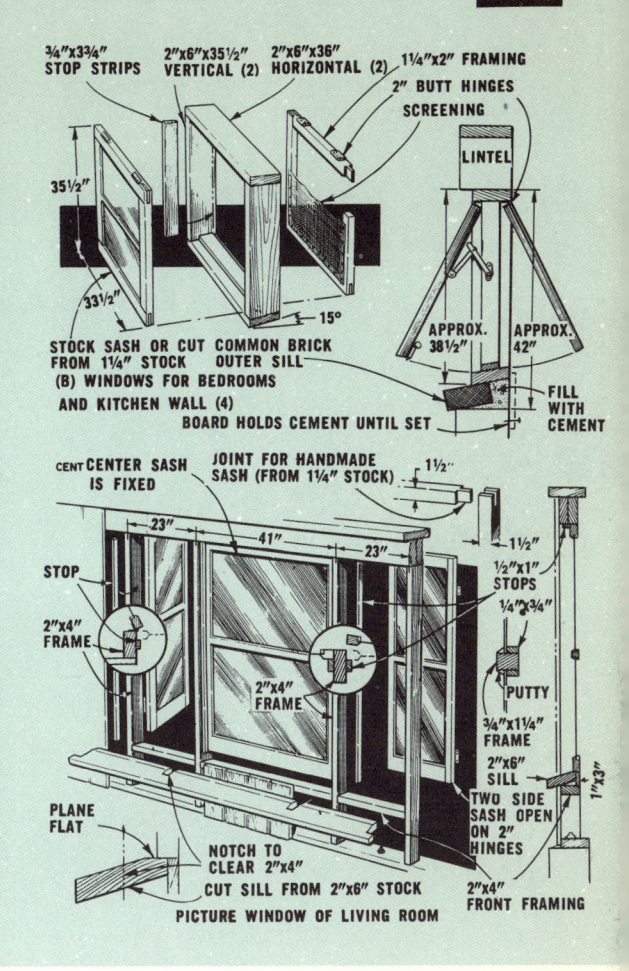

COAT of white cement paint is applied. It can be bought in colors if preferred. Simple window construction is apparent here.

SCREEN on inside is hinged to swing up. Window has lock at bottom and the storm sash adjuster at the side holds it open.

formed. The exposed two inches at the front of the sill was also covered, forming a beveled surface one inch high at the back edge.

The 4x6-in. beam, made up by splicing together two 2x6s, was then hoisted into place on the tops of the end pieces and supported and braced as necessary to hold it straight and level. After spiking this beam at the ends, even with the outer edge of the 2x6 supports, we were ready to place the 2x8-in. plate over it. This was set on two anchor bolts at each end and spiked securely to the beam all the way across. Care was taken to stagger the butt joints in both the beam and plate. The side and end plates were tied together at the corners by attaching 1/4x4x16-in. metal plates with two-inch lag screws.

Most of the front framing was then erected, leaving a generous opening so we could carry in the large sheets of wallboard for the partitions. Siding was then nailed on and we were ready to put up the rafters. After carefully checking the first assembled pair by trying them at various locations from end to end we used these as a pattern for the others. Because the rafters were to be exposed, we used the minimum number of crosspieces or collar beams, one for every second pair of rafters. In areas of heavy snowfall, one should use crosspieces on all rafters and still greater strength can be added by using a truss construction.

The other 16 pairs of rafters were then cut to shape, a job which made us very thankful that we had a portable electric handsaw. They were fitted together and assembled on the concrete floor, after which the ends were laid over the plate upside down and then swung up over for nailing into place. A spacing of 23½ in. on centers makes them come out even. However, if you used plywood on the roof, they must be spaced 24 in., leaving a smaller spacing next to the fireplace. After locating each pair and nailing the ends, boards are nailed diagonally across the upper surface to brace the rafters and give the assembly greater rigidity. Then the last pair at the chimney and the rafter on that side is marked for cutting, after which the ends butting the chimney must be supported by pieces of 2x2.

Over the rafters you can apply sheathing grade plywood, matched or unmatched lumber. We chose the latter, sawed at a local mill and planed only on

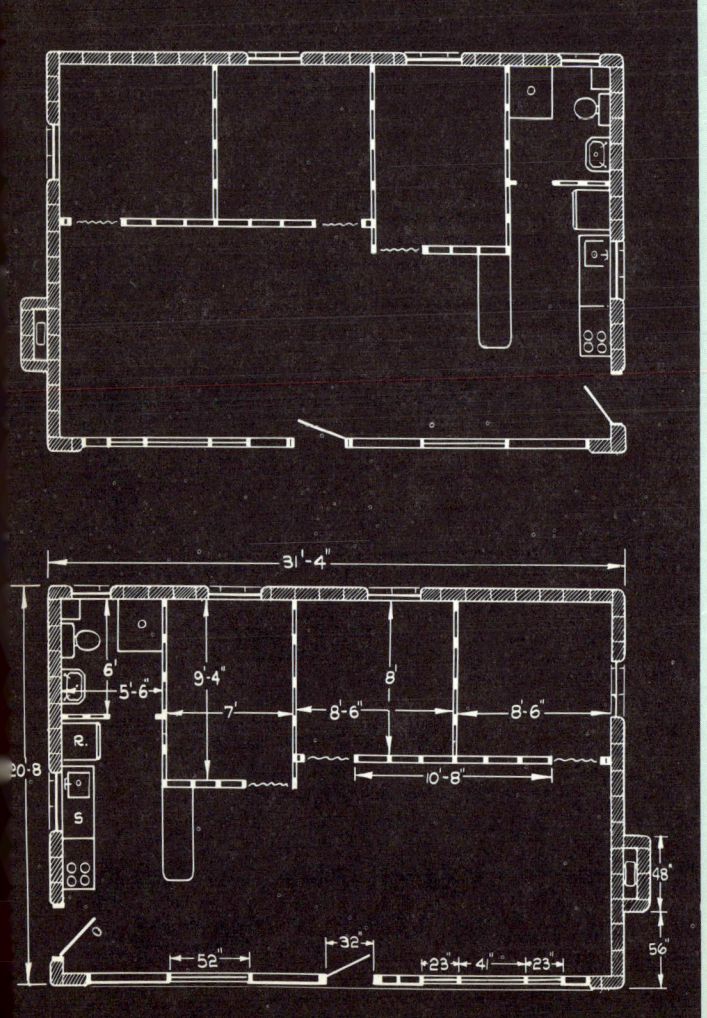

ALTERNATE floor plans appear below; bottom one is covered by text, photographs.

Calking

This magic material clings to wood, stone or metal; guards the home against rot and insects.

Calking is especially helpful where a wooden porch or garage joins the brick wall of your house.

Using putty knife or chisel, pry away rot and old compound around window frames.

For small repairs, calking compound is available in tubes for easy application.

Push the calking into all recesses, leaving the surface of compound convex.

Outside water faucets and pipes should be calked where they enter the house.

one side, chiefly because this was least expensive. Plywood would have saved some labor. The roof boards extend one inch beyond the ends of the rafters to cover the boxed ends.

Asphalt-saturated felt roofing paper was laid on the roofboards. This is fairly durable if secured with strips so the wind cannot get under it. It keeps out the rain until the asphalt strip shingles can be laid.

After the rafters were enclosed, both front and back, we found that some calking was necessary, especially at the back next to the wall. At this stage we also nailed the trim pieces, cut on a bandsaw from 2x8s, on each corner.

To make the cottage cooler in summer it is advisable to install a louver in one or both ends near the peak. These ventilators can be covered with cardboard or composition board when cold weather comes.

After putting in part of the concrete, we set the brick sills in place (14 on edge for all except the 20-in. bathroom window which took only 9). Next a board was nailed to the block wall on the inside, flush with the lower edge of the window frame. The frame was then removed, the space filled with concrete and the frame slid back in place. Two nails through each side of the 2x6 frames into the blocks fastened them permanently in place, after which a little calking compound sealed any cracks that remained.

Framing for all partitions was built of 2x4s which were placed on edge between the bedrooms and between the bedroom and bathroom. This saved two inches of space in each room and is about as sturdy as the usual method of construction. We used 2x2s against the block wall, securing them with toggle bolts. The partitions were constructed the same height as the wall plates for a neat appearance and to simplify the job of laying the joists for the bedroom and bathroom ceilings. Sheetrock plasterboard was used on the ceilings, Homasote on the walls.

Facing the fireplace with brick was not as difficult as we had anticipated because of the complete and well-illustrated instructions that were included with the fireplace unit. The brickwork was topped off with a mantel of pine. The added efficiency of the circulating air unit, not to mention the time saved in construction, more than compensated for the $50 to $75 the unit cost.

We were fortunate in being able to obtain good second-hand plumbing fixtures from a house-wrecking concern at about half the cost of new ones. The bathroom floor was left until this time because we wanted to set the soil pipe from the toilet and the drain pipes from the shower and lavatory in the concrete floor. A 6½-gallon, 120-volt electric water heater, set in the corner, provides plenty of hot water for ordinary usage. Check local regulations before installing a sewage disposal system. We buried a 600-gallon steel septic tank back of the cottage and ran a line of 4-in. field tile from this to a sizable dry well about 40 feet away. Under some conditions this might not be enough but we are fortunate in having well-drained soil.

Specifications for approved electrical wiring can be obtained from the local office of the company that supplies current to your community. This is the starting point in planning the wiring job. It is safest and in most areas it is required that you have the wiring inspected and approved before meter service will be provided. We installed a three-wire electric system to provide for the kitchen range. All other wiring throughout the cottage is No. 12 Romex stapled to the framing and provided with a third wire for grounding all outlets. The only overhead lights are over the dining table and the kitchen sink.

For inside painting, we used alkyd paints on the cinder block walls of the bedrooms and on the fireplace end of the living room, as well as on the Homasote partitions and sheetrock ceilings. A roller worked very nicely on the latter surfaces. On the kitchen end and on the cinder block sides of the bathroom, as well as outside, we used a cold water paint (Bondex or similar). •

LARGE-SCALE PLANS

and a bill of materials are available. Send $2 to MI Plans Service, Fawcett Place, Greenwich, Conn. Specify Plan No. HJ-27, Summer Cottage.